# RETHINKING
# Popular Culture and Media

EDITED BY ELIZABETH MARSHALL AND ÖZLEM SENSOY

KATHERINE STREETER

◆ A RETHINKING SCHOOLS PUBLICATION ◆

*Rethinking Popular Culture and Media*
Edited by Elizabeth Marshall and Özlem Sensoy

## A Rethinking Schools Publication

Rethinking Schools Ltd. is a nonprofit educational publisher of books, booklets, and a quarterly magazine on school reform, with a focus on issues of equity and social justice. To request additional copies of this book and/or a catalog of other publications, or to subscribe to *Rethinking Schools* magazine, contact:

**Rethinking Schools**
1001 East Keefe Avenue
Milwaukee, WI 53212
**800-669-4192**
**www.rethinkingschools.org**

Production Editor: Catherine Capellaro
Cover and book design: The Flynstitute
Cover and chapter head illustrations: Katherine Streeter
Curriculum Editor: Bill Bigelow
Proofreading: Lawrence Sanfilippo
Business Manager: Mike Trokan

Library of Congress Cataloging-in-Publication Data
Rethinking popular culture and media / edited by Elizabeth Marshall and Özlem Sensoy.
—1st ed.
      p. cm.
  Includes index.
  ISBN 978-0-942961-48-5
  1. Criticism—Study and teaching—United States.
  2. Social justice—Study and teaching—United States.
  3. Educational technology—Study and teaching (Elementary)—United States.
  4. Educational technology—Study and teaching (Secondary)—United States.
  5. Digital media.
  6. Internet in education.  I. Marshall, Elizabeth, 1968- II. Sensoy, Özlem.
      LB1027.R455 2011
      371.33—dc22
         2011000544

# Acknowledgements

We thank the editorial board of Rethinking Schools—Wayne Au, Linda Christensen, Terry Burant, Kelley Dawson Salas, Stan Karp, David Levine, Larry Miller, Bob Peterson, Stephanie Walters, and Jody Sokolower—for allowing us to compile and introduce this collection of articles. We are very honored to be "outsiders" editing a collection for Rethinking Schools. As such, we are grateful for the board's trust in us and for the generous feedback on our original proposal.

We would like to express our thanks to all of the contributing authors. Your work has greatly influenced our own teaching, and we deeply admire all of the fearless, insightful, compassionate, and critical educational insights you offer to readers.

Thank you to Katherine Streeter for the magnificent artwork on the cover as well as the illustrations throughout the book.

Many thanks to Catherine Capellaro, Mike Trokan, and Patrick Flynn for your expertise in organizing and orchestrating so many of the moving parts that are the machinery of publication. It goes without saying that we would be lost without your assistance.

Finally, we extend our profound appreciation to Bill Bigelow, without whom this project would not have been possible. The clarity and insight you bring to the struggles and possibilities of educating for a just world continue to challenge and to inspire us.◆

KATHERINE STREETER

# ◆ CONTENTS

## Part 1:
## Study the Relationship Among Corporations, Youth, and Schooling

## Part 2:
## Critique How Popular Culture and Media Frame Historical Events and Actors

## Part 3:
## Examine Race, Class, Gender, Sexuality, and Social Histories in Popular Culture and Media

## Part 4:
## View and Analyze Representations
## of Teachers, Youth, and Schools

## Part 5:
## Take Action for a Just Society

## Part 6:
## Use Popular Culture
## and Media to Transgress

# Introduction

◆ ELIZABETH MARSHALL AND ÖZLEM SENSOY

Few would disagree with the idea that good teachers ground curriculum in the lives of their students. But what happens when the lives of children and youth are thoroughly saturated by corporate influences that promote values of consumption, competition, hierarchy, sexism, homophobia, racism, and contempt for equality? What's an educator to do? *Rethinking Popular Culture and Media* seeks to answer these questions. The articles collected here, drawn from the *Rethinking Schools* archive, offer insightful analyses of popular culture and media and suggest ways to help youth and adults reflect on aspects of life that they may just take for granted—what Sut Jhally, founder of the Media Education Foundation, would describe as "getting the fish to think about the water."

KATHERINE STREETER

In many ways, popular culture is the Polaroid snapshot or Facebook photo page that documents our lives in the social world; it is a backdrop of day-to-day life. And its power is both diffuse and indisputable. From Disney to Barbie to MySpace, youth today navigate a range of popular culture and media. The reality that children and youth interact with a vast amount of media—books, toys, video games, advertisements, etc.—requires teachers to become aware of *and* fluent with the diverse popular cultural materials young people read, view, and consume.

Corporate interests and marketing activities aimed at youth are nothing new; however, young people today are the objects of a cor-

> **Popular culture is the Polaroid snapshot or Facebook photo page that documents our lives in the social world.**

porate media landscape that circulates messages with an intensity and range that is increasingly sophisticated. According to the Campaign for a Commercial-Free Childhood: "Children ages 2–11 see at least 25,000 advertisements on TV alone, a figure that does not include product placement. They are also targeted with advertising on the internet, cell phones, MP3 players, video games, school buses, and in school."[1] Similarly, a study published in 2010 by the Kaiser Family Institute reports that youth between the ages of 8 and 18 spend approximately 7.5 hours per day, seven days a week with media such as video games, TV, music, and books. It is important to note that time reading books has actually *increased* slightly rather than declined over the past 10 years—revealing some complicated connections between books and other texts.[2] And as the authors in this collection demonstrate, the relationship among pop culture, media, and corporations, more broadly, is a messy one.

Given the increasing amount of media with which youth interact, *Rethinking Popular Culture and Media* is an important collection largely written by and for teachers. The authors of these articles consider how and what popular cultural artifacts (such as toys) as well as popular media (like films and books) "teach" and the role that these materials have in the everyday lives of students.

The decision to pull together this collection came out of our own experiences in classrooms and as teacher educators. The articles in *Rethinking Schools* have framed our own work with children, youth, and adults as they offer examples that critically examine and reimagine popular culture and media in relationship to education. The articles collected here complicate the idea that popular culture is either bad or good and instead invite readers to look at familiar movies, books, games, and so on as spaces where meanings are made and contested. Authors in this collection complicate the idea that children and teens are naive, agent-less, or disengaged. Rather, children and youth in these articles are *actors* who view, read, watch, play, and often instruct their teachers about popular culture and media. Most importantly, this book illustrates that young people are capable of critical analyses that disrupt the limited representations of race, class, gender, and sexuality offered up in mainstream popular culture and media.

---

1 Campaign for a Commercial -Free Childhood. "Marketing to Children Overview." www.commercialfreechildhood.org/factsheets/overview.pdf. Retrieved 05/05/2010.

2 Rideout, V., Foehr, U. and Roberts, D. *Generation M2: Media in theLives of 8- to 18-Year -Olds.* Menlo Park, CA: Henry J. Kaiser Family Foundation, 2010.

## What Exactly Is Popular Culture?

"Popular culture" is a challenging term to define. Writing a book about popular culture is an even trickier proposition given that *culture* is constantly changing and renders what was once *popular* soon to be outdated and perhaps quaint. With this collection, we offer *an approach* to popular culture. Even though the stuff of popular culture becomes dated almost as quickly as it is produced, this book focuses on the questions educators ask and the pedagogies they use to approach popular culture and media.

**This book illustrates that young people are capable of critical analyses that disrupt the limited representations of race, class, gender, and sexuality offered up in mainstream popular culture and media.**

This book examines and takes on a variety of expressions of popular culture:[3]

- ◆ Popular culture can describe texts like Michael Jackson's *Thriller* album that are or were widely liked by many people;

- ◆ Popular culture is often used to refer to things that are less sophisticated or considered "low" culture. Adults often dismiss children's culture as innocent, crass, or dumbed down. For instance, popular series books produced for youth, such as the Nancy Drew mysteries, were not available in public library collections for decades because librarians dismissed them as popular texts that had little or no literary value;

- ◆ Popular culture is often synonymous with a consumer culture that is produced for mass consumption (Disney's animated films; McDonald's Happy Meal toys);

- ◆ Popular culture might also be defined as a place for creating new forms of expression as well as a vehicle for critique. In particular, mainstream popular culture and media offer a space where new meanings are made through tactics such as culture jamming. Culture jamming refers to the rewriting or reimagining of media such as corporate logos or advertisements in a way that subverts or overturns taken-for-granted ideas. Adbusters (www.adbusters.org provides numerous examples of this approach.

The articles in this collection help us to see the relationship between the many forms of popular culture and education.

---

3 Storey, J. *Cultural Theory and Popular Culture: An Introduction*. 3rd edition. Harlow, Essex: Pearson Education Limited, 2001.

## What Is the Relationship
## Between Popular Culture and Media?

Whereas media of previous generations may have referred to news-papers, magazines, and books, today's media include an explosion of online/global networking systems (Twitter, Facebook, Bebo, You-Tube), as well as a music culture that has moved beyond musical ex-change to include the marketing and selling of culture, lifestyle, and products. Cross-marketing between and among corporately structured partners has become the norm. Many movies (especially those target-ing young audiences) are released not simply as movies, but rather as carefully orchestrated campaigns of online, print, television promo-tions, soundtracks, clothing lines, toys, keychains—and in the case of Hannah Montana, even shoelaces and granola bars. Youth live in an in-creasingly complex world that holds potential for increasing participa-tion and citizenship via mediated culture (such as blogging and global networking) as well as increasing vulnerability to corporate maneuver-ing such as "embedded marketing." From one of the earliest examples of embedded marketing—Reese's Pieces in the 1982 blockbuster film *ET*—to more recent examples such as Coca-Cola's ongoing sponsor-ship of the Olympic Games and the "Coca Cola Olympic Flame," this increasingly sophisticated machinery demands that educators remain vigilant about the relationship between media, popular culture, and marketing.

In response to these challenges, the teachers in this collection share examples of their strategies to remain engaged. For example, in "Tuning In to Violence: Students Use Math to Analyze What TV Is Teaching Them," Margot Pepper leads her students in a data-collection activity of children's shows, after which they compile and analyze their data. Pepper's students learn the importance of noticing the pervasive-ness of particular kinds of media messages in their everyday environ-ment. Pepper writes that she wants students to be in "the habit of ask-ing 'why' about their world instead of merely consuming it—of making educated hypotheses then requiring multiple sources of supporting evidence."

### What to Do *with* Popular Culture and Media?

When we consider *youth* culture and the media that children, tweens, and teens find popular, the task of defining popular culture becomes even more difficult because as adults, we often dismiss what children and teens adopt as childish or in opposition to the "good" values of adults—as inferior to "adult" culture. Throughout this collection, read-ers are encouraged to think about popular culture and media in all its

complexity. For example, rather than simply critiquing "popular" or "kid" culture as anti-intellectual,
entertainment, or fluff to pass the time, we can ask
questions like the ones the authors in this collection
take up, including:

**When educators make the choice to critique what is "popular," whether it's Disney or Nike, they enter a high-stakes game in which power, privilege, and corporate interests are the rule.**

◆ How are youth making meaning of these popular
phenomena?

◆ What economic and political forces have helped
make a particular text, toy, film, or game popular?
How is it marketed? Where? To whom? For example, in "Why I Said
No to Coca-Cola," John Sheehan explains how his opinion about
advertising in schools shifted as his concerns about the long-term
consequences of advertising directly to students increased.

◆ How are youth *using* (revising, and/or resisting) popular culture and
media? What are the implications of this for concepts such as agency,
citizenship, and consumer action? For example, Antero Garcia
considers the importance of MySpace in the lives of his students in
his article "Rethinking MySpace." At the same time, he points out
that he finds it hard to reconcile wanting students to develop critical consciousness and connection by using a corporate-owned media
tool such as MySpace, which is owned by Rupert Murdoch's News
Corporation.

◆ How might teachers work with, and simultaneously critique, the
texts that youth find pleasurable? For example, in "*Seventeen*, Self-
Image, and Stereotypes," Bakari Chavanu guides students through
a content analysis of teen magazines, especially images of girls and
women. His goal was not to dissuade students from subscribing to
the magazines but rather to encourage the teens in his class to be
"critically conscious citizens rather than manipulated consumers."

◆ How are youth and adults using popular culture and media to
transgress or rethink their environments? In "Stenciling Dissent,"
students bring their own knowledge of street art as protest to a
class project Andrew Reed designed on the history of dissent in the
United States in which students created political graffiti that was
later displayed in the hallway of the school.

The articles in *Rethinking Popular Culture and Media* begin from the
premise that the "popular" in classrooms and in the everyday lives of
teachers and students is fundamentally political. Critiquing media is
not simply an intellectual activity but often a larger social standpoint

of resistance against corporate-produced popular culture. Steven Friedman and his students discover this in "Taking Action Against Disney"
when he and his students protested the working conditions of employees
in Central American factories that make Disney products. After Friedman published a list of "guilty companies" in the school's weekly newsletter, the school's director asked him to stop. He writes that he was told
that "by becoming a political activist, I was perilously close to muddying
my role as a neutral educator." Thus, when educators make the choice to
critique what is "popular," whether it's Disney or Nike, they enter into a
high-stakes game in which power, privilege, and corporate interests are
the rule. The articles in this collection make visible the limits and possibilities of teacher autonomy and the increasing role of corporations in
classrooms. They also highlight the challenges of facilitating dialogue
with students about the politics of popular culture and media.

## What to Do *About* Popular Culture and Media?

How can teachers resist the pedagogies and corporate interests of popular culture and media in which the social world is simplified in ways
that limit our understandings of complex social histories, identities,
and structural inequities? In Herbert Kohl's "The Politics of Children's
Literature" and Bill Bigelow's "Once upon a Genocide," we learn how
complex social histories such as segregation, genocide, and military interventions are often diluted and reorganized into simplistic plots of
good vs. evil that are common in popular culture and mainstream narratives of exceptionalism and meritocracy.

One of the key approaches to understanding the relationship between popular culture and media has been media literacy. Media literacy is a term that often comes up in educational contexts and has
several different meanings. As the *Rethinking Schools* editors point out,
teachers need to move beyond "what has come to be known as media
literacy....to delve into the tough issues that lurk underneath. In short,
these issues are commercialism and democracy." We agree that media
literacy needs to extend beyond content analyses. It should include a
critical examination of the production and circulation of media, as well
as analysis of the motivations for distribution.

The educators in this collection recognize the importance of using
and engaging with popular culture and media. We define this approach
as a *critical media literacy* approach.[4] It is increasingly hard to "protect"
children and youth from commercial messages and popular culture;

4 Kellner, D. and Share, J. "Critical Media Literacy, Democracy, and the Reconstruction of
   Education." In D. Macedo and S. R. Steinberg (Eds.), *Media Literacy: A Reader* (pp. 3-23). New
   York: Peter Lang Publishing, 2007.

these materials appear on cell phones, Facebook pages, billboards, and buses. In our view, students can become capable critics and revisers of culture who don't always need to be protected from popular culture and media.

**Teachers need to move beyond what has come to be known as media literacy to delve into the tough issues that lurk underneath. In short, these issues are commercialism and democracy.**

Writers here use a critical media perspective in which texts (including blogs, film, music, and so on) are up for critique to uncover power and commercialism as well as embedded messages. For instance, Barbara Ehrenreich critiques Disney princess products, but she also highlights how corporate power and interests obscure problematic capitalist dynamics. She writes, "Disney, which also owns ABC, Lifetime, ESPN, A&E, and Miramax, is rewarded with $4 billion a year for marketing the masochistic Princess cult and its endlessly proliferating paraphernalia."

In this and other articles collected here, teachers and students ask critical questions about the relationship between power, media, and schooling. In each of these articles the authors critique and rethink the connections among race, class, gender, sexuality, power, and schooling. From this framework, the articles in this book are grouped around five ways to do critical media literacy with popular culture and media. The articles do not fit neatly nor exclusively into each category, but the categories provide a useful organizational framework.

## Part 1:
## Study the Relationship Among Corporations, Youth, and Schooling

The line between education and big business has become increasingly blurry. The authors in this section draw our attention to the ways corporations use advertisements to sell and define what is "popular." Schools have also been targeted as a place to teach students brand loyalty through Scholastic book orders, "free" copies of *Sports Illustrated for Kids,* and corporate-sponsored curricula such as the "Feeling Good: More About You" program provided by Procter & Gamble (which includes a health instructor, "Feeling Good" girls' booklet, and sample pads and tampons all delivered in one class session). And it is not just Procter & Gamble that is out to get the "consumer in training"; it is also Colgate, Kellogg, DuPont, Anheuser-Busch, and Dow, to name just a few.

According to a Canadian national survey, many schools receive additional income by entering into exclusive product sale agreements.[5]

---

5 Hawkey, C. "Commercialization in B.C.'s Public Schools." *Teacher Newsmagazine,* 17 (6), 2005.

**This financial support from corporations rarely comes in the form of an anonymous donation; rather, teachers and students are bombarded with product placement within the school from corporations such as Coca-Cola and media conglomerates such as Fox.**

This financial support from corporations rarely comes in the form of an anonymous donation; rather, teachers and students are bombarded with product placement within the school from corporations such as Coca-Cola and media conglomerates such as Fox. In a time of ongoing school budgetary cuts, these relationships are increasingly complicated.

Corporations also seek to define the tastes of children and adolescents through how they market toys and other children's culture. Authors in this section point out how ideas created in a marketing boardroom such as "age compression" or the decision to package Disney princesses together have implications for teaching. Specifically, they question whether or not to take up these media as objects of curriculum as well as the pedagogical dilemmas that emerge when popular cultural texts enter the classroom.

### Part 2:
### Critique How Popular Culture and Media
### Frame Historical Events and Actors

Popular culture and media are an important place to critique the politics of seemingly straightforward storylines, plots, characters, and images. For many of us, popularized accounts of history are familiar. For example, *Schindler's List* is often used to teach about the Holocaust. The articles in this section examine the politics of popular historical children's literature, popularized biographies of Rosa Parks, Christopher Columbus, and Helen Keller, as well as children's films and toys.

Authors focus on the representation of history within popular children's picture books and novels, films such as Disney's *Mulan* and *Pocahontas*, and the popular American Girl dolls and books. Authors such as Debbie Reese and her colleagues point out misrepresentations in popular cultural texts such as Scholastic's "Dear America" series and the ways in which certain parts of a history are foregrounded (such as the "happiness" of Native American students in residential schools) while others remain in the background (such as the colonial legacy of genocide for indigenous peoples). In casting the government boarding schools in a positive light, popular narratives elide the effects of residential schooling on native peoples and the obligations to redress and remedy the history of colonization in North America and around the globe.

## Part 3:
## Examine Race, Class, Gender, Sexuality, and Social Histories in Popular Culture and Media

Popular culture and media relentlessly reproduce existing relationships between dominant and subordinate groups. In this way, culture produced for mass consumption seeks to erase difference and make certain sexist, racist, classist, and colonial representations seem natural. Because much of this representation is widely circulated as normal and natural, the authors in this section attempt to make visible the ideas about race, class, and gender that masquerade as authoritative and fixed. Authors challenge gender stereotypes and racist representations in various media locales such as music videos, movies, toys, and cartoons and connect these discussions to existing curricular goals. Contributors also offer a variety of strategies, including sending students on a toy store field trip, giving students surveys, and offering content analysis of popular texts, and guiding discussion questions. By sharing strategies and explanations for how this work occurs with students, the authors in this section do not simply uncover bias; they also illustrate how this type of work can occur with students as they model the kinds of critical engagements that can be taken up in classrooms.

> **Culture produced for mass consumption seeks to erase difference and make certain sexist, racist, classist, and colonial representations seem natural.**

## Part 4:
## View and Analyze Representations of Teachers, Youth, and Schools

From *Blackboard Jungle* to *Freedom Writers* to *High School Musical* and *Glee*, teachers and students are regular subjects of film and TV. These texts capture our shifting anxieties about adult/child relationships and about the desires we hold for teachers to "save" students. These are familiar stories in which a caring—usually white—teacher saves students in an under-resourced school. Kids in popular film and television are usually presented as uncivilized, uneducated, and in need of adult protection. The critiques offered in this section are important because they draw our attention to the political nature of schooling as a place of ideological struggle.

## Part 5:
## Take Action for a Just Society

Popular culture and media present an opportunity for teachers and students to take action in and beyond the classroom. In this section, authors describe the ways that teachers and students resist corporate

**In the articles collected here authors use a range of media—poetry, graffiti, film, and anime—to teach about and encourage resistance.**

incursions into everyday life as well as how educators might use popular culture and media to examine issues such as exploitation, violence, power, and privilege. One of the most interesting examples is Ann Pelo and Kendra Pelojoaquin's "Why We Banned Legos" and the resulting backlash their article received from Fox News and other right-wing outlets. The authors begin with the assumption that even young children are "political" and that they, too, can understand and question inequity. Their story illustrates how doing critical media literacy from a social justice orientation often aligns with "being political," but in reality it draws attention to the false neutrality of schooling. As such, the best "defense" is to anchor resistance work in a strong theoretical and conceptual framework. We believe that this collection offers such a grounding for any critical media literacy and resistance work teachers may want to take up in their classrooms.

### Part 6:
### Use Popular Culture and Media to Transgress

In this section, the authors examine how popular culture and media provide the space and materials to break the rules and challenge the status quo. Media such as zines, fan fiction, blogs, graffiti, and so on offer avenues to represent transgressive ideas and identities. To provide just one example, on fan fiction sites authors, illustrators, and filmmakers revise familiar storylines and images from popular cultural texts.

In the articles collected here authors use a range of media—poetry, graffiti, film, and anime—to teach about and encourage resistance. Renée Watson uses poetry with a group of middle school students to explore the realities of racism and police brutality in the Bronx. Watson reminds readers that "for centuries poets and writers have put ink to paper to celebrate, encourage, heal, challenge, teach, and even chastise their world." She introduces students to Willie Perdomo's "41 Bullets off Broadway" about Amadou Diallo, a 23-year-old Guinean immigrant, who in 1999 was shot 19 times when police fired 41 bullets at him. Watson ties this to the contemporary 2006 murder of African American Sean Bell, a 23-year-old; police shot 50 bullets at the unarmed Bell and his two friends. The middle school students create their own poems about Sean Bell that put to paper the marginalized perspectives and experiences of kids of color as they are consistently targeted by law enforcement.

## Conclusion

Popular culture, then, is also a way for adults, children, and teens to reposition themselves, from cogs in the machine to social actors intent on jamming, resisting, and/or rewriting the status quo. In this way, the authors give us examples of a critical media literacy in which critique makes way for revision and protest and where students and teachers have access to and power over the everyday media we consume, read, and view.

While corporations have quickly jumped to the blackboard to school youth in lessons of consumption, in many ways educators have been playing catch-up. The realities of the classroom and school politics—not to mention the spotlight on standardized testing that often results in more heat than light—make doing critical media literacy work challenging. We believe this collection of essays offers strong conceptual critiques and relevant pedagogical strategies for educators at every level to engage with the popular. ◆

# Part 1:
# Study the Relationship Among Corporations, Youth, and Schooling

KATHERINE STREETER

# Moving Beyond Media Literacy

◆ THE EDITORS OF RETHINKING SCHOOLS

The press reports regularly on mergers or buyouts of one media/telecommunications company or another. Educators, like many people, often pay little attention to such stories. Their concern is focused on the more obvious manifestations of media influence, such as infestations of Pokémon cards or infatuations with the newest video game.

Yet what happens at the top of corporate media, that is, who controls our media, directly influences the lives of students and classrooms. Concern needs to move beyond what has come to be known as "media literacy." We need to delve into the tough issues that lurk underneath. In short, those issues are commercialism and democracy.

The defining reality about the media is that the tremendous power of communications technology—from radio to the internet—has been placed in corporate hands for commercial purposes and private profit. Even where substantial public resources (e.g., the airwaves, the academic/governmental creation of the internet) were indispensable to the development of media networks, corporate power has been allowed to subjugate the networks so as to serve corporate ends.

## Commercialism

Commercialism increasingly infects every public (and "private") space, making the values of the market the dominant criteria by which everything is judged. The new corporate media giants play a central role in this "hypercommercialism." A movie is no longer just a movie—but an international corporate campaign that shapes the consciousness of hundreds of millions of people. Toy figurines are "given" away at the local fast-food place, glowing "reviews" of the movie are broadcast over TV networks owned by the corporation that produced the movie, and a plethora of paraphernalia hits the market, from trading cards to interactive video games.

The amount spent on the promotion of products ranges into the billions. According to Robin Templeton, former program director of the anticommercialism group UNPLUG, "A greater proportion of the GNP is spent on advertising than on education." Schools, once relatively free of overt advertising influence but now increasingly deprived

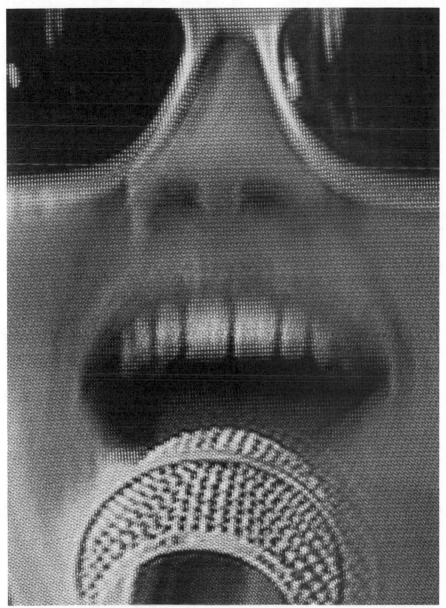

JOSEPH BLOUGH

of resources, find it necessary to flash brand names and logos in front of students on everything from commercially produced curriculum to field house scoreboards.

Behind such commercialism stand deeper issues of private profit and corporate control—the driving forces of economic and social life. School-based activities, such as annual No-TV weeks, are important beginnings. But ultimately, critical media literacy

**The tools of social dialogue and mass communication are too important to be privately deformed in order to better sell deodorant or $100 Nike shoes (not to mention selling presidents).**

has to question the values and social structures that lead media to serve private profit rather than public interest.

## Democracy

In his book *Rich Media, Poor Democracy,* media scholar Robert McChesney writes that the concentration of a few global media empires among a tiny number of people threatens the very notion of informed public discourse and participatory democracy. A media system forced to serve consumption and profit is not compatible with an informed citizenry. Complementing this is an electoral system that also serves private interests. The same 1 percent of the U.S. population that owns 40 percent of U.S. wealth has a similarly disproportionate influence on the electoral process. McChesney puts it this way: "The corporate media cement a system whereby the wealthy and powerful few make the most important decisions with virtually no informed public participation."

The tools of social dialogue and mass communication are too important to be privately deformed in order to better sell deodorant or $100 Nike shoes (not to mention selling presidents). At a minimum, a public/educational sector of media should exist free of profit interests and substantially supported by the government so that democratic debate could exist independently of corporate power. Unfortunately, given cutbacks in public funding of public radio and television, the opposite is happening.

Educators have a particular responsibility to take up media issues. We see the impact of the media on young minds. We know the potential of quality dialogue and study in schools free of commercial influence. We understand the threat that public institutions—such as public schools and public television and radio—now face from profiteers and free market ideologues.

Addressing the various topics surrounding media and corporate power is not easy. Yet given their importance, we have no choice. ◆

# Why I Said No to Coca-Cola

◆ JOHN SHEEHAN

In the late 1990s, a consortium of three Colorado school districts approved one of the most lucrative beverage contracts in the nation at that time. The vote on the 10-year, $27.7 million pact with Coca-Cola was unanimous—almost. I was the only one of the consortium's 17 board members to vote against it.

Why was I opposed? The reasons are not simple, and indeed, the issue is not a simple one. I started out relatively supportive of the use of advertising in schools, as long as it was done "judiciously." But gradually, I changed my opinion. Now I can no longer accept the notion of our schools becoming brokers for advertising space or, worse yet, middlemen in the merchandising of products directly to our students. It is better, in my opinion, to walk away from the short-term opportunity for money than to open our schools to the long-term consequences that come with the dollars. I list my concerns below.

**Public schools should be a respite from the constant onslaught of advertisers. And there is no such thing as opening the floodgates just a little bit.**

## Education and Marketing Are Like Oil and Water

Public education has an agenda that is already crowded enough. When we become marketers and distributors, we confuse our mission. I worry about a time when our educational goals might be influenced or even set by private companies targeting our students with their own narrow messages. And before you think I am simply being paranoid, consider some of the advertisements from companies that already specialize in marketing to students in schools. "School is . . . the ideal time to influence attitudes, build long-term loyalties, introduce new products, test-market, promote sampling and trial usage, and—above all—to generate immediate sales," says an ad for clients of Lifetime Learning Systems. "Reach him in the office," an ad for Modern Talking Picture Service Inc. says, above a photo of a 5-year-old Asian American boy dressed in a three-piece suit and armed with a briefcase, "His first day job is kindergarten . . . . If he's in your target market, call us." How long will it be before these messages become our message?

## We Are Opening the Floodgates of Consumerism

We have all become inured to the constant barrage of advertising, but for me, consumerism is a real problem. The pressure to buy and measure our success in life through the things we acquire is overwhelming. Education should offer a way for students to seek a good life that means more than just wealth. It saddens me to see our schools become part of this marketing machinery. Public schools should be a respite from the constant onslaught of advertisers. And there is no such thing as opening the floodgates just a little bit. The driving force behind the marketing machine is immense. Once in the door, businesses will be ceaseless in their efforts to gain more ground. In our high schools, Coca-Cola has already won the opportunity to put 20 Coke machines in each building. Our contract with the company alludes to the idea that Coke sales in the lunchroom could become a reality if the U.S. Department of Agriculture were to sanction Coke products within the federal lunch program.

## Businesses Are Targeting a Captive Audience

There is something unethical, in my opinion, about viewing our captive audience of students as targets for current and future marketing efforts. These students are captive only because our schools have been entrusted with the responsibility of educating them. Taking financial advantage of this unique situation is a breach of that trust.

## Letting Our Legislators and the Public Off the Hook

Yes, schools need money, but turning to commercial sales for income is a cop-out. It sends the message to our voters and legislators that we can let them off the hook—that advertising and sales of consumer products can fill the gap when it comes to supporting education. My state ranks pitifully low in funding for public schools, but when we sign up with corporate giants like Coke, we are sending the message that a multimillion-dollar market is ours for the taking. What incentive is there for our legislators to rethink their priorities? Most of the decisions school boards make are not grand decisions that have a huge and immediate impact; they are incremental. The decision to sign a contract with Coca-Cola is also incremental. Today, we feel reasonably safeguarded from abuses in advertising and sales. But let's put things in context. I have already heard from our administration that this decision is no big deal because schools already sell soda. Some 20 years ago or so, an administrator decided to put a vending machine in the building to raise a little loose change. Do you suppose anyone saw that decision as the harbinger of a multimillion-dollar marketing arrangement among three major Colorado school districts and Coca-Cola? I doubt it. And I can't imagine what things might look like 20 years from now. ◆

---

*John Sheehan is the former vice president of the school board of Douglas County, Colorado. Reprinted with permission from the* American School Board Journal, *October 1999.* © *National School Boards Association.*

# Coping with TV

## *Some lesson ideas*

◆ BOB PETERSON

"One thousand and ninety-five hours!" Elizabeth shook her head in disbelief as she announced to the class the amount of time she would "have for herself" each year if she reduced her TV watching from five to two hours a day.

"That's over 45 days of time!" added Dennis, as he quickly figured it out on the calculator. The class brainstormed what a kid could do with that much time—learn to juggle or to play a musical instrument, read scores of books, write his or her own book, get good at a sport. Of course, several in the class proudly proclaimed that if they had that much extra time, they'd do what they liked best to do—watch TV.

For years I chose to ignore TV, on the one hand blaming it for many of my students' problems, but on the other feeling it was beyond my control. Yet I came to realize that because of TV's negative impact on children, we must teach children how to cope with television. At La Escuela Fratney, the kindergarten through 5th grade school where I teach, the staff decided to tackle the problem head-on and sponsor an annual No-TV Week. Our goal was not only to decrease the amount of TV students watch, but also to increase their skills in critically analyzing television and other media.

## Limiting the Habit

Students need to recognize that TV watching can develop into an addiction. Students often are familiar with the word "addiction" and link it to drugs. The anti-TV addiction commercials available on video from the activist group Adbusters are useful for sparking discussion of TV addiction (see resources). The commercials show entranced children watching television, and explain how the children are addicted. In follow-up discussions, students can explore the meaning of addiction, different types, and how people overcome their addictions.

Statistics can be helpful. According to Nielsen Inc., children watch on average about 24 to 28 hours of television per week. The average 5-year-old will have spent 5,000 hours in front of the TV before entering kindergarten, more time than he or she will spend in conversation with his or her parents for the rest of their lives and longer than it would take to get a college degree.

Part of Fratney's success at reducing kids' TV watching was because we worked closely with our students' families. No-TV Week is not aimed just at students and staff but also at family members. During the week, everyone—staff, students, and family members—are asked to voluntarily pledge not to watch TV.

To prepare students for the week, teachers try to raise the students' awareness of how much time they spend watching television. Students keep a weeklong log of the TV they watch, including the names and times of the programs.

Some of the teachers then have each child tabulate the number of hours they watched TV, making comparisons and reflecting on the differences. Some classes rank their favorite shows

HENRIK DRESCHER

and discuss why they are popular. For older students, the No-TV Week can be tied to math lessons. The students figure out the average hours of TV watched daily, weekly, annually, or from the time they were 5 years old to age 18.

Some classes prepare "No-TV Week Survival Kits" with alternative home activities such as playing games, going on a bicycle ride, making cookies, or reading a book. One year my class coordinated a schoolwide campaign to come up with 500 things to do instead of watching TV. Another year my 5th

**How are problems solved? Who does most of the talking? What race, gender, and age are the characters on the shows —or commercials? How many instances of violence does one observe? How many put-downs are there?**

**"There always are pretty ladies next to new cars. It must be so men come in to look at them."**

graders went to each class and surveyed the students about the types of media/communication devices in their homes—from TVs to computers, from phones to video games. They tallied the data, figured out the percentages, and made bar graphs to display the survey's results.

Because many children have difficulty conceptualizing "life before TV," I have children interview a family member or friend who grew up without television. Questions include: How did your life change after you got a television set? What did you do instead of watching TV?

Parent response to No-TV Week has ranged from wildly enthusiastic, to highly supportive, to nonchalant. Although most of the families fall in the middle, there are a number who tell wonderful stories about how the week forced them to reconsider their television habits. One parent, for example, explained how previously her family had always watched TV during dinner. Although she didn't like the habit, she wasn't sure how to change it. After the No-TV Week, she said, she felt confident enough to ban the television during dinner and call for family conversation instead. Another parent said that after the week, she started a practice of telling her kids at breakfast several times a week that it would be a No-TV Day. A third parent said her children even ask for No-TV evenings because they like to play games with Mom and Dad.

## Critique

After the first No-TV week, parents suggested we put more emphasis on helping children critique and analyze television. They were concerned not only about the shows but also about the commercials.

The teachers started by focusing on commercials. On the average, children see 20,000 TV commercials a year—more than 350,000 by the time they are 18, according to Action for Children's Television. One of my homework assignments asks students to "Add up the Ads" and to keep track of all the TV ads they see in one night—both the number and the minutes. This gives the children an understanding of how commercials saturate our lives and gets them to begin thinking how the television industry rests on advertising dollars.

For one lesson plan on commercials, teachers recorded certain commercials and later watched them with their students. Teachers posed the question "What messages are sent by the commercial and why?" They also explained the difference between implicit and explicit messages. After watching and discussing various commercials, students wrote about the ads' explicit and implicit messages. As Maria noted,

"You seem to be always happy if you eat that cereal." John concluded: "There always are pretty ladies next to new cars. It must be so men come in to look at them."

TV shows can be critiqued in the same way. I have recorded segments of cartoons and sitcoms to show in class. We analyze the messages and ask: How are problems solved? Who does most of the talking? What race, gender, and age are the characters on the shows or commercials? How many instances of violence does one observe? How many put-downs are there? As a follow-up homework assignment, students interview a family member about the positive and negative messages of TV shows. One parent answered, "Children tend to believe that violence is the way to solve problems, like in violent TV shows." Another responded, "TV has a bad effect because it absorbs much of the brain."

How much of our kids' brains TV will "absorb" is an open question. But media literacy projects like our No-TV Week present the question for discussion and allow collective reflection on one of the most powerful influences on our children's lives. ◆

*Bob Peterson teaches at La Escuela Fratney in Milwaukee and is an editor of* Rethinking Schools *magazine.*

## No-TV Resources

**www.tvturnoff.org**
This nonprofit organization promotes the national TV Turnoff Week each April and September. Includes quotations, statistics, and teaching ideas.

**www.whitedot.org**
A thoughtful collection of articles about TV and its effect on children.

**www.adbusters.org**
Produces an excellent print magazine and the DVD *The Production of Meaning,* which includes startling "commercials" about TV addiction and overconsumption. Also sponsors a "digital detox" week.

# Seventeen, Self-Image, and Stereotypes

◆ BAKARI CHAVANU

Silently reading an article about the images of women in advertising, one of my 11th-grade female students looked up and snarled: "This media literacy stuff is making me mad. Now when I open my copy of *Seventeen* magazine, I can't look at it in the same way. I just renewed my subscription to it and now I can hardly stand it."

I smiled and sympathized with what it meant to have her illusions of something shattered, but I honestly felt a little proud of the positive impact my advertising unit was having on my students.

Many of my students are walking advertisements and consumers of media. They purchase T-shirts, hats, and backpacks embossed with the ubiquitous Nike swoosh. They sport images of their favorite heavy metal bands and sports teams. They enter class talking of the latest episode of *Dawson's Creek*. Typically, they will have accumulated 22,000 hours of television viewing by the time they graduate from high school, which is twice the amount of time they will have spent in school. They will have seen 350,000 television commercials by the age of 17.

We may not admit it, but our students are often more influenced by the popular media outside our classrooms than they are by the novels and textbooks we often must bribe them to read. Thus, media literacy can play a necessary role in helping our students become critically literate and reactive to the powerful influence of television, video games, commercial advertising, popular magazines, and movies.

## The Role of Commercial Advertising

As part of my 11th-grade class, I did a media literacy unit on advertising. The purpose of the unit was to help students consider more critically the role and influence of media, particularly the pervasive and intrusive nature of advertising, and how it conveys certain values, messages, and ideas that often perpetuate sexist, racist, and pro-capitalist points of view.

The unit took seven weeks, covering topics from the image of women in advertising to what the Center for Media Literacy calls the "Myths of the Image Culture" (for example: "your body is not good

THE FLYNSTITUTE

enough" and "the 'good life' consists of things that require lots of money"). In this article, I want to outline my general orientation and to focus in particular on how we analyzed the images of women in advertising.

To begin the unit, I surveyed the students about their media interests and habits. Then, using the resource "What's Wrong with Advertising?" (see page 27), the students developed and performed satirical skits. One group of girls, for example, did a "commercial" about trendy and expensive tennis shoes, showing how advertising tells us that you're not cool unless you wear certain articles of clothing. A racially mixed group of students did a skit about rap videos, showing how advertising perpetuates racial (African Americans as musicians and athletes), gender (women as sex objects, men as businesspeople), and class (middle-class whites as social norm) stereotypes.

**Sadly, these images are part of a culture in which one out of five women has a serious eating disorder such as anorexia; where adolescent girls increasingly have problems with low self-esteem; and where blacks, especially women, have historically had serious problems and prejudices concerning the lightness and darkness of their skin.**

**Ads will have you believe that no one is disabled and everyone is heterosexual; that a woman's body is in constant need of improvement; that women need to look young, "beautiful," made up, sprayed up, very thin, and perfectly groomed.**

After one or two skits were performed each day, I presented a few commercials I recorded. We watched and critiqued television commercials, speculating on how they were constructed, what messages they conveyed, and what various techniques advertisers used to sell products. For instance, a frozen food product commercial opens with a black-and-white shot of frozen fish sticks on a cooking pan. With no music to accompany this shot, viewers are asked if they would rather have the "usual frozen food" or would they rather have a "real meal"? We next get a colorful shot accompanied with alluring music of a steamy hot Swanson beef and vegetable dinner—"a real meal." I presented this commercial a second time without sound and asked students to identify what they saw and noticed about the editing. I replayed the ad again with sound only so students could notice the role music and voice-over narration plays in advertising.

After a moment of silent reflection, one of my students, China, spouted: "Shoot, there's no real difference between the two products. One's no better than the other. They both are frozen foods." Other students chimed in: "A real meal is not a frozen dinner!"

"How do they try to convince you that the foods are different?" I asked.

"Through the editing and the upbeat sound," one student responded. Because this critique of media was new to many students, they were reluctant to admit advertising's influence on their own values and decisions as consumers. So when one student boasted that the media had no influence on him, I spontaneously asked the students to name their favorite cars. They had no problem spouting off the makes and models. Then I asked them to consider how they knew the best cars when most of them hadn't even driven those cars. They had to admit they knew of the cars because they were advertised in many of the commercials and magazines they encountered on a daily basis.

## Images of Women

This preliminary analysis of commercials helped prepare students for a presentation of Jean Kilbourne's classic work *Killing Us Softly 4: Advertising's Images of Women*. I had shown this video in past years as part of my women in literature and society unit. But watching it as part of a media unit, students were better able to comprehend Kilbourne's analysis.

*Killing Us Softly* is an engaging and even humorous analysis of how images and ads shape our values. Ads, Kilbourne points out, not only

# What's Wrong with Advertising?

Ads lie about the quality of products and services by touting benefits and hiding drawbacks.

Advertising may encourage materialism, greed, and selfishness. That, in turn, may make people less supportive of spending for critical social needs such as schools and healthcare.

Ads encourage a brand-name mentality: buying on the basis of the maker rather than the quality or price of the product.

Advertising may encourage people to care more about their own and others' appearances than about the character, talents, and personalities.

Advertising fosters dissatisfaction, envy, and insecurity.

Advertising projects unrealistic images of our society: You're not cool unless you drive an expensive car; to be an adult means drinking alcohol.

Corporate sponsorship may undermine objectivity and influence the content of exhibits at science and art museums.

Advertising promotes alcohol and tobacco addictions, which kill half a million people in the United States annually.

Advertising perverts our culture by turning every event into a sales event. Examples include the Federal Express Orange Bowl and the Macy's Thanksgiving Parade, with Disney character floats.

Commercial messages and corporate logos degrade the dignity of government agencies, museums, and "noncommercial" radio and TV stations.

Advertising steals our time. The average person in the United States will spend almost three or more years of his or her waking life just watching television commercials.

Advertising implies that there is an easy solution to everything, from having friends to being healthy.

Ubiquitous advertising—on billboards, in the sky, and on the phone—means that we can hardly ever escape the annoyance of commercial messages.

Advertising materials in schools undermine objective education.

Ads increase the prices of many products—both because of the cost of the ads and the higher-value image that the ads cultivate.

---

*Excerpt from:* Marketing Madness, *by Michael F. Jacobson and Laurie Ann Mazur (1995).*

sell products; they also sell ideas about romance, sex, success, beauty, and power. Ads, she says, "will have you believe that women in the real world are all white and under 40; that no one is disabled and everyone is heterosexual; that a woman's body is in constant need of improvement; that women need to look young, 'beautiful,' made up, sprayed up, very thin, and perfectly groomed."

Sadly, these images are part of a culture in which one out of five women has a serious eating disorder such as anorexia; where adolescent girls increasingly have problems with low self-esteem; and where blacks, especially women, have historically had serious problems and prejudices concerning the lightness and darkness of their skin. If I had had more time, I would have shown students Kathe Sandler's work *A Question of Color*, which examines color prejudice in and outside African-descended communities. Sandler shows how this prejudice is significantly shaped by media presentations of beautiful white women and light-skinned women of color who usually must have the features of white models.

Because some of the material was new to them, I had students watch *Killing Us Softly* without taking notes. I wanted to make sure they could give it their undivided attention. The next day, I presented students with a page of typed notes from Kilbourne's presentation and we discussed the notes. Then students broke into groups and looked through magazines they had brought to class, tearing out images that illustrated the arguments Kilbourne makes in her presentation.

As students, especially the young women, presented the magazine ads, they talked of how no one they knew could possibly acquire the physical appearance of the models. And they began to articulate how women, and even men, are sexualized in the ads in order to sell products.

During one presentation, one male student leaned back in his chair and complained: "I think this stuff is going a little too far. I don't look at women's magazines, so how can I be influenced by them?" Looking over at him at his desk, I responded: "Well, think about what it means to have that magazine picture of model Tyra Banks [in an alluring bathing suit] on the front of your notebook." When he smiled back, I asked him and his classmates to consider how such images might influence their idea of beauty or the type of girls or guys they might choose to date. I further reminded them that advertisers don't want potential consumers thinking critically about what is flashed at them on television or what is shown to them in magazines and on billboards. It's important that these corporate commercial images are received as a common, unquestioned part of culture. Finally, I asked them why companies would spend billions of advertising dollars if they have no effect on the buying habits and values of consumers?

To reinforce Kilbourne's analysis, I used another activity I found on the Media Literacy Clearinghouse website. This activity has students critically examine *Seventeen* magazine.

First students read an article, "How *Seventeen* Undermines Young Women," by Kimberly Phillips, published in the January 1993 *Extra!*, a bimonthly magazine published by the media watch group FAIR (available at www. fair.org/index.php?page=1560). Students were asked to investigate Phillips' claim that *Seventeen* "reinforces the cultural expectations that an adolescent woman should be more concerned with her appearance, her relations with other people, and her ability to win approval from men than with her own ideas or her expectations for herself." Since most students are familiar with this publication, and some girls subscribe to it, the unit had particular relevance.

I then gave a single copy of *Seventeen* or a similar publication, such as *YM* (*Young and Modern*), to groups of four or five. Next, I gave the groups two survey sheets asking them to conduct a page count of the number of advertisements, articles, quizzes, celebrity profiles of males and females, makeup tricks and techniques, beauty features, and fashion pieces found in the magazine. Next, they were to list the theme or focus of these items.

As students flipped through pages, heads popped up and some squirmed in their seats. Sample comments included: "You can hardly find the articles in this magazine."

"Mr. Chavanu, there's an ad on almost every page of this magazine." I had to remind students to use the table of contents to find the articles buried in the publication. Almost every group had to ask me if at least one or more items in *Seventeen* was an ad or an article. It was often difficult to tell the difference.

Typical student responses to this activity included:

> I think this survey is good for women because it will help them to see these magazines are not good at boosting one's self-image. I stopped reading them because I could never be what they expected me to be.

> Well, I now realize that young girl magazines only focus on looks, and not on being smart or achieving your goals. [They] never mention schooling or jobs—just malls and cosmetics.

**Although I don't necessarily want my students to cancel their subscriptions to *Seventeen*, I do want them to see themselves as critically conscious citizens rather than manipulated consumers.**

> This survey was a waste because I already know how "us teenagers" are portrayed and should supposedly be or act.

This latter response is important because it reflects how not all students were comfortable with these insights. Clearly, the unit had challenged their assumptions and caused them to question their own sense of identity.

On the other hand, some students were already critical of how the media stereotypes groups of people. I challenged them to think more deeply about the implications of certain media representations in influencing not only buying habits, but also the ways they give support to a capitalist economy in which a small sector of rich people make huge profits off an unsuspecting consumer class.

These last two activities on women in advertising would later be tied to a couple of the essay-writing projects students could choose from as part of the media unit. One project, for instance, required students to research and write an essay in which they compared *Seventeen* with one or more noncommercial magazines, both by and for girls. This assignment led one student to do a class reading from her journal about her statistical analysis, which showed that *Seventeen* lacked the racial diversity found in *Vibe*, another popular teen magazine.

Although I don't necessarily want my students to cancel their subscriptions to *Seventeen*, I do want them to see themselves as critically conscious citizens rather than manipulated consumers. And, at least with a few of my students, I know I succeeded. As my student Alicia Seibel wrote in her essay: "Throughout the last 30 years, teenage girls have depended on magazines like *Seventeen* to help through times of need, but I've realized that the magazine doesn't do a good enough job. It lowers the self-esteem of teens and makes them think they aren't good enough."◆

---

*Bakari Chavanu is a freelance writer and photographer. He taught high school English for 12 years, including a course in popular culture and media.*

## Resources

**The Colour of Beauty**
Documentary film by Elizabeth St. Philip (NFB, 2010). Available online at http://www.nfb.ca/film/colour_of_beauty

**Western Eyes**
Documentary film by Ann Shin (NFB, 2000). Available online at www.nfb.ca/film/western-eyes

**Killing Us Softly 4: Advertising's Image of Women**
Documentary film featuring Jean Kilbourne (Media Education Foundation, 2010).

**A Question of Color**
Documentary film by Kathe Sandler, St. Clair Bourne, and Luke Harris (California Newsreel, 1993).

# Rethinking MySpace

*Using social networking tools
to connect with students*

◆ ANTERO GARCIA

The time stamp on my email program shows that the last MySpace message I received was Wednesday, 3:08 a.m., during my off-track vacation. Logging on to the site, I read the message that apparently could not wait to be sent until a more humane hour: "hey garcia, i was wondering if u could tell me what work im missing from both of ur classes so i can make it up during these days . . . and since i will be taking some interssesion classes i was wondering if u are ever going during vacation to school so i could give it to u."

ERIC HANSON

Preparing to reply to the email, I paused and wondered if being able to connect with students at all hours is really a part of a culturally relevant education experience.

I am in my third year at Manual Arts High School, a year-round school in South Central Los Angeles. Blocks away from the freeway and the University of Southern California, Manual Arts is in a low-income community; African Americans make up 20 percent of the student body, the remaining 80 percent is Latino. In order to deal with overcrowding, the students are separated into three different tracks. Although I've never been interested in the social and networking sites that now flood the internet, sites such as MySpace, Facebook, and Twitter have become too prominent in my students' lives to ignore. As an educator constantly searching for ways to use popular culture in my

**I hope to sway students to use MySpace to spread messages and bulletins to fellow schoolmates— to take "ownership" of the mass media and to use MySpace to create a difference in the school atmosphere.**

classroom, I decided to make MySpace part of my teaching repertoire.

At the heart of MySpace is its ability to connect individuals into a greater social web. Initially, I had envisioned my page to be a place to post assignments, suggest discussion questions, and respond to student questions. Today, I've come to use the site for much more, whether communicating with students or tracking down those who may be habitually absent. Several former students have contacted me through the page; one invited me to one of her concerts. One student had me walk her step-by-step through the online SAT registration—one MySpace message at a time—and I've even been invited to a quinceañera via MySpace.

More interestingly, students have contacted me as a way of circumscribing the bureaucracy of an overcrowded school. Several have used the site for me to help them inquire about fee waivers for college admissions tests and college applications. Though such information is available at our school's college center, traveling to campus while our track is on vacation and talking one's way past the security guard at the front door is not easy. Although the site was supposed to be purely an outside resource, it's become intertwined with the daily welfare of my students as they negotiate the school environment.

There are currently more than 100 million accounts registered at MySpace. Yet going to the main page is an underwhelming experience for the uninitiated user. I didn't see the appeal of the myriad ads on the site for bands and films, or of the list with small photos of recently registered users. Only in accessing a member's page did the site start to make sense.

Each member's page can be customized. It has a space to upload pictures or maintain a blog, and it allows visitors to leave comments and send messages.

Most of my students spend time tweaking their individual MySpace pages, perhaps to play popular songs or customize their page's appearance. Much like a pair of sneakers or the logo bejeweled on one's belt, a student's MySpace page is a reflection of his or her personality. In addition, students' status within the school community can be measured in terms of how many "friends" are connected to a given user; while my account struggled to attract a couple dozen initial friends, many of my students boast of hundreds of "friends."

MySpace does not function in lieu of activities that occur at school. Being able to contact students in a manner that they are comfortable with helps encourage classroom participation. Two frequent users, for instance, are chronically absent at school and often ask for the assignments missed. In addition, students who are often most reticent to speak in class are much more vocal through the online messaging format. Because of MySpace, difficult-to-reach students seek out advice, explain extenuating circumstances behind absences, and generally find a way to participate in the class curriculum—all outside of the school.

In creating the MySpace page for my classes, I initially found that students were hesitant to send "friend requests," which allowed them to be connected to my site. The dilemma, apparently, was that I might pry into a student's page, and perhaps learn about activities that would not be endorsed in an English class. I've spoken with a colleague who also uses MySpace with her students. She occasionally peruses her students' profiles to make sure they are staying out of trouble and are doing OK outside the classroom. Although I understand her concerns, I started this site at the beginning of the year, when I was still gaining the trust of my students. Because of this, I told students that I would refrain from perusing their sites. I will send messages to students who I know are receptive to getting online messages, but I do not look at, scrutinize, or judge the content on my students' pages.

In addition, as an English teacher, I have a feeling that some students are reluctant to use the messaging feature that is an integral part of MySpace. Some students resort to a minimalist form of letter writing when asking me a question: "Garcia, what is the homework?" or "How do I register for the SAT?" Some students adopt typical online conventions and jargon; their messages are rife with smiley symbols, nonstandard English spelling, and random words and letters capitalized. I have yet to interfere with students' online writing style. As a developing teacher, I am unsure if students' messaging vernacular is something I should be concerned about. After all, these students are writing outside of the classroom, which is never a bad thing. Further, in working with my seniors on résumés, cover letters, and interview techniques, I am confident that they are becoming proficient in using the most appropriate language for the setting. While spelling and grammar are issues that need to be honed and improved within the classroom, the word choice and format of students' messages suggest that students are actively questioning the tone and audience to whom their messages are addressed.

The use of MySpace is not without controversy. The increased attention from shows like the "To Catch a Predator" series on NBC's *Dateline*, along with general wariness about personal contact with students, often causes other teachers and friends to raise an eyebrow when we discuss the site. In my opinion, this site allows students to more easily contact me with class questions and to have a wealth of resources at their fingertips; however, others may see it as crossing a legitimate line between students and teachers. This is one reason why, from my syllabus to the first Back-to-School Night, I've made parents aware of the MySpace page and have invited them to contact me with any questions or concerns.

Though many of my students do not have computers or regular internet access at home, they have demonstrated an amazing resourcefulness in being able to regularly send messages and update their MySpace pages. These students know how to get around the school's blocking program to access MySpace while at school. They also go to the local library, or to friends' houses. In not expecting my students to have computers, my students are also not expected to have or excel in the same kinds of computer literacy skills taught in other schools. For me, this is a class issue; MySpace is a way to cross one of the many barriers between my students and an equal, fair education. In addition, while I could simply create an official, school-associated website for my students, the use of MySpace is an endorsement of youth culture. My students can identify with and easily navigate the site. A school website, though it could convey the same information as the MySpace page, would likely receive less traffic due to the stifling formality associated with a school-sanctioned site.

Nonetheless, I find it hard to reconcile that I'm using the services of a Fox-owned company. (Rupert Murdoch's News Corporation bought MySpace in 2005 for just over $500 million.) I struggle with the contradiction of wanting my students to develop a critical consciousness about wealth and power in the world—and to resist injustice—at the same time that I use the corporate-owned media tools that appeal to my school's community.

Although I regularly update homework and class assignments on my page, I have also begun placing information for upcoming activities that I think would interest my students. Unsure whether students were actually looking at the information on my site, I was pleasantly surprised when one of my students returned from our two-month break and said she went to hear Luis Rodriguez speak at a local book festival. Later, another student expressed interest in an event I had mentioned on the site, about the street artist Banksy. This was one of the first steps in using the page to extend my English class outside of the traditional classroom, and I continue to search for ways to use my MySpace site beyond a resource for homework and classwork postings.

A culminating 12th-grade English project looms on the horizon as a means to integrate the site into my curriculum. While collaborating with the students' government teacher to look at medical and social epidemics, we've asked students to create a positive "social epidemic" on our school's campus. For most students, the assignment is daunting. Successfully completing it involves spreading an idea or belief to as many students as possible. I hope to sway students to use MySpace to spread messages and bulletins to fellow schoolmates—to take "ownership" of the mass media and to use MySpace to create a difference in the school atmosphere.

**"i get it" was one of those moments that, as a new teacher, I cling to and strive for.**

And that student who sent me a MySpace message at 3:08 a.m.? After lengthy message exchanges, I still felt unsure whether I was getting through to him, and I worried that MySpace might actually be hurting my ability to communicate with students. However, a week after I'd sent a final, lengthy message, I received a reply: "GARCIA!!! I am so sorry for not answering before, really i didnt want to leave u without an answer . . . but i couldnt send messages nor read them . . . i also wanted to leave u a message in ur voice mail but i lost ur # . . . yeah ur response makes sence to me . . . i get it . . . thank u very much . . . u rock"

Though the gratitude expressed in the student's message is nice, it's not what I found most fulfilling about the exchange. Three words validated all of the work I had put into the messaging system. "i get it" was one of those moments that, as a new teacher, I cling to and strive for. It was a moment of success and perhaps an ironic step toward equity, using the machinery of the right-wing media.◆

---

*Antero Garcia is an English teacher at Manual Arts High School in South Central Los Angeles. He is also a doctoral student at the University of California, Los Angeles and a 2010 teaching fellow with the Department of Education.*

# Six, Going on Sixteen

*Fighting "age compression"*
*and the commercialization of childhood*

◆ GERALYN BYWATER McLAUGHLIN

"I saw you on My Space!"
"Yesterday after school Trina and Shayla got in a catfight over Brandon!"
"My butt is hot!"
"I got his phone number!"
"She thinks she's cuter than me."

These comments may or may not raise an eyebrow in any middle school classroom, but the year they became a common occurrence in my kindergarten and 1st-grade classroom threw me for a loop. It was just a few years ago, and at that time I had been teaching for 18 years. My combined kindergarten and 1st-grade classroom was in a small, urban K-8 school serving about 165 students from a mix of cultures and classes. The student population is about 45 percent black, 27 percent Hispanic, and 23 percent white. That particular school year was one of the most challenging I have experienced. The social dynamics were a constant source of stress and strife for my students, my families, my assistant teacher, and for me. At the end of a particularly frustrating day I described the situation to my principal: "We have two middle schools in our school. The middle school and the K-1!"

In a nutshell, that is how the year felt. The problems I encountered, mostly around the over-sexualization of my students, caught me off guard and utterly unprepared. I had 5-year-old girls vying for the attention of the "coolest" 1st-grade boy. They would push to be near him at the sand table, and groan audibly if I didn't place them in his book group. Students in the class thought of each other as "boyfriend" and "girlfriend." Freeze dance and soul train, which are usually a big hit and lots of fun, had a new dimension as students danced out the social scenarios they had seen in music videos. Performer Chris Brown was the ultimate favorite, though 50 Cent and others were also on the scene. My 5-, 6-, and 7-year-olds played out and talked about "being in the club" and "drinking Heineken." They wrote about the music world in their journals and turned the block area into a radio station. Sometimes they used the hollow blocks to build a stage to perform on. Small cylindrical blocks were their microphones. This type of play was OK

HENRIK DRESCHER

with me, except who was "in" and who was "out" was a constant social battle.

There was another aspect of this that had a negative impact on our classroom community, and that was the idea of certain kids wearing the "right" sneakers. This was among a group of boys, but the rest of the class was affected. It was something we had class meetings about, and tried to minimize the negative effects of, but it was a continuous struggle.

**Child development experts now work with marketing firms to optimize the impact of commercials according to the developmental stage of the target audience.**

One morning, as they walked up the stairs to our second-floor class-room, a kindergarten boy and a 1st-grade boy got in a pushing and hitting fight because the younger boy said he was wearing "Carmelo Anthonys" and the older boy said, "No, those are Jordans." Another boy, whose mom refused to buy expensive sneakers, had repeated melt-downs (crying, throwing things, yelling) when other boys arrived at school with new sneakers, stylish shirts or outfits, or big plastic gold rings.

One day in June, things crystallized for me as the three K-1 classes rode a big yellow school bus on our annual trip to the Farm School, in Athol, Mass. The Farm School is an important part of our school culture. Everyone in the school visits the working farm at least once a year, and starting in 4th grade students get to sleep over. The K-1 students were excited. The school bus was happily buzzing with kids talking to each other about the farm, the animals they would see and hold, what they had in their lunchbox—general happy kid talk. Then, the bus driver decided to put on the radio. I was very near the back, so I had a good vantage point. The music pumped for just a few seconds, but the mood in the bus changed dramatically. All of a sudden kids popped up in their seats and checked out who else heard the song. They knew the song, but I didn't. I saw and felt the change in energy. They were looking for other kids who were "in the know" and related to that teen-age/grown-up world of popular music. They weren't talking about the farm anymore. My assistant teacher and I exchanged knowing glances and sighed. We understood this is what we had been struggling with the whole year, the negative effect of mainstream media on our young students—the way it was taking away their chance to just be little kids excited about a day at the farm.

Throughout the year, I tried many strategies to counteract the neg-ative impact that all of these complicated factors were having on our ability to live, learn, and laugh. We had class meetings and made rules. I partnered students with classmates they didn't usually work with; had lunch meetings with the powerful core group; set up a series of lunch meetings for my most involved girls to meet with our counselor; talked a great deal to moms and grandmothers; devoted some of my weekly newsletters for families to this topic; brought back some of my former students to help create a positive counterculture; brainstormed with families and colleagues; cried and yelled. Some strategies helped, but it was an ongoing, uphill battle.

We made it through the year. That June I remember meeting with the rest of the staff at our end-of-the-year retreat. I shared my struggles and my determination to get a better handle on what felt to me like a crisis in the early childhood realm. I had consulted with colleagues throughout the year, and some of them knew what I had been up against. Others were amazed, shocked, and saddened. One friend and colleague made a suggestion that ended up being the best and most transformative advice I've received in a long time. She told me about Diane Levin, a professor at nearby Wheelock College, and she suggested I enroll in the two-day summer media institute, called Media Madness: The Impact of Sex, Violence, and Commercial Culture on Children and Society.

> **I knew that one huge goal was to find ways to bring back childhood— making even more time in the day for creative and imaginative play.**

I learned from Diane how the corporate world deliberately targets vulnerable children. I learned how child development experts now work with marketing firms to optimize the impact of commercials according to the developmental stage of the target audience and how the toy market has dramatically changed since children's television was deregulated in 1984. I also learned about "age compression." In Levin's book, *So Sexy, So Soon,* she describes age compression this way:

> "Age compression" is a term used by media professionals and marketers to describe how children at ever younger ages are doing what older children used to do. The media, the toys, the behavior, the clothing once seen as appropriate for teens are now firmly ensconced in the lives of tweens and are rapidly encroaching on and influencing the lives of younger children. In addition, there is a blurring of boundaries between children and adults, as demonstrated by the similarities in clothing marketed to both groups by the fashion industry. Age compression is especially disturbing when it involves sexual behavior. Children become involved in and learn about sexual issues and behavior they do not yet have the intellectual or emotional ability to understand and that can confuse and harm them. (pp. 69-70)

Here's a true story that helps illustrate my experience with age compression. It was the first day of kindergarten, fall of 2005. I had brought my class to the cafeteria for lunch. The students were assigned seats at one of our 10 round tables. I sat down next to a 5-year-old girl who was beginning to eat her lunch. "That's the popular table," she said matter-of-factly as she gestured over her shoulder. I was taken aback, but followed her finger to see where she was pointing. I looked again at her and asked: "Popular? What do you mean by that?" "Oh, you know, they have nice clothes," she explained. I thought about that for a moment, and since it was the first day she'd ever been in school, I asked, "Where did you learn about that?" Without a moment's hesitation she answered, "The Disney Channel."

On the upside, my school is a pilot public school, so we have autonomy over curriculum. Despite No Child Left Behind and the current high-stakes testing frenzy that have sadly turned many kindergartens into heavily academic 1st grades, our 5-, 6-, and 7-year-olds still get to play with blocks and playdough. They love to dress up, play with puppets, cuddle the baby dolls, and draw hearts. And they have time to play. Even the "coolest" kids will sing "The Pizza Song" and "Make New Friends." "Can we sing it in a round?" they'll ask. Also, I have students for two years, so I have time each summer to think more about them and what they need and what I can do. I was determined to have a better handle on the issues, find more strategies for the classroom, and extend my small one-on-one conversations to begin a broader community conversation.

As the new school year began, I knew that one huge goal was to find ways to bring back childhood—making even more time in the day for creative and imaginative play. I also wanted to encourage kids to turn off their screens and become more connected with the natural world, their classmates, and their own selves. To this end, I titled my fall curriculum unit Garden Friends: Taking Care of Each Other and Taking Care of the Earth. I had studied gardens with young children before, but this time I had an added goal of reducing the influence of screen messages. I knew from experience that one excellent antidote to screen addiction is nature. Children are fascinated by it. It's also affordable and available, even in our urban school. We got our hands dirty and looked closely at snails and spiders. We also spent time in those first few weeks explicitly practicing positive problem-solving skills. At the media institute, Diane had described "problem-solving deficit disorder" and "compassion deficit disorder," two critical social problems that are affecting our children as a direct result of current media and popular culture. These terms described beautifully the issues that I had felt firsthand in my classroom. I realized I needed to be even more explicit and deliberate in my problem-solving lessons, activities, and discussions. For example, I needed to teach some of my young students how to look at each other's faces and interpret others' reactions and what words to use to solve conflicts. Throughout the school year I used my weekly letter to families to let them in on our struggles, conversations, and solutions. Families are on the front line in the battle against corporate encroachment into children's lives and I wanted them to stay connected with our work at school. I knew their support was one important factor in our growing success. Here is an excerpt from a November letter to families:

I added baby dolls to the dress-up area, and watched and listened as the week unfolded. Monday and Tuesday had children claiming baby dolls as their own, and conflicts and tears arose. On Wednesday morning, with 8th-grader Darren's help, we did a skit about the baby dolls. Darren pretended to play with a doll and our student teacher pretended to snatch the doll so she could play. I pretended to add fuel to the fire, making the situation even worse by yelling and stomping my feet. The students laughed at how silly we looked, then helped brainstorm ways to be safe and take care even when we disagree. For example: stay calm; take a deep breath; count to 10; use nice words like, "Can I please use that?"; or try playing Rock, Paper, Scissors.

**Picture a child playing with wooden blocks. She builds a tower, pretending the smallest blocks are the people. As she plays, another child joins and builds nearby. Someone gets the idea to connect their two buildings, and they decide to turn them into a hotel and a parking garage.**

By Friday, our project time was more satisfying and productive. John pretended his baby needed surgery and Jared was the skillful doctor. Keisha pretended she was a childcare worker taking care of a few babies. I overheard Jennifer listing the symptoms of her baby as Louisa (the doctor) listened closely, nodding her head and asking questions about the baby. When conflicts arose, I saw students trying our techniques.

In the spring my curriculum theme was Imagine, Pretend, and Play. I designed the unit to celebrate and highlight children's ability to be in charge of their own learning as they create stories, invent problems, and evolve as powerful individuals. I wanted all students to know that pretend play is important and to practice making choices that involve imagining, pretending, and playing. They would learn how to create their own entertainment and that many things can be used for play— rocks, sticks, dirt, cardboard boxes, scraps of fabric, and unmatched socks, for example. We focused our literacy work on reading stories that celebrate imagination, such as *Roxaboxen*, by Alice McLerran. I found related poems to recite and songs to sing. The students had special journals to record and reflect about their play. I had students practice describing how they felt while they were engaged in their chosen activity. We invited our families for a special breakfast and exhibition as we displayed our accomplishments. I shared with families a quote from Susan Linn's wonderful book *The Case for Make Believe: Saving Play in a Commercialized World* to help illustrate my curriculum decisions: "The ability to play is central to our capacity to take risks, to experiment, to think critically, to act rather than react, to differentiate ourselves from our environment, and to make life meaningful." (p. 19)

One student stands out in my mind. In his early years, he had been exposed to a great deal of media. He was literally tuned in to the teen-age/grown-up world and had trouble making friends his own age. I struggled to find ways for him to be comfortable and happy at school. During the Imagine, Pretend, and Play curriculum he found some of his happiest school moments. He used recycled materials to build his own skate park and used found objects (boxes and bottles) to make his own drum set. He worked on and perfected these projects over a number of weeks. One day, when reflecting, he said, "I was pretending I was downtown. I had the bass drum, the solo drum, and the high drum." He added: "It was hard to get the pretending into me. Once I started, I felt good."

Along with changes I made in my own classroom, I also worked with my colleagues and the school as a whole. A few of us formed a small media work group where we could meet and share ideas and resources. We wrote front-page newsletters to the community. Every Friday our school sends a newsletter home. It includes a front-page letter, usually written by the principal, but often written by other staff members, occasionally a parent and sometimes even a student. Besides the front-page letter, there are columns written by each of the 10 classroom teachers, hot topics, and more. Our school uses our Friday newsletters as a place to share ideas, reflect, inform, pose questions, and stimulate conversations. Here are some excerpts from one newsletter:

> The trouble is that media-linked toys limit children's play. Children need to play creatively. They need to invent. They practice problem-solving as their play evolves. Picture a child playing with wooden blocks. She builds a tower, pretending the smallest blocks are the people. As she plays, another child joins and builds nearby. Someone gets the idea to connect their two buildings, and they decide to turn them into a hotel and a parking garage. Their play continually evolves as they share ideas, make decisions and solve problems. They end feeling powerful and satisfied.

> Media-linked toys, however, lead children to imitate the scripts they have seen. How often have you seen children playing "Power Rangers," "Cheetah Girls," or some other show? The boys have to be violent and the girls have to be sexy. That's what they see, so that's what they play. When children act out the scripts from TV shows or movies, they aren't in control of their play. They aren't creating, they are imitating. This isn't a satisfying kind of play.

In December, we sent home an excellent resource to all our families. It was TRUCE's Toy Action Guide. Teachers Resisting Unhealthy

Children's Entertainment (TRUCE) is a group of national educators actively working to raise awareness about the negative effect of violent and stereotyped toys and media on children. They are supporting

> **"Turnoff Week is the best thing ever."**

teachers and parents in their efforts to promote healthy play. Their free and downloadable guide is a powerful tool for parents. The guide helps parents understand healthy play and how it is a critical part of healthy development. It helps them understand how open-ended and simple toys are actually better than the glitzy electronic toys that are expensive and limiting to problem-solving and creativity. The guide lists books, articles, organizations, and websites for further support. Again, parent response was overwhelmingly positive, though a few parents lamented that it was hard to find good toys at the stores that are convenient to shop at. Even toys such as wooden blocks and generic puppets can be hard to find, and they can be expensive.

Those comments spurred me to work on opening our Toy Lending Library. I asked around for donations and found some underused materials already in the school. IKEA donated a set of shelves and bins, and even some great creative toys. I got donations from other stores and parents. The library became a hit. Once a child in one class borrowed a set of blocks, puppets, or a marble run, other students wanted to do the same. It was a big project to undertake and organize, but it has proven to be a fun resource and conversation starter. The Toy Lending Library also helps counter our country's consuming culture, since the toys are not purchased but shared within the community.

A simpler schoolwide initiative was the Family Game Night we had in January. The entire school community was invited to come for a potluck dinner and games. It was an "unplugged" night with no remote controls, video games, or electronic gadgets. Many staff members volunteered to oversee a wide range of games. We had fun playing Twister, Uno, bingo, blackjack, charades, and more. The biggest hit was a fast-paced card game called Spoons, led by our middle school humanities teacher. Even families who usually play board games at home were excited. "We usually only get to play with our small family. It was so much fun to play with so many people." "When can we have the next Game Night?" I was asked excitedly the next day by parents, students, and staff.

In February, we had a Family Council Meeting on the topic of media influences. Our media work group facilitated the evening, and more than 30 parents and staff gathered to share information and strategies to combat the media onslaught that we felt was attacking the well-being of our children and families. One idea that stemmed from the meeting was for our school to celebrate "TV Turnoff Week."

The National Turnoff Week coincided with spring break, so we chose a week in May that worked better for us. In the weeks leading up to our Turnoff Week, we launched a campaign to build enthusiasm. For many people, it isn't easy to just turn off screen entertainment. You have to prepare for it. You have to schedule other entertainment and a plan for what you will do. Students throughout the school brainstormed alternatives. At our Friday Share (a weekly community gathering of the entire school community) we dedicated one entire assembly to the event. Teachers did funny skits about kids who played too many video games and watched too much TV. We recited poems and sang songs about turning off our TVs. In the end, Turnoff Week was a great success. More than 50 students and staff from kindergarten to 8th grade successfully turned off their screen entertainment for one week, and many others watched less than usual. However, it was the conversations that were the most important indicator of the event's success. In classrooms from kindergarten through 8th grade, classes talked about why we were having the event and how media impacts our lives. In the end, we heard from students who read more and played more outside instead of watching TV. They did puzzles, picked dandelions, got better at basketball, and helped their grandmothers. Parents thanked us, saying things such as "Turnoff Week is the best thing ever." They played more with their kids and got projects done around the house. Some parents noticed their children slept better and were thinking about keeping the screen entertainment off during the weekdays. Five days after the Turnoff Week ended, one 5th-grader said to me, "I watched my first show last night," meaning she'd gotten out of the TV habit.

More good news is that the conversations have continued. Parents and colleagues send each other links to related news stories. For example, the Feb. 2009 *Scientific American Mind's* cover story, "The Serious Need for Play," has been making the rounds. The staff is hosting another unplugged Family Game Night this year, and the Family Council will have a follow-up meeting about media influences. In the weekly newsletter, a "Portraits of Play" column documents how our students engage in imaginative play.

A few years ago I felt hopeless. Now, armed with more information and support from colleagues, families, and key organizations, I am hopeful and empowered. The students are better supported in their efforts to learn how to just be kids. I know that I am not alone when I join successful letter-writing crusades from Campaign for a Commercial-Free Childhood, which among other successes has pressured Scholastic to remove the highly sexualized Bratz doll merchandise from their school book fairs and book clubs. I gain inspiration from the Alliance for Childhood, which works to educate policy makers about the benefits of child-centered play, and from places such as Quebec, which bans all advertising to children younger than 13 under the Quebec Consumer Protection Act. And finally, I'm inspired by parents who share stories.

Children are complex, and pop culture and media are not the sole cause of their troubles. However, protecting them from a corporate world that forces them to grow up too soon, and promoting their creative play are two giant leaps in the right direction. ◆

*A classroom teacher for 19 years, Geralyn Bywater McLaughlin is now the director of the nonprofit organization Empowered by Play. She is on the steering committee of Teachers Resisting Unhealthy Children's Entertainment (TRUCE), an active member of Campaign for a Commercial-Free Childhood (CCFC), and a founding teacher of the Mission Hill School in Roxbury, Massachussetts. She is also the mother of 6-year-old twin sons.*

## Resources

**Books for young children that encourage imaginative play:**

**Come Out and Play** by Maya Ajmera and John D. Ivanko (Charlesbridge Pub., 2001).

**Fix-It** by David McPhail (Unicorn, 1984).

**Mud Is Cake** by Pam Muñoz Ryan (Hyperion Books for Children, 2002).

**Roxaboxen** by Alice McLerran (HarperCollins, 1991).

**Songs by Brady Rymer:** "Water, Sand, Blocks, and Clay" and "Instead of Watching My TV"

**Books for teachers and parents:**

**The Case for Make Believe** by Susan Linn (The New Press, 2008).

**Consuming Kids** by Susan Linn (The New Press, 2004).

**Last Child in the Woods** by Richard Louv (Algonquin Books of Chapel Hill, 2006).

**So Sexy, So Soon** by Diane E. Levin and Jean Kilbourne (Ballantine, 2008) www.sosexysosoon.com.

**Taking Back Childhood** by Nancy Carlsson-Paige (Hudson Street Press, 2008).

**Teaching Young Children in Violent Times: Building a Peaceable Classroom** by Diane E. Levin (Educators for Social Responsibility, 1994 and 2003).

**Organizations/Websites:**

www.empoweredbyplay.org

www.allianceforchildhood.org

www.commercialfreechildhood.org

www.truceteachers.org (Teachers Resisting Unhealthy Children's Entertainment).

# Bonfire of the Disney Princesses

◆ BARBARA EHRENREICH

Contrary to the rumors I have been trying to spread for some time, Disney Princess products are not contaminated with lead. More careful analysis shows that the entire product line—books, DVDs, ball gowns, necklaces, toy cell phones, toothbrush holders, T-shirts, lunch boxes, backpacks, wallpaper, sheets, stickers, etc.—is saturated with a particularly potent time-release form of the date-rape drug.

We cannot blame China this time, because the drug is in the concept, which was spawned in the Disney studios. Before 2000, the Princesses were just the separate, disunited heroines of Disney animated films—Snow White, Cinderella, Ariel, Aurora, Pocahontas, Jasmine, Belle, and Mulan. Then Disney's Andy Mooney got the idea of bringing the gals together in a team. With a wave of the wand ($10.99 at Target, tiara included) they were all elevated to royal status and set loose on the world as an imperial cabal, and have since busied themselves achieving global domination. Today, there is no little girl in the wired, industrial world who does not seek to display her allegiance to the pink- and purple-clad Disney dynasty.

Disney likes to think of the Princesses as role models, but what a sorry bunch of wusses they are. Typically, they spend much of their time in captivity or a coma, waking up only when a Prince comes along and kisses them. The most striking exception is Mulan, who dresses as a boy to fight in the army, but—like the other Princess of color, Pocahontas—she lacks full Princess status and does not warrant a line of tiaras and gowns. Otherwise the Princesses have no ambitions and no marketable skills, although both Snow White and Cinderella are good at housecleaning.

And what could they aspire to, beyond landing a Prince? In Princessland, the only career ladder leads from baby-faced adolescence to a position as an evil enchantress, stepmother, or witch. Snow White's wicked stepmother is consumed with envy for her stepdaughter's beauty; the sea witch Ursula covets Ariel's lovely voice; Cinderella's stepmother exploits the girl's cheap, uncomplaining labor. No need for complicated witch-hunting techniques—pin-prickings and dunkings—in Princessland. All you have to look for is wrinkles.

STEPHEN KRONINGER

Feminist parents gnash their teeth. For this their little girls gave up Dora, who bounds through the jungle saving baby jaguars, whose mother is an archeologist, and whose adventures don't involve smoochy rescues by Diego? There was drama in Dora's life too, and the occasional bad actor like Swiper the fox. Even Barbie looks like a suffragist compared

**Even Barbie looks like a suffragist compared to Disney's Belle. So what's the appeal of the pink tulle Princess cult?**

**Sex—and especially some middle-aged man's twisted version thereof— doesn't belong in the pre-K playroom.**

to Disney's Belle. So what's the appeal of the pink tulle Princess cult?

Seen from the witchy end of the female life cycle, the Princesses exert their pull through a dark and undeniable eroticism. They're sexy little wenches, for one thing. Snow White has gotten slimmer and bustier over the years; Ariel wears nothing but a bikini top (though, admittedly, she is half fish.) In faithful imitation, the 3-year-old in my life flounces around with her tiara askew and her Princess gown sliding off her shoulder, looking for all the world like a London socialite after a hard night of cocaine and booze. Then she demands a poison apple and falls to the floor in a beautiful swoon. Pass the Rohypnol-laced margarita, please.

It may be old-fashioned to say so, but sex—and especially some middle-aged man's twisted version thereof—doesn't belong in the pre-K playroom. Children are going to discover it soon enough, but they've got to do so on their own.

There's a reason, after all, why we're generally more disgusted by sexual abusers than adults who inflict mere violence on children: We sense that sexual abuse more deeply messes with a child's mind. One's sexual inclinations—straightforward or kinky, active or passive, heterosexual or homosexual—should be free to develop without adult intervention or manipulation. Hence our harshness toward the kind of sexual predators who leer at kids and offer candy. But Disney, which also owns ABC, Lifetime, ESPN, A&E, and Miramax, is rewarded with $4 billion a year for marketing the masochistic Princess cult and its endlessly proliferating paraphernalia.

Let's face it, no parent can stand up against this alone. Try to ban the Princesses from your home, and you might as well turn yourself in to Child Protective Services before the little girls get on their Princess cell phones. No, the only way to topple royalty is through a mass uprising of the long-suffering serfs. Assemble with your neighbors and make a holiday bonfire out of all that plastic and tulle! March on Disney World with pitchforks held high! ◆

---

*Barbara Ehrenreich is the author of numerous books, including* Nickel and Dimed: On (Not) Getting By in America. *This article is reprinted, with permission, from the Dec. 24, 2007, issue of* The Nation.

# Sweatshop Accounting

*A high school teacher shares lessons on economic justice with his business education students*

◆ LARRY STEELE

JORDIN ISIP

My students are out of their seats again. They're digging into backpacks, flipping down the collars of their Old Navy T-shirts, and pulling off their shoes, looking for those little "Made In" tags. Made in China. Made in Vietnam.

"Hey, I was made in Vietnam," says Allan.

The students stick yellow Post-it notes on a big map of the world, marking the countries where their stuff was made. In five minutes, the Post-its obscure the coast of China, plus the Philippines, Malaysia, Indonesia and other low-wage countries where people struggle to live on as little as $1 per day.

This isn't social studies class. It's business education. The students are examining the connections between their habits as consumers and working conditions in the countries where the goods are made. I teach students who hope to be future business leaders, and these connections (often ignored in business education classes) are the central focus of our classroom work.

Today's high school students can take classes their parents never considered until college, like marketing, economics, and international finance. But this 21st-century curriculum needs to be taught as more than a set of technical skills. In our $31 trillion global economy, business decisions affect billions of people. That's why I think it's more important than ever for business education to connect economic skills with the values of democracy, social justice, and environmental sustainability.

That's what my accounting students are doing as they analyze the pattern of yellow Post-It notes on our classroom map. I ask them what they think the pattern shows.

"Use what you've learned about accounting," I say.

Allan waves his hand. "Companies are cutting their salary expenses," he says. "They can do it by hiring people in developing countries who will work for not much money."

Allan sees the connection between the numbers on the income statement he is studying and people on the other side of the planet. That's because I supplement our textbook and its columns of worksheet numbers with readings, role plays, videos, discussions, and writing about social responsibility. As we learn how the numbers work, we also take time to look for the people behind the numbers.

## Sweatshop Accounting

My students are learning what our accounting textbook calls "the language of business." As they gain fluency, they start talking about debits and credits, business transactions, and financial reports. It's a cross-cultural language spoken by businesspeople worldwide. The key word in this language is "profit."

"When we format a company's income statement, where do we report net profit?" I ask the class.

After some near-miss answers, Mei Li says, "It goes on the bottom line."

"Right. And what is the bottom line?" I ask her.

"It's total sales minus total expenses," she answers.

"Spoken like an accountant," I say. "But I'm looking for a broader meaning. What does the phrase mean in general? Like, 'The bottom line is you need a college education to get a middle-class job?'"

More near misses, then Mei Li ventures, "The most important thing?"

Bingo.

I want students to think critically about what can happen when profitability becomes the most important thing. Decisions based on business considerations often are presented as if they are "value neutral"—just part of doing business. Nothing could be further from the truth. I use a lesson called "Sweatshop Math," from *Rethinking Globalization*, edited by Bill Bigelow and Bob Peterson, to illustrate the human consequences when business managers focus too narrowly on the bottom line.

**It's more important than ever for business education to connect economic skills with the values of democracy, social justice, and environmental sustainability.**

To help visualize people living and working in other countries, we watch "Sweating for a T-Shirt," a video by Medea Benjamin and Global Exchange. Then, the students read short vignettes from *Rethinking Globalization* about the lives of workers in low-wage countries.

Using information from the reading, the students label maps of the world with summaries of local working conditions, wage rates, and hours worked. For example, one vignette tells about workers in El Salvador who "get paid 29 cents for each $140 Nike NBA shirt they sew. The drinking water at the factory is contaminated. Women raise their babies on coffee and lemonade because they can't afford milk."

As the students cut and paste labels for their maps, I help them reflect about what they know. Their ideas usually echo views they've heard before.

"If somebody takes a job it's their own choice. It must be better than what they were doing before," says Rob.

"They should go on strike," says Brian.

We talk about the loss of traditional jobs, suppression of labor unions, and the pressures of global competition.

"This is making me uncomfortable," says Alicia. "Maybe I don't want to be in business if you have to take advantage of people."

"So, let's use our business skills to see if we could give those workers a better deal," I say.

We visit www.cleanclothes.org (the Clean Clothes Campaign) to get some real-life accounting data. The site has a photo of a $100 athletic shoe labeled with all the costs that go into its retail price, including production costs, advertising, and profit for the company that owns the brand name. Soon, the students are transferring the data to Excel spreadsheets and using the program to make colorful bar charts.

Brian is shocked. On his chart the 40 cent bar representing factory worker wages is barely visible. There's a long, $13.50 bar for the brand-name company, and an even longer $50.00 bar that goes to the retail store. With such a visible and familiar example the students immediately see options for more equitable distribution of income.

"They could pay the factory workers twice as much and it would barely dent the shoe company's share," says Brian.

"Or cut advertising expense by not paying Michael Jordan so much to wear the Nike logo," adds Linh.

"Reduce the retail store's costs," says Desiree. "That's the biggest cost."

I remind Desiree that with her knowledge of fashion, she might want to work in retail sales. "Your paycheck would be part of the retail store's costs. How would you feel about taking a cut in salary?"

"Oh no! They won't be taking it out of my pocket," she says.

Desiree gets a laugh from her classmates. But the students are beginning to see that global economic connections involve decisions that challenge their own values.

## Mom and Pop vs. the Big Box Store

After looking at how financial decision-making affects people in faraway countries I want my students to see how doing business by the numbers also changes lives in our own communities. So, as my advanced accounting students study the ownership rights of corporate shareholders, we take time to compare and contrast the interests of shareholders with the interests of local communities. In a unit I call Mom & Pop vs. the Big Box, we read about competition between neighborhood "mom-and-pop" stores and the world's biggest "big box" store, Wal-Mart Stores Inc.

We read parts of the Walmart Annual Report. It says the corporation's "job is to see how little we can charge for a product." It describes exciting career opportunities for its workforce of diverse, respectful, well-trained "associates," including 300,000 outside the United States.

Quang is impressed when he finds a list of Walmart financial contributions to Boys' & Girls' Clubs, the United Way, and other local charities in neighborhoods near Walmart stores. I ask him to create a "local citizenship" ratio to compare the amount Walmart spends on community relations with its total sales for a typical store. Quang is less impressed when his calculator shows a ratio that's a tiny fraction of 1 percent.

Next, we compare the company's self-portrait with one of the many critical reports about Walmart's business practices around the world. As an example, here is a quote from the website of Walmart

Watch (www.walmartwatch.com), an organization that encourages consumers to shop at stores offering employees "good jobs with living wages":

> There are two ways to cut costs. You can reduce waste and inefficiency. That's great. It's what makes the market system go 'round. But you can also cut costs by putting them off onto someone or something else.... You can muscle down your suppliers' prices, so they have to move production to poor communities and pay wages that won't support a decent life. You can hire part-time workers with no benefits and give them no training. Our taxes and insurance fees will pay for their health care. ...You can pressure towns for tax breaks and free roads and water lines and sewers. The other taxpayers will pick up the bill. You can pay only a fraction of the real costs of materials and energy. Nature will eat the damage. This kind of cost cutting not only imposes injustices on others, it also undermines the market economy. It distorts prices so consumers cannot make rational decisions. It rewards bigness and power, rather than real efficiency.

**After several rounds of bidding, virtually all of the countries discover that they have been competing in a "race to the bottom"—a race that destroys social and environmental values rather than promoting them.**

This statement and the company's annual report provide a great opportunity to compare and contrast texts. The Walmart Watch text describes how Walmart creates low prices by avoiding costs for labor, health insurance, and the environment. The costs don't go away, but the company leaves them out of its own accounting. It makes them "external costs," or "externalities," that will be paid later, or by someone else. Walmart avoids taking responsibility for externalities. Our textbook doesn't mention this concept. It might be considered too advanced for a beginning course. I think it's pretty basic, so I introduce it here and return to the concept again and again.

The next day I hand out role-play instructions for a make-believe community meeting, including short character sketches I put together. In this role play, students play Walmart executives, city planning officials, shop owners, shoppers, neighborhood residents, and potential store employees.

When we're ready to begin, I shout, "Action!"

City Planner Mei Li introduces the key speaker.

Quang stands up to make his presentation to the community. He unrolls a large sheet of paper representing the plan for a 100,000-square-foot Walmart Super Store.

"We want to build this great store across the street from the Martin Luther King Mall. It will sell everything you need, at low, low prices!"

My students shop at Martin Luther King Mall. They visit African American-owned hairstyling boutiques, a dollar store owned by a Vietnamese family and a dozen tiny restaurants and shops.

"Hey, wait a minute," says Alicia. "My friend's aunt owns a deli sandwich shop on that street. What if all her customers start going to Walmart? She'll go out of business."

"Forget those raggedy stores at King Mall," says bargain-shopper Desiree. "I want to go to one store with good prices. It's convenient."

"Yeah, and they might hire minimum-wage teenagers," says Rob.

Many of the shoppers and residents agree. Some say they've shopped at the local stores all their lives, but even they are impressed by Quang's promise of low prices for everything they need.

Later, reflecting about what we learned during the role play, the students realize that most of their opinions were based on personal considerations. Nobody stood up and cited Walmart's income statement to show the connection between low prices and low wages. Nobody argued consciously about externalities, although some students were getting at it when they mentioned shopkeepers that might go out of business if the supercenter opened. Next time, I'll find a more concrete way for students to correlate their concerns with the financial considerations affecting their community. Maybe I'll cast someone as a labor activist. Nevertheless, the make-believe community meeting reflected real life. It was clear that by focusing narrowly on a low-cost business model, discount stores like Walmart—and discount shoppers—would sacrifice important social values.

## Full-Cost Accounting

What if the accounting system changed to include, rather than exclude, social and environmental costs? From the European Union to Japan to the U.S. Environmental Protection Agency, government agencies and innovative businesses are experimenting with ways to do this. They call it "environmental accounting," or "full-cost accounting."

I want my students to get a taste of how full-cost accounting could work, so I announce that it is snack time. We share slices of crisp, juicy apples, taken from two paper plates labeled "Local Organic," and "Imported." Then, I ask the students to discuss their ideas about the costs to bring each type of apple to the table.

We chart the entire life cycle of the apples, listing all the various costs involved in growing, transporting, and marketing the product. Dividing into small groups, some for organic apples and some for imported varieties, the students compete to see who can make the longest, most complete list of costs. In a second column, the students mark

## Ambushed by Fox

When Fox News called me to request a television interview about my "Sweatshop Accounting" curriculum, I sensed an ambush. A news producer in New York explained that the questions would be about teachers who use math problems based on real-world situations to push their own social and political values. She said Fox would be "completely objective" and cover "both sides of the story." I didn't trust her.

"Sweatshop Accounting" introduces lots of controversial social, political, and economic issues. That's intentional. Best practices demand that we teach students to evaluate multiple sources and perspectives, think critically, and develop their own opinions.

Fox News apparently did not agree. On the day of the interview, the news crew arrived in my classroom. They set up lights. A serious reporter in a dark suit asked me his question: "Isn't it true that you create math problems to push your own political agenda?" He repeated this question again, and again, and again. It was, in fact, his only question.

So I repeated my answer again, and again: "My personal opinions aren't important. I teach students how to develop their own views." Fox aired about four seconds of my interview.

What's the moral of this story? Some people don't *like* critical thinking. Also, anyone who is "media literate" knows that news networks, reporters, teachers—everyone, in fact—speak from their own experiences and perspectives. Responsible citizens know how to evaluate diverse viewpoints objectively.

—Larry Steele

an "I" for costs they think are included in the price of the apple, or an "E" for costs they think are externalized.

I hear debates about water, organic fertilizer, and pesticides.

"Where do imported apples come from?" I ask.

"Australia!" "Mexico!" "Chile," they answer.

"Then don't forget the fuel for long-distance transportation, and the exhaust and traffic jams," I remind them.

We consolidate the group lists on the white board. The organic and imported lists look pretty similar—land, water, farmworker labor, a store. But the students begin to find differences, too.

"You can use a truck to get Washington apples to the store, but you need a ship for apples from Australia," says Ramiro.

"Organic fertilizer doesn't pollute, but nonorganic ones might pollute," says Grace.

The groups think most of the costs, even highways and seaports, are included in the price of an apple.

"Diesel fuel taxes pay for highways. The store includes that in the price of the apple," says Rob.

But we find some externalities, too. Businesses don't pay for more air pollution when they burn more fuel. They don't pay if chemical pesticides get into groundwater. If companies were held fully accountable for these costs, they would have stronger reasons to adopt better practices.

Apples provide an accessible example. Full-cost accounting gets far more complicated in industries like forestry, mining, or energy. I ask for some general conclusions and trigger a short debate.

"Companies will have to pay for the damage they do instead of leaving their mess for somebody else to clean up," says one student.

"Yeah, but that will make everything more expensive," argues another.

We try to reconcile these two views and realize that the costs wouldn't change; they'd just be assigned to specific products. That would make their prices more realistic.

"If my business had to pay for all the social and environmental costs, I'd try to treat people and the planet better," says Rushawn.

## Driven by the Market

Do corporate executives really *want* to promote social justice and environmental sustainability? Maybe there is something in the rules that stops them. The "Transnational Capital Auction" activity from *Rethinking Globalization* reveals part of the answer. Student teams role-play as representatives of poor countries trying to attract foreign investment. They must bid against each other to win new factories and jobs.

As business students, my students know what investors want: lower costs and higher profits. They quickly learn how to play the game.

"Build your factories in our country!" they say. "Our people are happy to work for $1 per day. We don't allow unions. We'll cut your taxes. Forget about environmental regulations!" Within reason, country-teams that compromise social and environmental conditions to reduce business expenses win the prize of foreign investment. After several rounds of bidding, virtually all of the countries discover that they have been competing in a "race to the bottom"—a race that destroys social and environmental values rather than promoting them.

When the game is over, we talk about why countries enter the race at all.

"Everybody needs jobs," says Irene.

"If they don't have money for their own facto-ries, they've got to get it somewhere," says Henry.

Those are the traditional answers. But our es-sential question was: Is there something in the rules that forces a competition to make things worse?

I explain the concept of "fiduciary responsibility." Corporate exec-utives, bankers, investment advisors, and many kinds of businesspeople are responsible for managing the money invested by other people. Gen-erally, this means increasing the "return on investment" by increasing profits. It means people who are rich enough to have disposable income to invest get richer. People who aren't get their salaries squeezed.

"It's the bottom line again," says Mei Li.

"That's why we won the game," says Rob, whose country now al-lows child labor and pays starvation wages. "We cut their costs so they could make bigger profits."

There are many reasons for poverty and ecological decline. As we reflect about what we learned from the Transnational Capital Auction, we talk about all the different ways people struggle to improve their lives. Political parties struggle for democracy against the temptation of corruption. Workers fight to organize unions. Teachers prepare stu-dents for more complex jobs.

But as business students, we are studying the financial rules that guide the entire game. I want the students to think critically about whether those rules are creating outcomes we truly desire.

**What can we see if we look at the lives of people behind the financial numbers?**

## National Accounting

The U.S. government uses a system of national accounting to measure the performance of the entire country. To understand this, I ask my students to visit the website of the U.S. Bureau of Economic Analysis (http://www.bea.gov). They download a table of numbers that shows the historical size of U.S. gross domestic product (GDP), the dollar val-ue of all goods and services produced in the country. Using graph paper or Excel spreadsheets, they create bar charts that show how GDP has skyrocketed during our lifetimes to $11 trillion per year. Government leaders, economics textbooks, media commentators, and many teach-ers agree that the growth of the GDP means our lives are getting better and often equate "growth" with "progress."

A lesson called "What's Up with GDP?" at the website of Facing the Future (www.facingthefuture.org) illustrates the distorted picture we get by equating success with higher production. Students role-play as citizens of a make-believe town called Salmon Bay, Alaska. Facing the Future publishes an inexpensive curriculum guide called *People and the Planet* that includes instructions and materials for this activity and many others.

Most folks in Salmon Bay earn their living by fishing, but the town also has bankers, lawyers, business owners, retail workers, and the CEO of an oil company. Henry, the banker, passes out everyone's monthly salaries in colored-paper $100 bills. We tape the bills together into chains—shorter ones for the fishing people and longer ones for the professionals and CEO. We use the total income of everyone in Salmon Bay to represent the town's GDP.

Then disaster strikes. A truck hits the oil pipeline running through Salmon Bay, the oil spills, and a thin film flows over the waters of the bay. The fish die. The fishers lose their jobs. People get sick as oil contaminates the water supply.

But the spill boosts business for some companies.

Desiree reads an "after-spill" card from the curriculum guide that tells what happens, for example, to retail business owners:

> We are sorry to say that some oil workers and fishers are out of work and are now spending less at the grocery store, movie theaters, and gas stations. However, the good news is that hotels and restaurants have been very busy since the spill, as there are many officials in town reviewing and monitoring the cleanup operations. We are experiencing a 50 percent increase in business. Doctors are busy. Lawyers are busy. The oil company CEO spends millions on cleanup, and gets a bonus for her performance.

After the oil spill, Henry adjusts pay envelopes for everyone in town. We again measure Salmon Bay's GDP, represented by totaling everyone's colored-paper $100 bills. Allan announces the bottom line: "The GDP *increased!*"

This isn't what the students expected. Because traditional GDP measures only economic transactions in dollars and cents but leaves out human suffering and environmental damage, the economy of Salmon Bay looks better *after* the oil spill.

As always, we remind ourselves of the essential question for this class: What can we see if we look at the lives of people behind the financial numbers? We would see the wrong picture if we used only dollars and cents to account for the success of life in Salmon Bay.

Next year I plan to use more lessons from Facing the Future. They recently published a useful student reading guide titled *Global Issues & Sustainable Solutions* that supports the People and the Planet curriculum. This set would help balance any business education curriculum.

## Redefining Progress

Like full-cost accounting for companies, some economists support full-cost accounting for the national economy. If we want to account for the things that truly make our lives better, what important things could we measure?

> **Students discover that it balances many of the "important values" they listed with more traditional economic indicators.**

After reading about labor struggles, watching videos about environmentally sustainable development, and role-playing as economic decision makers, my students now can list dozens of important values: job security, clean water, fair pay, health care, safe food, a sustainable future. I scramble to list them all on the white board.

Then we discuss the concept of the Genuine Progress Indicator (GPI) (See www.wikipedia.org for an explanation). GPI is an alternative to the GDP index. The students discover that it balances many of the "important values" they listed with more traditional economic indicators. For example, the GPI includes the value of unpaid childcare and housework. It subtracts, rather than adds, the expense of cleaning up pollution.

We print out a chart showing historical growth of the GPI and compared it to our earlier charts of historical GDP. The traditional measure of U.S. economic success is increasing faster and faster. But when pollution, crime, natural resource exploitation, and other social and environmental factors are included, the GPI shows that our lives are improving more slowly.

I hope this lesson is a challenge to my business education students. It shows that there are alternative ways to measure social progress and well-being that could be used to help guide social decision making.

## The View from the Corner Office

My students are out of their seats again. They're looking out the 40th-floor windows of a "Big Four" accounting firm, the local office of one of the world's four predominant accounting companies. From this height they can see container ships from China unloading at the Port of Seattle. They can see the homeless shelter down the street from the King County jail. They can see the snow-capped Olympic Mountains 35 miles away across Puget Sound.

The young associate accountants who meet us are plugged-in and enthusiastic. Their clients are medium-sized businesses and large corporations. It's a people-oriented profession, they say. Everyone has a laptop computer with wireless connection to their colleagues, plus links to accounting rules and tax laws in every country of the world.

They love the variety, pay, and perks of their jobs. The best news is that Big Four firms often recruit business school students during their senior year of college.

Study accounting, pass the CPA exam, and you could start your career earning $30 to 40,000, with great upward potential, according to the American Institute of Certified Public Accountants (AICPA).

Some of my students will find a place in corporate accounting. Some may start their own accounting practices and help small businesses or individuals. Many will use their knowledge of accounting principles to be informed investors and consumers—and perhaps activists. Whatever paths they choose, I hope they have the courage to ask the critical questions that lurk behind every financial decision: When we measure success in terms of dollars and cents, who do our decisions affect, and how?◆

*Larry Steele is a business education and social studies teacher at Franklin High School in Seattle. Before changing careers he was a corporate affairs director in the international air cargo industry. The student voices in his article represent the general classroom discussion, and are not direct quotes. All students' names have been changed.*

### Resources

**Rethinking Globalization** edited by Bill Bigelow and Bob Peterson (Rethinking Schools, 2002).

**Global Issues & Sustainable Solutions: Population, Poverty, Consumption, Conflict, and the Environment** by Devin Hibbard, Gilda Wheeler, and Wendy Church (Facing the Future, 2004).

### Websites

**www.worldbank.org/data**
World Bank: Size of the Economy by Country

**www.cia.gov/library/publications/the-world-factbook/index.html**
Central Intelligence Agency: The World Fact Book

**www.cleanclothes.org**
Clean Clothes Campaign

**www.walmartwatch.com**

**www.bea.gov**
Bureau of Economic Analysis: U.S. Economic Accounts

**www.aicpa.org**
American Institute of Certified Public Accountants: Career Resources

**http://myfootprint.org**
Ecological Footprint Quiz

**www.facingthefuture.org**

# My Year with Nike

*A story of corporate sponsorship, branding, and ethics in public schools*

◆ RACHEL CLOUES

I taught 4th grade in Beaverton, Oregon, which also happens to be the corporate headquarters of Nike, the biggest (some would say most notorious) shoe company in the world. One year, Nike selected our school to participate in a new elementary health and fitness program. Ours was a Title I school, where most kids are learning English and live in low-income homes.

Nike presented its education program as an opportunity we couldn't refuse, especially as field trip money was scarce. They were aggressive—in daily emails and phone calls—about "partnering" with us. They would foot the bill for four field trips, including the buses. They would help us meet the state physical fitness standards. And our school would receive money for each hour spent at the Nike Campus, to be used for new P.E. equipment.

STEPHEN KRONINGER

The offer smelled of marketing and public relations to me, but our school chose to participate with little hesitation. The staff had varying levels of discomfort with the proposal, but it involved free field trips, so most people greeted it with enthusiasm. Had I refused, I would have been faced with the daunting task of planning and funding at least four alternative field trips so my students wouldn't

**At one point, Nike group leaders escorted the students directly from a nutrition class into a huge auditorium. Nike employees handed each child a can of soda and students spent the next hour watching not-yet-released Nike commercials.**

rise up against me when they were the only 4th-grade class left behind.

This wasn't the first time I had questioned my school's corporate connections. The previous teaching year I had refused to participate in our school's McTeacher's Night fundraiser. This program, incredibly, invited teachers and school administrators to work behind the counter at the local McDonald's, luring students and their families to purchase a fast-food dinner. Aside from its demoralizing title, McTeacher's Night countered almost everything I was trying to teach my students about healthy lifestyles, nutrition, and their own ecological impact. It was fairly easy for me to boycott McTeacher's Night as it was not during school hours. But Nike's proposed program included at least four daytime excursions, a total of 12 school hours.

During my year with Nike, a particular irony haunted me: Along with many other giant corporations, Nike operates exploitative sweatshops that keep communities poor and voiceless in some of the very countries from which my students' families have migrated. These companies perpetuate injustice in developing countries by paying workers a minimum wage that is not a living wage. In addition, workers can be exposed to dangerous conditions, independent unions are outlawed or attacked, and environmental regulations, when they exist at all, are not enforced.

I couldn't help but think about these issues as I found myself interpreting for and escorting students through the pristine headquarters of a company that covers up social and environmental injustice with landscaped gardens and expensive ads.

## A Swoosh for Every Child

A few days before the first field trip, 100 blue shirts with white swooshes were delivered to our classroom doors. At Nike's request, all the children remembered to wear their new shirts. When the big day arrived, the excitement in the buses must have been audible for miles. "Wouldn't it be great if we could get them this excited on the first day of school?" one colleague yelled through the din. "Imagine if we could give all the kids T-shirts with our school name and mascot!"

Driving slowly through the guarded gates, we looked onto impeccably landscaped gardens full of colorful flowers and bubbling fountains. Nike employees from the Global Apparel Department were waiting for us, all smiles and cheers. Dressed from head to toe in Nike sports attire, they seemed genuinely enthusiastic about meeting the 4th graders. The kids were divided into small groups and quickly led away to what seemed like all corners of the immense campus.

Despite glossy literature and detailed schedules, it turned out that no one in charge actually had experience working with large groups of schoolchildren. At one point, Nike group leaders escorted the students directly from a nutrition class into a huge auditorium.

**Poor schools, like mine, seem especially vulnerable to states of dependency on this kind of corporate largesse.**

Nike employees handed each child a can of soda and students spent the next hour watching not-yet-released Nike commercials. They sent the teachers and most of the volunteer employees to the cafeteria for lunch, leaving 100 students in the auditorium with only a few Nike representatives. When we asked the program directors why the students were watching commercials, they told us it would help "rev them up" for their upcoming soccer game. Looking back, I wonder how we could have sat, albeit uneasily, through that catered lunch while they showed our students ads. I remember feeling powerless to say or change anything in that unfamiliar and imposing setting.

To their credit, Nike employees responded to our feedback (and my outrage) that neither soda nor commercials were appropriate for a health and fitness program. On our next field trip, students were served juice and trail mix for a snack, and there was no screen watching. This didn't do much for my first impression of the program, though, nor quell my conviction that this was indeed a marketing and PR ploy.

## Fun and Excitement

Each subsequent visit to Nike was full of fun and exciting activities like swimming, hip-hop dancing, rock climbing, yoga, and tennis. Many of my students were able to try things they might not have had a chance to do otherwise, and there wasn't a single child who didn't enjoy some aspect of our year with Nike. I was pleased the children were able to try these sports and get almost individual attention from the enthusiastic Nike employees.

At the same time, I watched as our students were indoctrinated into a corporate culture, experiencing the lovely Nike Campus without being asked to consider where Nike products are made, who makes them, and under what conditions.

Branding the children was a not-so-hidden agenda of Nike's "partnership" with my school. After every field trip, Nike sent each student home with a plastic bag full of trinkets and gifts—all emblazoned, of course, with the Nike swoosh. The children grabbed the gift bags as they were tossed onto the bus, arguing over the quantity and color of the items. I was reminded of scenarios where well-meaning but naive charities throw toys or candy to children in poor countries. It felt pa-

**In an era of increased budget crises, schools are frequently pressured into working with corporate sponsors.**

tronizing, and at the same time I felt like nothing I could possibly do for my students could ever live up to the Nike gifts and the Nike Campus experience. Poor schools, like mine, seem especially vulnerable to states of dependency on this kind of corporate largesse.

### Sizing Up Nike's "Partnership"

At one point in the year the director of the Nike education program came to our school to give a career talk to students. As he was leaving, he noticed a teacher's Adidas shoes. "I see you're not wearing Nikes," he said to her in front of her students: "We'll have to do something about that. What size do you wear?" My colleague has not yet received new shoes, but the true purpose for the "partnership" was clearly exposed—marketing Nike products.

There were times during the school year—between the four much-anticipated "Nike Day" field trips and "Nike Career Day"—when, in frustrated desperation, I tried to counterbalance the one-sided perspective my students were getting from Nike. During a math lesson, for example, my class surveyed, graphed, and discussed where their sneakers were made, and I pieced together an advertising unit focusing on persuasive techniques in the media. I wanted to teach my class to think more critically about the commodities they buy and the media's influence on their choices. Ultimately, I wanted them to see Nike from a fuller, less glamorous perspective. But I didn't have the tools or the support to take either of those projects to any great depth. I also was not comfortable using Nike as an example for critical study. I worried that people at our school would view it as "inappropriate."

My year with Nike was certainly not all bad. There were many positive opportunities for the students, nice volunteers, and responses from Nike to many of the comments we gave them throughout the school year (even though we never received evaluation forms nor were offered a formal feedback session).

In an era of increased budget crises, schools are frequently pressured into working with corporate sponsors like Nike. But we don't have to give in to a corporation's every demand. Some districts across the United States have outlawed partnerships with certain corporations whose products are deemed unhealthy for students, like soft drink companies. In our case, if Nike representatives had met with teachers, students, and parents to design a program, it might have set a better precedent for the year. At a minimum, schools or school districts should develop guidelines for relationships with corporations so that when they are approached by a business they are prepared and more likely to get their needs met. Whatever schools decide, there must be plenty of opportunity for honest discussion and careful decision-making, always asking: What is *really* in the best interest of students?

Ultimately, the benefits Nike received from the education program—if only in advertising and generating brand loyalty—far outweighed the benefits received by our school. If there is a genuine interest in supporting our community and our school, as Nike claims, they could undoubtedly afford to donate money with no commercial strings attached. They could encourage their employees to volunteer in existing community groups or schools.

I would gladly welcome into my classroom any volunteers who could read with my students—Nike shoes and all. ◆

---

*Rachel Cloues taught 4th grade for eight years and worked as an elementary science resource teacher for two years. She is currently a teacher/librarian in a K-8 public school in the San Francisco Unified School District.*

# Part 2:
# Critique How Popular Culture and Media Frame Historical Events and Actors

KATHERINE STREETER

# The Politics of Children's Literature

*What's wrong with the Rosa Parks myth?*

◆ HERBERT KOHL

Issues of racism and direct confrontation between African American and European American people in the United States are usually considered too sensitive to be dealt with directly in the elementary school classroom. When African Americans and European Americans are involved in confrontation in children's texts, the situation is routinely described as a problem between individuals that can be worked out on a personal basis. In the few cases where racism is addressed as a social problem, there has to be a happy ending.

This is most readily apparent in the biographical treatment of Rosa Parks, one of the two names that most children associate with the Civil Rights Movement, the other being Martin Luther King Jr.

The image of "Rosa Parks the Tired" exists on the level of a national cultural icon. Dozens of children's books and textbooks present the same version of what might be called "Rosa Parks and the Montgomery Bus Boycott." This version can be synthesized as follows:

> Rosa Parks was a poor seamstress. She lived in Montgomery, Alabama, during the 1950s. In those days there was still segregation in parts of the United States. That meant that African Americans and European Americans were not allowed to use the same public facilities such as restaurants or swimming pools. It also meant that whenever the city buses were crowded, African Americans had to give up seats in front to European Americans and move to the back of the bus.
>
> One day on her way home from work Rosa was tired and sat down at the front of the bus. As the bus got crowded she was asked to give up her seat to a European American man, and she refused. The bus driver told her she had to go to the back of the bus, and she still refused to move. It was a hot day, she was tired and angry, and she became very stubborn.
>
> The driver called a policeman, who arrested Rosa.
>
> When other African Americans in Montgomery heard this, they became angry too, so they decided to refuse to ride the buses until everyone was allowed to ride together. They boycotted the buses.
>
> The boycott, which was led by Martin Luther King Jr., succeeded.

Rosa Parks was one of the first women in Montgomery to join the National Association for the Advancement of Colored People (NAACP) and was its secretary for years.

© 2011 JOSEPH CIARDIELLO

> Now African Americans and European Americans can ride the buses together in Montgomery.
>
> Rosa Parks was a very brave person.

This story seems innocent enough. Rosa Parks is treated with respect, and the African American community is given credit for running the boycott and winning the struggle. On closer examination, however, this version reveals some distressing characteristics that serve to turn a carefully planned movement for social change into a spontaneous outburst based upon frustration and anger.

The following annotations on the previous summary suggest that we need a new story, one not only more in line with the truth but also one that shows the organizational skills and determination of the African American community in Montgomery and the role of the bus boycott in the larger struggle to desegregate Montgomery and the South.

## Correcting the Myth

### 1. Rosa Parks was a poor, tired seamstress. She lived in Montgomery, Alabama, during the 1950s.

Rosa Parks was one of the first women in Montgomery to join the National Association for the Advancement of Colored People (NAACP) and was its secretary for years. At the NAACP she worked with chapter president E. D. Nixon, who was also vice president of the Brotherhood of Sleeping Car Porters. Parks learned about union struggles from him. She also worked with the youth division of the NAACP, and she took a youth NAACP group to visit the Freedom Train when it came to Montgomery in 1954. The train, which carried the originals of the U.S. Constitution and the Declaration of Independence, was traveling around the United States promoting the virtues of democracy. Since its visit was a federal project, access to the exhibits could not be segregated. Parks took advantage of that fact to visit the train. There, she and the members of the youth group mingled freely with European Americans who were also looking at the documents. This overt act of crossing the boundaries of segregation did not endear Parks to the Montgomery political and social establishment.

Parks' work as a seamstress in a large department store was secondary to her community work. In addition, as she says in an interview in *My Soul Is Rested*, she had almost a life history of "being rebellious against being mistreated because of my color." She was well known to African American leaders in Montgomery for her opposition to segregation, her leadership abilities, and her moral strength. Since the 1954 *Brown v. Board of Education* decision, she had been working to desegregate the Montgomery schools. She had also attended an inter-

racial meeting at the Highlander
Folk School in Tennessee a few
months before the boycott. Highlander was known throughout
the South as a radical education
center that was overtly planning
for the total desegregation of the
South. At that meeting, which
dealt with plans for school desegregation, Parks indicated that she
intended to participate in other
attempts to break down the barriers of segregation. To call Rosa
Parks a poor, tired seamstress and
not talk about her role as a community leader is to turn an organized struggle for freedom into
a personal act of frustration. It
is a thorough misrepresentation
of the Civil Rights Movement
in Montgomery and an insult to
Parks as well.

EBONY MAGAZINE | NATIONAL ARCHIVES ID: 306-PSD-65-1882 (Box 93)

**Rosa Parks
in 1955 at an
organizational
meeting with
Dr. Martin
Luther King Jr.**

**2. In those days there was still
segregation in parts of the
United States. That meant that
African Americans and European Americans were not
allowed to use the same public facilities.**

The existence of legalized segregation in the South during the 1950s is
integral to the story of the Montgomery bus boycott, yet it is an embarrassment to many school people and difficult to explain to children
without accounting for the moral corruption of the majority of the European American community in the South.

Locating segregation in the past is a way of avoiding dealing with
its current manifestations and implying that racism is no longer a major
problem.

Describing segregation passively ("There was still segregation"
instead of "European Americans segregated facilities so that African
Americans couldn't use them") also ignores the issue of legalized segregation, even though Parks was arrested for a violation of the Alabama
law that required segregation in public facilities. It doesn't talk overtly
about racism. And it refers to "parts" of the United States, softening the

tone and muddying the reference to the South.

I've raised the question of how to expose children to the reality of segregation and racism to a number of educators, both African American and European American. Most of the European American and a few of the African American educators felt that young children do not need to be exposed to the violent history of segregation. They worried about the effects such exposure would have on race relations in their classrooms and especially about provoking rage on the part of African American students. The other educators felt that, given the resurgence of overt racism in the United States, allowing rage and anger to come out was the only way African American and European American children could work toward a common life. They felt that conflict was a positive thing that could be healing when confronted directly and that avoiding the horrors of racism was just another way of perpetuating them. I agree with this second group.

**3. Whenever the city buses were crowded, African Americans had to give up seats in front to European Americans and move to the back of the bus.**

Actually, African Americans were never allowed to sit in the front of the bus in the South in those days. The front seats were reserved for European Americans. Between five and ten rows back, the "colored" section began. When the front filled up, African Americans seated in the "colored" section had to give up their seats and move toward the back of the bus. Thus, for example, an elderly African American would have to give up his or her seat to a European American teenager at the peril of being arrested.

**4. One day on her way home from work Rosa was tired and sat down at the front of the bus.**

Parks did not sit at the front of the bus. She sat in the front row of the "colored" section. When the bus got crowded she refused to give up her seat in the "colored" section to a European American. It is important to point this out as it indicates quite clearly that it was not her intent, initially, to break the segregation laws.

At this point the story lapses into the familiar and refers to Rosa Parks as "Rosa." The question of whether to use the first name for historical characters in a factual story is complicated. One argument is that young children will more readily identify with characters presented in a personalized and familiar way. However, given that it was a sanctioned social practice in the South during the time of the story for European Americans to call African American adults by their first names as a way of reinforcing the African Americans' inferior status (African Americans could never call European Americans by their first names without breaking the social code of segregation), it seems unwise to use that practice in the story.

**This story of collective decision-making, willed risk, and coordinated action is more dramatic than the story of an angry individual who sparked a demonstration.**

In addition, it's reasonable to assume that Parks was not any more tired on that one day than on other days. She worked at an exhausting full-time job and was also active full-time in the community. To emphasize her being tired is another way of saying that her defiance was an accidental result of her fatigue and consequent short temper. Rage, however, is not a one-day thing, and Parks acted with full knowledge of what she was doing.

**5. As the bus got crowded she was asked to give up her seat to a European American man, and she refused. The bus driver told her she had to go to the back of the bus, and she still refused to move. It was a hot day, she was tired and angry, and she became very stubborn. The driver called a policeman who arrested Rosa.** This is the way that Parks, in her book *My Soul Is Rested,* described her experiences with buses:

> I had problems with bus drivers over the years because I didn't see fit to pay my money into the front and then go to the back. Sometimes bus drivers wouldn't permit me to get on the bus, and I had been evicted from the bus. But, as I say, there had been incidents over the years. One of the things that made this [incident] . . . get so much publicity was the fact that the police were called in and I was placed under arrest. See, if I had just been evicted from the bus and he hadn't placed me under arrest or had any charges brought against me, it probably could have been just another incident.

In the book *Voices of Freedom* by Henry Hampton and Steve Fayer, Parks describes that day in the following way:

> On Dec. 1, 1955, I had finished my day's work as a tailor's assistant in the Montgomery Fair Department Store and I was on my way home. There was one vacant seat on the Cleveland Avenue bus, which I took, alongside a man and two women across the aisle. There were still a few vacant seats in the white section in the front, of course. We went to the next stop without being disturbed. On the third, the front seats were occupied and this one man, a white man, was standing. The driver asked us to stand up and let him have those seats, and when none of us

> moved at his first words, he said, "You all make it light on yourselves and let me have those seats." And the man who was sitting next to the window stood up, and I made room for him to pass by me. The two women across the aisle stood up and moved out.
>
> When the driver saw me still sitting, he asked if I was going to stand up and I said, "No, I'm not."
>
> And he said, "Well, if you don't stand up, I'm going to call the police and have you arrested."
>
> I said, "You may do that."
>
> He did get off the bus, and I still stayed where I was. Two policemen came on the bus. One of the policemen asked me if the bus driver had asked me to stand and I said yes.
>
> He said, "Why don't you stand up?"
>
> And I asked him, "Why do you push us around?"
>
> He said, "I do not know, but the law is the law and you're under arrest."

Mere anger and stubbornness could not account for the clear resolve with which Parks acted. She knew what she was doing, understood the consequences, and was prepared to confront segregation head-on at whatever sacrifice she had to make.

**6. When other African Americans in Montgomery heard this, they became angry too, so they decided to refuse to ride the buses until everyone was allowed to ride together. They boycotted the buses.**

The connection between Parks' arrest and the boycott is a mystery in most accounts of what happened in Montgomery. Community support for the boycott is portrayed as being instantaneous and miraculously effective the very day after Parks was arrested. Things don't happen that way, and it is an insult to the intelligence and courage of the African American community in Montgomery to turn their planned resistance to segregation into a spontaneous emotional response. The actual situation was more interesting and complex. Not only had Parks defied the bus segregation laws in the past, according to E. D. Nixon, in the three months preceding her arrest at least three other African American people had been arrested in Montgomery for refusing to give up their bus seats to European American people. In each case, Nixon and other people in leadership positions in the African American community in Montgomery investigated the background of the person arrested. They were looking for someone who had the respect of the community and the strength to deal with the racist police force as well as all of the publicity that would result from being at the center of a court challenge.

**The idea that only special people can create change is useful if you want to prevent mass movements and keep change from happening.**

This leads to the most important point left out in popularized accounts of the Montgomery bus boycott. Community leaders had long considered a boycott as a tactic to achieve racial justice. Of particular importance in this discussion was an African American women's organization in Montgomery called the Women's Political Council (WPC). It was headed by Jo Ann Gibson Robinson, a professor of English at Alabama State University in Montgomery, an African American university. In 1949, Gibson was put off a bus in Montgomery for refusing to move to the back of an almost-empty bus. She and other women resolved to do something about bus segregation.

The boycott was an event waiting to take place, and that is why it could be mobilized over a single weekend. Parks' arrest brought it about because she was part of the African American leadership in Montgomery and was trusted not to cave in under the pressure everyone knew she would be exposed to, not the least of which would be threats to her life.

This story of collective decision-making, willed risk, and coordinated action is more dramatic than the story of an angry individual who sparked a demonstration; it is one that has more to teach children who themselves may one day have to organize and act collectively against oppressive forces.

**7. The boycott, which was led by Martin Luther King Jr., succeeded. Now African Americans and European Americans can ride the buses together in Montgomery. Rosa Parks was a very brave person.**

The WPC, E. D. Nixon, and others in Montgomery planned the boycott. Martin Luther King Jr. was a new member of the community. He had just taken over the Dexter Avenue Baptist Church, and when Nixon told him that Parks' arrest was just what everybody was waiting for to kick off a bus boycott and assault the institution of segregation, King was reluctant at first. However, the community people chose him to lead, and he accepted their call. The boycott lasted 381 inconvenient days, something not usually mentioned in children's books. It did succeed and was one of the events that sparked the entire Civil Rights Movement. People who had been planning an overt attack on segregation for years took that victory as a sign that the time was ripe, even though the people involved in the Montgomery boycott did not themselves anticipate such a result.

## Concluding Thoughts

What remains then, is to retitle the story. The revised version is still about Rosa Parks, but it is also about the African American people of Montgomery, Alabama. It takes the usual, individualized version of the Rosa Parks tale and puts it in the context of a coherent, community-based social struggle. This does not diminish Parks in any way. It places her, however, in the midst of a consciously planned movement for social change, and reminds me of the freedom song "We Shall Not Be Moved," for it was precisely Parks' and the community's refusal to be moved that made the boycott possible.

When the story of the Montgomery bus boycott is told merely as a tale of a single heroic person, it leaves children hanging. Not everyone is a hero or heroine. Of course, the idea that only special people can create change is useful if you want to prevent mass movements and keep change from happening. Not every child can be a Rosa Parks, but everyone can imagine herself or himself as a participant in the boycott. As a tale of a social movement and a community effort to overthrow injustice, the Rosa Parks story opens the possibility of every child identifying herself or himself as an activist, as someone who can help make justice happen. ◆

---

*Herbert Kohl is an educator and author of numerous books. He writes the "Good Stuff" column for* Rethinking Schools *magazine.*

# Once upon a Genocide

*Columbus in children's literature*

◆ BILL BIGELOW

Children's biographies of Christopher Columbus function as primers on racism and colonialism. They teach youngsters to accept the right of white people to rule over people of color, of powerful nations to dominate weaker nations. And because the Columbus myth is so pervasive—Columbus' "discovery" is probably the only historical episode with which all my students are familiar—it inhibits children from developing democratic, multicultural, and anti-racist attitudes.

Almost without exception, children's biographies of Columbus depict the journey to the New World as a "great adventure" led by "probably the greatest sailor of his time." It's a story of courage and superhuman tenacity. Columbus is brave, smart, and determined.

VICTOR MAYS/Random House

**Columbus kneels in pious glory in de Kay's *Meet Christopher Columbus*.**

But behind this romanticized portrayal is a gruesome reality. For Columbus, land was real estate and it didn't matter that other people were already living there; if he "discovered" it, he took it. If he needed guides or translators, he kidnapped them. If his men wanted women, he captured sex slaves. If the indigenous people resisted, he countered with vicious attack dogs, hangings, and mutilations.

On his second voyage, desperate to show his royal patrons a return on their investment, Columbus rounded up some 1,500 Taíno Indians on the island of Hispaniola and chose 500 as slaves to be sold in Spain. Slavery did not show a profit as almost all the slaves died en route to Spain or soon after their arrival. Nonetheless, he wrote, "Let us in the name of the Holy Trinity go on sending all the slaves that can be sold."

Columbus decided to concentrate on the search for gold. He ordered every Indian 14 years and older to deliver a regular quota of gold. Those who failed had their hands chopped off. In two years of the Columbus regime, perhaps a quarter of a million people died.

This article follows Columbus as he sails through eight children's biographies (see box at right), comparing the books with the historical record, then analyzing how these accounts may influence young readers.

## Portrait of Columbus

Why did Columbus want to sail west to get to the Indies? The answer offered to children in today's books hasn't changed much since I was in 4th grade. I remember my teacher, Mrs. O'Neill, asking our class this question. As usual, I didn't have a clue, but up went Jimmy Martin's hand. "Why do men want to go to the moon?" he said triumphantly. Mrs. O'Neill was delighted and told us all how smart Jimmy was because he answered a question with a question. In other words: just because—because he was curious, because he loved adventure, because he wanted to prove he could do it—just because. And for years I accepted this explanation (and envied Jimmy Martin).

In reality, Columbus wanted to become rich. It was no easy task convincing Queen Isabella and King Ferdinand to finance this highly questionable journey to the Indies, partly because his terms were outrageous. Columbus demanded 10 percent of all the wealth returned to Europe along the new trade route to Asia (where Columbus thought he was headed)—that's 10 percent of the riches brought back by everyone, not just by himself. And he wanted this guaranteed forever, for him, for his children, for their children, in perpetuity. He demanded that he be granted the titles "Viceroy" and "Admiral of the Ocean Sea." He was to be governor of all new territories found; the "admiral" title was hereditary and would give him a share in proceeds from naval booty.

As for Queen Isabella and King Ferdinand, curiosity, adventure, and "exploration" were the last things on their minds. They wanted the tremendous profits that could be secured by finding a western passage to the Indies.

The books acknowledge—and even endorse—Columbus' demands and readily admit that securing "gold and spices" was an objective of the Enterprise. "Of course [Columbus] wanted a lot! What was wrong with that?" James de Kay's *Meet Christopher Columbus* tells 2nd graders. But this quest for wealth is downplayed in favor of adventure. "Exploration" meant going to "strange cities" where "many wonderful things" could be seen. (de Kay) Travel was exciting: Columbus "felt the heady call of the open sea. 'I love the taste of salt spray in my face,' he told a friend, 'and the feel of a deck rising and falling under my feet....'" (Monchieri)

According to these eight biographies, the major reason Columbus wants to sail west is because of his deep faith in God. Columbus thought "that the Lord had chosen him to sail west across the sea to find the riches of the East for himself and to carry the Christian faith to the heathens. His name was Christopher. Had not the Lord chosen his name-sake, Saint Christopher, to carry the Christ Child across the dark water of a river?" (D'Aulaire)

Religion, curiosity, adventure—all those motives are given preference in the Columbus biographies. But each of these motives pales before the Spanish empire's quest for wealth and power. In burying these more fundamental material forces, the Columbus books encourage students to misunderstand the roots of today's foreign policy exploits. Thus students are more likely to accept platitudes—"We're involved in the Middle East for freedom and democracy"—than to look for less altruistic explanations.

## The Kind and Noble Columbus

None of the biographies I evaluated—all still on the shelves of school and public libraries and widely available—disputes the ugly facts about Columbus and the Spanish conquest of the Caribbean. Yet the sad irony is that all encourage children to root for Columbus. "It was lucky that Christopher Columbus was born where he was or he might never have gone to sea." (Fritz) "There once was a boy who loved the salty sea." (D'Aulaire) Some of the books, particularly those for younger readers, refer to Columbus affectionately, using his first name. Unlike the people he will later exterminate, Columbus is treated as a real human being, one with thoughts and feelings. "When Christopher Columbus was a child, he always wanted to be like Saint Christopher. He wanted to sail to faraway places and spread the word of Christianity." (Osborne)

The series title of Robert Young's *Christopher Columbus and His Voyage to the New World* sums up the stance of most biographies: "Let's Celebrate."

**Books Reviewed in this Article**

**Christopher Columbus and His Voyage to the New World (Let's Celebrate Series)** by Robert Young (Silver Press, 1996).

**Meet Christopher Columbus** by James T. de Kay and John Edens (Random House, 2001).

**Christopher Columbus** by Jan Gleiter, Kathleen Thompson, and Rick Whipple (Ideals, 1995).

**Columbus** by Ingri and Edgar Parin D'Aulaire (Doubleday, 1955, 1996).

**Where Do You Think You're Going, Christopher Columbus?** by Jean Fritz (G. P. Putnam's Sons, 1997).

**Christopher Columbus (Why They Became Famous Series)** by Lino Monchieri, trans. by Mary Lee Grisanti (Silver Burdett, 1985).

**The Story of Christopher Columbus: Admiral of the Ocean Sea (Famous Lives Series)** by Mary Pope Osborne and Stephen Marchesi (Dell, 1997).

**Christopher Columbus: The Intrepid Mariner (Great Lives Series)** by Sean J. Dolan (Fawcett Columbine, 1989).

The books cheer Columbus on toward the Indies. Each step on the road to "discovery" is told from his point of view. When Columbus is delayed, this is the "most unhappy part of his great adventure." (de Kay) Every successful step is rewarded with exclamation marks: "Yes, [the Queen] would help Columbus!" (Osborne) "After all these years, Columbus would get his ships!" (de Kay)

Columbus' devout Christianity is a theme in all the books—and is never questioned. The most insistent of these, and the worst of the lot in almost every respect, is Sean J. Dolan's *Christopher Columbus: The Intrepid Mariner.* By the second page in Dolan's reverent volume we're reading about Columbus' attachment to his leather-bound Bible. Dolan is constantly dipping us into the admiral's thoughts. Usually these meditations run deep and pious: "[He] believed that the awe-inspiring beauty that surrounded him could only be the handiwork of the one true God, and he felt secure in his Lord and Savior's protection. If only my crewmen shared my belief, Columbus thought." And this is only on the third page—Dolan's narrative goes on like this for 114 more. The reader is practically strangled by Columbus' halo.

Jean Fritz's *Where Do You Think You're Going, Christopher Columbus?* is the only book somewhat skeptical about religion as a motive. Fritz tells her readers that Queen Isabella "was such an enthusiastic Christian that she insisted everyone in Spain be a Christian too.... Indeed, she was so religious that if she even found Christians who were not sincere Christians, she had them burned at the stake. (Choir boys sang during the burning so Isabella wouldn't have to hear the screams.)"

This is pretty strong stuff, but the implied critique would likely be lost on the book's targeted readers, upper elementary students.

The close association between God and Columbus in all the books, with the possible exception of Jean Fritz's, discourages children from criticizing Columbus. "Columbus marveled at how God had arranged everything for the best," the D'Aulaires write. Well, if God arranged everything, who are we, the insignificant readers, to question?

No book even hints that the Indians believed in their own God or gods who also watched over and cared about them. The Columbus expedition may be the first encounter between two peoples—Us and Them—where children will learn that "God is on our side."

## Evils? Blame the Workers

Columbus' journey across the Atlantic was not easy, according to most of the books, because his crew was such a wretched bunch. The sailors are stupid, superstitious, cowardly, and sometimes scheming. Columbus, on the other hand, is brave, wise, and godly. These characterizations, repeated frequently in many of the books, protect the Columbus myth; anything bad that happens, like murder and slavery, can always be blamed on the men. Columbus, the leader, is pure of heart.

Taken together, these portrayals serve as a kind of anti-working-class pro-boss polemic. "Soon [Columbus] rose above his shipmates, for he was clever and capable and could make others carry out his orders." (D'Aulaire) Evidently, ordinary seamen are not "clever and capable," and thus are good merely for carrying out the instructions of others. "Soon [Columbus] forgot that he was only the son of a humble weaver," the D'Aulaires write, as if a background as a worker were a source of shame. The books encourage children to identify with Columbus' hardships, even though his men worked and slept in horrible conditions while the future admiral slept under a canopy bed in his private cabin. The lives of those who labored for Columbus are either ignored or held in contempt.

INGRI AND EDGAR PARIN D'AULAIRE/Doubleday

**Columbus "calm and alone," in *Columbus* by the D'Aulaires.**

## The "Discovery"

At the core of the Columbus myth—and repeated by all eight books—is the notion that Columbus "discovered" America. Indeed, it's almost as if the same writer churned out one ever so slightly different version after another.

James T. de Kay describes the scene in *Meet Christopher Columbus*:

The sailors rowed Columbus to the shore. He stepped on the beach. He got on his knees and said a prayer of thanks.

Columbus named the island San Salvador. He said it now belonged to Ferdinand and Isabella.

He tried to talk to the people on San Salvador. But they could not understand him.

Of course he couldn't understand them, either. But de Kay attributes the inability to understand solely to the Indians. Is it these Indians' implied ignorance that justifies heavily armed men coming onto their land and claiming it in the name of a kingdom thousands of miles away? In *Christopher Columbus and His Voyage to the New World*, Robert Young doesn't even tell his young readers of the people on these islands. Young's Columbus found "lands" but no people; in illustrations we see only palm trees and empty beaches.

Why don't any of the books ask students to think about the assumptions that underpinned this land grab? Naively, I kept waiting for some book to insert just a trace of doubt: "Why do you think Columbus felt he could claim land for Spain when there were already people living there?" or "Columbus doesn't write in his journal why he felt entitled to steal other people's property. What do you think?"

This scene of Columbus' first encounter with the Indians—read in school by virtually every child—is a powerful metaphor about relations between different countries and races. It is a lesson not just about the world 500 years ago, but also about the world today. Clothed, armed, Christian, white men from a more technologically "advanced" nation arrive in a land peopled by darker-skinned, naked, unarmed, non-Christians—and take over. Because no book indicates which characteristic of either group necessitates or excuses this kind of bullying, students are left alone to puzzle it out: Might makes right. Whites should rule over people who aren't white. Christians should control non-Christians. "Advanced" nations should dominate "backward" nations. Each and every answer a student might glean from the books' text and images invariably justifies colonialism and racism.

In Columbus' New World "adventures," the lives of the Indians are a kind of "muzak"—insignificant background noise. Only one book, *Where do You Think You're Going, Christopher Columbus?*, tries to imagine what the Indians might have been thinking about the arrival of the Spaniards. Still, the point here seems more to gently poke fun at Columbus and crew than to seriously consider the Indians' point of view: ". . . if the Spaniards were surprised to see naked natives, the natives were even more surprised to see dressed Spaniards. All that cloth over their bodies! What were they trying to hide? Tails, perhaps?" Jean Fritz's interior monologue for the Indians makes fun of the explorers but in the process trivializes the Indians' concerns.

Not a single Columbus biography ever asks children: "What might the Indians have thought about the actions of Columbus and his men?"

The silent Indians in Columbus stories have a contemporary consequence. The message is that white people in "developed" societies have consciousness and voice, but Third World people are thoughtless and voiceless objects. The books rehearse students in a way of looking at the world that begins from the assumption that they are not like us. A corollary is that we are more competent to determine the conditions of their lives—their social and economic systems, their political alliances, and so on. Intervention in Vietnam, subversion of the government headed by Salvador Allende in Chile, the invasions of Grenada and Panama, the attempted overthrow by proxy of the Nicaraguan and Angolan governments: Our right to decide what's best for *them* is basic to the conduct of U.S. foreign policy. As most children's first exposure to "foreign policy," the Columbus myth helps condition young people to accept the unequal distribution of power in the world.

VICTOR MAYS/Random House

**Whose side do you feel you're on in this illustration from *Meet Christopher Columbus* by de Kay?**

## Theft, Slavery, and Murder

Columbus' genocidal policies toward the Indians were initiated during his second journey. The three books aimed at children in early elementary grades, Gleiter and Thompson's *Christopher Columbus*, de Kay's *Meet Christopher Columbus*, and Young's *Christopher Columbus and His Voyage to the New World*, all conveniently stop the story after his first journey. The Columbus myth can take root in young minds without the complications of the slavery and mass murder to come.

After his first trip, Columbus returned to a hero's welcome in Spain. He also arrived telling all kinds of lies about gold mines and spices and unlimited amounts of wealth. The admiral needed royal backing for a second trip, and had to convince his sponsors that the islands contained more than parrots and naked heathens.

During his second voyage, in February of 1495, Columbus launched the slave raids against the Taínos of Hispaniola. Four of the eight books I reviewed—the ones aimed at older children—admit that Columbus took Indians as slaves. (Monchieri, Fritz, Osborne, and Dolan) Their critique, however, is muted. No account tells children what slavery meant for its victims. One of the books, Monchieri's *Christopher Columbus*, says that taking slaves was "a great failing of Columbus....He saw nothing wrong with enslaving the American Indians and making them work for Spanish masters....Missionaries protested against this policy, but they were not listened to." End of discussion.

Mary Pope Osborne in *The Story of Christopher Columbus: Admiral of the Ocean Sea*, writes that "this terrible treatment of the Indians was Columbus' real downfall." Still, Osborne is unable to offer even this minimal critique of the admiral without at the same time justifying his actions: "Since Columbus felt despair and disappointment about not finding gold in the Indies, he decided to be like the African explorers and try to sell these Indians as slaves." (Osborne) Neither book ever describes the character of slave life—or slave death.

The other two biographies offer Columbus' justifications for taking slaves: "African explorers were always sending Africans back to Spanish slave markets, Columbus told himself. Besides, the natives were all heathens. It wasn't as if he were selling Christians into slavery." (Fritz) Dolan at one point blames it all on the men: "Given the attitude of the men at large, however, [Columbus] had little choice but to give his approval to the slaving sorties."

Imagine, if you will, Nazi war crimes described in this way—nothing about the suffering of the victims, tepid criticism of the perpetrators, the horrendous crimes explained by the rationalizations of Hitler and his generals. How long would these books last in our schools?

From the beginning, locating gold was Columbus' primary objective. In one passage, not included in any of the children's books, Columbus wrote: "Gold is a wonderful thing! Whoever owns it is lord of all he wants. With gold it is even possible to open for souls the way to paradise." Two of the eight authors, Fritz and Dolan, describe Columbus' system for attempting to extract gold from the Indians. Dolan writes that Columbus instituted "a system of forced tribute: Each Indian was to provide a certain amount of gold each year. Penalties for failure to comply with this rule included flogging, enslavement, or death." Nothing here about cutting people's hands off, which is what Columbus did, but still it's pretty explicit. Fritz writes simply that Indians who didn't deliver enough gold "were punished." She concludes that "between 1494 and 1496 one-third of the native population of Hispaniola was killed, sold, or scared away." The passive voice in Fritz's version—"was killed, sold, or scared away"—protects the perpetrators: Exactly who caused these deaths?

More significantly, these accounts fail to recognize the Indians' humanity. The books' descriptions are clinical and factual, like those of a coroner. What kind of suffering must these people have gone through? How did it feel to have their civilization completely destroyed in just a few years? What of the children who watched their parents butchered by the Spanish gold seekers? These books show no passion or outrage—at Columbus or at the social and economic system he represented. This devastation happened to several hundred thousand human beings, maybe more. Why don't the writers of these books get angry?

I find the most "honest" books about Columbus' Enterprise—those that admit slavery and other crimes—the most distressing. They lay out the facts, describe the deaths, and then move on to the next paragraph with no look back. These books foster a callousness toward human suffering—or is it simply a callousness toward people of color? Apparently students are supposed to value bravery, cunning, and perseverance over a people's right to life and self-determination.

INGRI AND EDGAR PARIN D'AULAIRE/Doubleday

A racist drawing in the D'Aulaires' *Columbus*, still on the shelves of many libraries. The authors state that some of the Indians were cannibals who ate their enemies, but offer no historical evidence.

## Contempt for Native Resistance

Given that Columbus biographies scarcely consider Indians as human beings, it's not surprising that native resistance to the Spaniards' atrocities is either barely acknowledged or treated with hostility. Gleiter and Thompson's *Christopher Columbus* notes that in future trips Columbus "fought with the natives." In a sentence, Lino Monchieri writes, "The Indians became rebellious because [Columbus] compelled them to hand over their gold." At least here the author credits the Indians with what might be a legitimate cause for revolt, though offers no further details. Mary Pope Osborne buries the cause of resistance in nonexplanatory, victimless prose: "But the settlers had run into trouble with the Indians, and there had been a lot of fighting."

Some writers choose to portray Indian resistance not as self-defense, but as originating from the indigenous people's inherently violent nature. In *Meet Christopher Columbus*, "unfriendly Indians" surprise the innocent Spaniards: "Suddenly more than 50 Indians jumped out from behind the trees. They had bows and arrows. They attacked the men. The men fought back." Thus, Indian resistance to the Spaniards' invasion and land grab is not termed "freedom fighting," but instead is considered "unfriendly." The violence of the Spaniards is described as self-defense. Note that in this quote, the Spaniards are "men" and the Indians are, well, just Indians.

The books that bother to differentiate between groups of Indians single out the Caribs for special contempt. Caribs are presented as cannibals, even though no historical evidence exists to corroborate such a claim. The Caribs lived on islands "so wild and steep, it seemed as if the waterfalls came tumbling out of the clouds. The Indians who lived there were wild too. They were cannibals who ate their enemies." (D'Aulaire)

In Dolan's *Christopher Columbus: The Intrepid Mariner*, Columbus sends an armed contingent to "explore" the island that today is St. Croix. Because Caribs attack the Spaniards, Dolan considers this resistance sufficient to label the Caribs as ferocious. In fact, according to the eyewitness account of Dr. Diego Alvarez Chanca, the Indians attacked only when the Spaniards trapped them in a cove. In today's parlance, the Caribs were "radicals" and "extremists"—in other words, they tenaciously defended their land and freedom.

The books condition young people to reject the right of the oppressed to rebel. We have a right to own their land, and they should not protest—at least not violently. Those who do resist will be slapped with a pejorative descriptor—cannibal, savage, communist, militant, radical, hard-liner, extremist—and subdued. The Columbus biographies implicitly lead students to have contempt for contemporary movements for social justice. Obviously, they leave children ill-prepared to respect current Indian struggles for land and fishing rights.

## Columbus' Legacy

I expected each book to end with at least some reflection on the meaning of Columbus' voyages. None did. In fact, only one book, *Meet Christopher Columbus*, even suggests that today's world has anything to do with Columbus: Thanks to the admiral, "Thousands of people crossed the ocean to America. This 'new world' became new countries: the United States, Canada, Mexico, Brazil, and many others."

It's much simpler for the authors to ignore both short- and long-term consequences of Columbus' Enterprise. Instead of linking the nature of Columbus' Spain to 20th century America, each book functions as a kind of secular Book of Genesis: In the beginning there was

Columbus—he was good and so are we.

This is a grave omission. In addition to the genocide of native peoples in the Caribbean, the most immediate effect of Columbus' voyages was the initiation of the Atlantic slave trade between Africa and America.

Colonialism and slavery: This was the "new world" Columbus did not so much discover as help to invent. In the emerging commercial ethos of his society, human beings were commodities whose

JOHN C. AND ALEXANDRA WALLNER

value was measured largely in monetary terms. The natural environment was likewise cherished not for its beauty but for the wealth that could be extracted. Columbus' Enterprise and the plunder that ensued contributed mightily to the growth of the nascent mercantile capitalism of Europe. His lasting contribution was to augment a social order that confronts the world in commercial terms (how much is it worth?), and that appreciates markets rather than cultures.

**In this typical illustration, young Chris sits and dreams— a sympathetic image to young readers today. From *A Picture Book of Christopher Columbus*, by David A. Adler (New York: Holiday House, 1992).**

## Asking Why?

Why are Columbus biographies characterized by such bias and omission? I doubt any writers, publishers or teachers consciously set out to poison the minds of the young. The Columbus story teaches important values, some would argue. Here was a young man who, despite tremendous adversity, maintained and finally achieved his objectives. Fear and narrow-mindedness kept others from that which he finally accomplished.

But in the Columbus biographies, these decent values intermingle seamlessly with deep biases against working-class people, people of color, and Third World nations. The blindness of writers and educators to these biases is simply an indication of how pervasive they are in the broader society. The seeds of imperialism, exploitation, and racism were planted with Columbus' first trans-Atlantic Enterprise—and these seeds have taken root.

Without doubt, ours is a very different world than Spanish America in the 15th and 16th centuries, but there is a lingering inheritance: the tendency for powerful groups to value profit over humanity; racial and cultural differences used to justify exploitation and inequality; vast disparities in living conditions for different social classes; economically and militarily strong nations attempting to control the fates of weaker nations. Hence, life amidst injustice in today's United States inures many of us to the injustice of 500 years earlier. Characteristics that appear to someone as natural and inevitable in the 21st century will likely appear as natural and inevitable in the descriptions of the world five centuries ago.

## The Biographies' Pedagogy

The Columbus stories encourage passive reading, and never pose questions for children to think about. Did Columbus have a right to claim Indian land in the name of the Spanish crown? Were those Indians who resisted violently justified in doing so? Why does the United States commemorate a Columbus Day instead of a Genocide Day? The narratives require readers merely to listen, not to think. The text is everything, the

# Dear Diary...

**I, Columbus: My Journal, 1492-3**
Edited by Peter and Connie Roop, illustrated by Peter E. Hanson (Walker and Co., 1990).

Diaries are a seductive form of literature. "This is the real thing," we imagine as we sit down to read. A silent bargain is struck with the writer: You let me into your private thoughts and I'll try to look at the world through your eyes.

This is the danger of the Roops' book. *I, Columbus* invites children into the colonialist mind—and leaves them there. The very structure of the book encourages children to view colonial conquest from the standpoint of the white European conqueror. Youngsters buddy up to Columbus and ride along on his "voyage to the unknown," as the Roops call it.

Clearly the book is intended to foster an admiration for Columbus. The Roops write in their acknowledgments: "Most of all we express our awe of Columbus himself, a man with a vision and the determination to accomplish it."

The Roops selected passages from Columbus' journal that portray him at his most appealing. Indeed the Roops' Columbus is more saint than conqueror. For example, on first encounter with the indigenous people of Guanahaní the Roops' Columbus is strict with his crew and kind to the Indians: "I warned my men to take nothing from the people without giving something in exchange." They neglect to include a passage from Columbus' journal that foreshadows his massive slave raids: "They [the Indians] should be good servants and of quick intelligence, since I see that they very soon say all that is said to them...."

reader nothing. Not only are young readers conditioned to accept social hierarchy—colonialism, racism, and classism—they are also rehearsed in an authoritarian mode of learning.

By implication, in this review essay I suggest the outlines of a more truthful history of Columbus and the "discovery" of America. First, the indigenous peoples of America must be accorded the status of full human beings with inalienable rights to self-determination. The tale of "discovery" needs to be told from their perspective as well as from that of the Europeans. Although there is little documentation of how the Indians interpreted the Spaniards' arrival and conquest, readers could be encouraged to think about these events from the native point of view. Columbus' interior monologue should not be the only set of thoughts represented in the story.

The Roops' October 14 diary entry acknowledges that Columbus "captured" Indians, but fails to include a later passage from that day that places this act in a broader context. Columbus wrote: "…I caused [the Indians] to be taken in order to carry them off that they may learn our language and return. However, when Your Highnesses so command, they can all be carried off to Castile or held captive in the island itself, since with fifty men they would be all kept in subjection and forced to do whatever may be wished."

Columbus' captives resist, by attempting to escape, sometimes successfully. The Roops edit this resistance out of their book, as they also omit Columbus's further kidnappings. On November 12, Columbus describes the kidnap of "seven head of women, small and large, and three children."

As in the traditional myth, *I, Columbus* largely ignores the Taíno people. On October 29, Columbus enters Taíno homes that "were well swept and clean, and their furnishing very well arranged; all were made of very beautiful palm branches."

None of this appears in the Roop version. And on December 16, Columbus says of the Taínos, "They are the best people in the world and beyond all the mildest." Again, none of this appears in the Roop version. Columbus even refers to some Taíno leaders, like the Hispaniola *cacique* (leader), Guacanagarí, by their given names. The Roops' Indians have no names.

*I, Columbus* follows the same cheerleading pattern as other biographies. However, unlike other biographical accounts, the journal structure more easily excuses the Roops from prompting students to question the myth. We're only letting Columbus tell his own story, they can claim. Even more effectively than other biographies, the Roops' diary silences the perspectives of the "discovered."

—BILL BIGELOW

A more accurate tale of Columbus would not simply probe his personal history but would also analyze the social and economic system he represented. And children might be asked to think about how today's world was shaped by the events of 1492. Above all, young readers must be invited to think and critique, not simply required to passively absorb others' historical interpretations.

Until we create humane and truthful materials, teachers may decide to boycott the entire Columbus canon. The problem with this approach is that the distortions and inadequacies characterizing this literature are also found in other children's books.

A better solution is to equip students to read critically these and other stories—inviting children to become detectives, investigating their biographies, novels, and textbooks for bias. In fact, because the Columbus books are so bad, they make perfect classroom resources to learn how to read for social as well as for literal meaning. After students have been introduced to a critical history of Columbus, they could probe materials for accuracy. Do the books lie outright? What is omitted from the accounts that would be necessary for a more complete understanding of Columbus and his encounters with native cultures? What motives are given Columbus, and how do those compare with the actual objectives of the admiral and the Spanish monarchs? Whom does the book "root" for, and how is this accomplished? What role do illustrations play in shaping the view of Columbus? Why do the books tell the story as they do? Who in our society benefits and who is hurt from these presentations?

Teachers could assign children to write their own Columbus biographies—and some of these could be told from Indians' points of view. Or youngsters might take issues from their own lives suggested by the European invasion of America—fighting, fairness, stealing, racism—and write stories drawn from these themes.

Significantly, to invite students to question the injustices embedded in text material is implicitly to invite them to question the injustices embedded in the society itself. Isn't it about time we used the Columbus myth to allow students to begin discovering the truth? ◆

---

*Bill Bigelow is the curriculum editor of Rethinking Schools.*

## Resources

**A People's History of the United States** by Howard Zinn (Harper Perennial, 2003).

**A People's History for the Classroom** by Bill Bigelow and the Zinn Education Project (Rethinking Schools, 2008)

**The Conquest of Paradise: Christopher Columbus and the Columbian Legacy** by Kirkpatrick Sale (Knopf, 1990).

**The African Slave Trade: Precolonial History 1450-1850** by Basil Davidson (Little, Brown, 1961).

# The Truth About Helen Keller

*Children's books distort her life*

◆ RUTH SHAGOURY

The "Helen Keller story" that is stamped in our collective consciousness freezes her in childhood; we remember her most vividly at age 7 when her teacher, Annie Sullivan, connected her to language through a magical moment at the water pump. We learned little of her life beyond her teen years, except that she worked on behalf of people with disabilities.

But there is much more to Helen Keller's history than a brilliant deaf and blind woman who surmounted incredible obstacles. Helen Keller was a socialist who believed she was able to overcome many of the difficulties in her life because of her class privilege—a privilege not shared by most of her blind or deaf contemporaries. "I owed my success partly to the advantages of my birth and environment," she said. "I have learned that the power to rise is not within the reach of everyone." More than an icon of American "can-do," Helen Keller was a tireless advocate of the poor and disenfranchised.

Helen Keller was someone who worked throughout her long life to achieve social change; she was an integral part of many important social movements in the 20th century. Her life story could serve as a fascinating example for children, but most picture books about Helen Keller are woefully silent about her life's work. It's time to start telling the truth about Helen Keller.

## Covert Censorship: Promoting the Individual

*"The world is moved not only by the mighty stories of heroes, but also by the aggregate of the tiny pushes of each honest worker."* —Helen Keller

In the last decade, there has been a surge in literature for children that depicts people who have worked for social change. On a recent search for nonfiction picture books that tell the stories of those involved in social activism, I found scores of books—beautifully illustrated multicultural texts. Initially, I was delighted to be able to share these books with kids in my neighborhood and school. But as my collection grew, so did my frustration.

One problem with many of the books is that they stress the individual rather than the larger social movements in which they worked. In his critique of popular portrayals of the Rosa Parks story, educator and author Herb Kohl argues convincingly that her role in the Montgomery bus strike is framed again and again as that of a poor, tired seamstress acting out of personal frustration rather than as a community leader in an organized struggle against racism. (See "The Politics of Children's Literature," on page 68 in this volume.)

Picture books frame the stories of many other key community leaders and social activists in similar ways. In *It's Becoming Political*, activist and educator Patrick Shannon careful analyzes the underlying social message of books for young readers: "Regardless of the genre type, the authors of these books promoted concern for self-development, personal emotions, self-reliance, privacy, and competition rather than concern for social development, service to community, cooperation toward shared goals, community, and mutual prosperity."

I first became interested in the activist work of Helen Keller when I read James Loewen's *Lies My Teacher Told Me: Everything Your American History Textbook Got Wrong*. Loewen concludes that the way that Helen Keller's life story is turned into a "bland maxim" is lying by omission. When I turned to the many picture books written about her, I was discouraged to discover that books for young children retain that bland flavor, negating the power of her life work and the lessons she herself would hope people would take from it. Here is a woman who worked throughout her long life as a radical advocate for the poor, but she is depicted as a kind of saintly role model for people with disabilities.

## Images of Helen Keller in Picture Books

For the purposes of this investigation, I chose six picture books published from 1965 through 1997, which are the most readily available from bookstores and websites. Four of the six covers depict the famous moment at the well where Annie, her teacher, spells "water" into Helen's hand. This clichéd moment is the climax of each book, just as it is in the movies made about her life. To most people, Helen remains frozen in time in her childhood. According to these picture books, she is to be remembered for two things after she grew up: her "courage" and her "work with the blind and deaf."

**Four of the six covers depict the famous moment at the well where Annie, her teacher, spells "water" into Helen's hand. This clichéd moment is the climax of each book, just as it is in the movies made about her life.**

*Young Helen Keller, Woman of Courage* is typical. The first 29 pages bring us to Helen, age 12, who can read and write "and even speak." The last page, page 30, sums up the remaining 66 years of her life:

> When Helen was 20, she did something that many people thought
> was impossible. She went to college. Annie went with her to help her
> study. Helen spent her life helping blind and deaf people. She gave
> speeches and wrote many books. Helen Keller died on June 1, 1968.
> But people all over the world still remember her courageous, helpful
> life.

But courage to do what? The statements that sum up her "courageous accomplishments" are ambiguous and confusing. "She gave speeches and wrote books." What were they about? What did she do that was so courageous?

None of the children's books I reviewed mentioned that in 1909 Helen Keller became a socialist and a suffragist—movements that framed most of her writing. "I felt the tide of opportunity rising and

**Helen Keller was not afraid to ask tough, "impolite" questions: "Why in this land of great wealth is there great poverty?" she wrote in 1912.**

longed for a voice that would be equal to the urge sweeping me out into the world," she wrote.

Nor do those books tell readers that Helen Keller's publishing options dwindled because she wrote passionately for women's voting rights and against war and corporate domination. In order to promote the social justice she believed in, she decided she would take lessons to improve her speaking voice so that she could publicly speak out against injustice. This was true courage. Even after three years of daily work, her voice was uneven and difficult to control. Though she was embarrassed by her speaking voice and terrified of the crowds, Helen Keller boldly went on the lecture circuit. She later wrote that it felt as if she were going to her own hanging: "Terror invaded my flesh, my mind froze, my heart stopped beating. I kept repeating, 'What shall I do? What shall I do to calm this tumult within me?'"

The picture books omit the courage that took Helen Keller farther away from her home to visit poverty-stricken neighborhoods in New York City, where she witnessed the horror of the crowded, unhealthy living conditions in tenement buildings. Outraged about the child labor practices she encountered, she began to educate herself about efforts to organize unions and the violence that organizers and strikers faced. She wrote angry articles about the Ludlow Massacre, where, in an attempt to break a miners' strike, the Colorado National Guard shot 13 people and burned alive 11 children and two women.

The Ludlow Mine belonged to the powerful millionaire John D. Rockefeller, and Rockefeller had paid the wages of the National Guard. When newspapers hesitated to publish her articles, Helen Keller spoke out publicly against Rockefeller: "I have followed, step by step, the developments in Colorado, where women and children have been ruthlessly slaughtered. Mr. Rockefeller is a monster of capitalism," she declared. "He gives charity in the same breath he permits the helpless workmen, their wives and children to be shot down."

Helen Keller was not afraid to ask tough, "impolite" questions: "Why in this land of great wealth is there great poverty?" she wrote in 1912. "Why [do] children toil in the mills while thousands of men cannot get work, why [do] women who do nothing have thousands of dollars a year to spend?"

This courage to speak out for what she believed in is also ignored in the picture book *Helen Keller: Courage in the Dark*. Here, her achievements are summed up on the final page:

Helen's story has been retold over and over. She has been the subject of books, plays, films, and television programs. The United States Postal Service has dedicated a stamp to her. And an organization with her name works to help blind people. Helen Keller's life was filled with silence and darkness. But she had the courage and determination to light her days.

LIBRARY OF CONGRESS

**Helen Keller and Annie Sullivan, 1888.**

This is courage at its blandest—and most passive.

Notice that Helen herself is simply an icon—a "subject" of the media, the name behind an organization, and of course, best of all, an image on a stamp!

What a contrast to Helen Keller's own commitment to an active, productive life. When she wrote her autobiography in 1929, Keller declared, "I resolved that whatever role I did play in life, it would not be a passive one." Children don't learn that Helen Keller not only supported organizations to support blind people, she also supported radical unions like the Industrial Workers of the World, becoming a Wobbly herself. Nor do they learn of her support for civil rights organizations like the NAACP and that W. E. B. DuBois printed news of her financial donations and the text of her letter of support in the organization's publication. "Ashamed in my very soul, I behold in my beloved south-land the tears of those oppressed, those who must bring up their sons and daughters in bondage to be servants, because others have their fields and vineyards, and on the side of the oppressor is power."

At one time, the two best-selling picture books on Helen Keller listed at amazon.com were: *A Picture Book of Helen Keller* (Adler) and *A Girl Named Helen Keller* (Lundell). The theme of passive courage is at the center of both these books as well. At least in Lundell's book, Helen is credited with some action. After focusing on her childhood for 42 of the book's 44 pages, the author sums up Helen Keller's life with the following list:

## Helen Keller Chronology

**David Adler's best-selling** *A Picture Book of Helen Keller* **includes an ending chronology, typical of the dates that other authors include about Helen Keller's life:**

**1880** Born on June 27 in Tuscumbia, Alabama.

**1882** As a result of illness, became deaf and blind.

**1887** Met Anne Sullivan.

**1900** Entered Radcliffe College.

**1924** Began to work for the American Foundation for the Blind.

**1936** Anne Sullivan died on October 20.

**1946** Visited injured soldiers.

**1964** Received the Presidential Medal of Freedom from President Lyndon Johnson.

**1968** Died on June 1.

**There are a few dates I would add to this chronology that highlight her lifelong commitment to social justice:**

**1903** *The Story of My Life* is published—first in a series of articles in the *Ladies' Home Journal*, and then as a book.

**1907** Helen writes a groundbreaking article for the *Ladies' Home Journal* in an effort to prevent blindness among infants caused by the mothers' venereal disease. (She rallies forces to convince the medical establishment to treat children's eyes at birth with a cleansing solution as a regular procedure.)

**1908** Publication of *The World I Live In*.

**1909** Becomes a socialist and a suffragist.

**1912** Publicly speaks out in favor of birth control, and in support of Margaret Sanger's work.

**1914** Demonstrates with the Woman's Peace Party to call for peace in Europe; after the demonstration, she makes an impassioned speech for pacifism and socialism in crowded Carnegie Hall.

**1915** Writes articles publicly denouncing Rockefeller as a "monster of capitalism," responsible for the Ludlow Massacre (at his coal mine in Ludlow, Colorado), where men, women, and children were killed in a bloody confrontation between strikers and the militia.

**1916** Openly supports the Industrial Workers of the World.

**1917** Donates money to the National Association for the Advancement of Colored People (NAACP) and writes a supportive article in the *NAACP Journal*.

**1918** Helps found the American Civil Liberties Union to fight for freedom of speech.

**1919** Stars in *Deliverance*, a silent movie about her life; supports Actors Equity Union's strike by refusing to cross the picket line to attend the opening.

**1924** Campaigns for Robert LaFollette, a Progressive running for president as a third-party candidate.

**1929** Publication of *Midstream: My Later Life*.

**1948** Visits "the black silent hole" that had once been Hiroshima and Nagasaki and recommits herself to the antiwar movement.

**1961** Suffers first stroke; retires from public life.

In her life, Helen wrote five books. She traveled many places. She met kings and presidents. She spoke to groups of people around the world. Most of the work she did was to help people who were blind or deaf. She was a warm and caring person. People loved her in return. The life of Helen Keller brought hope to many.

**At the core of her commitment was being part of work for social change with others, taking part in rallies, marches, meeting with friends to talk politics and to strategize.**

Helen Keller herself would probably be horrified by this vague and misleading representation of her life's work. She spoke to groups of people around the world—ah, but what did she say? Lundell doesn't hint that she said things like, "The future of America rests on the leaders of 80 million working men and women and their children. To end the war and capitalism, all you need to do is straighten up and fold your arms." Lundell is equally vague about the content of her books, neglecting to mention essays such as "How I Became a Socialist" or books such as *Out of the Dark: Essays, Letters, and Addresses on Physical and Social Vision* (1913).

Lundell's synopsis of Keller's accomplishments focuses on the famous people—"kings and presidents"—she met in her life. But at the core of her commitment was being part of work for political change with others, taking part in rallies, marches, meeting with friends to talk politics and to strategize. "I have never felt separated from my fellow men by the silent dark," she wrote. "Any sense of isolation is impossible since the doors of my heart were thrown open and the world came in." She showed that connection to her fellow workers in her actions again and again.

One fascinating example occurred in 1919, when Keller starred in *Deliverance*, a silent movie about her life. Helen supported the Actors Equity Union's strike by refusing to cross the picket line to attend the opening—and by joining a protest march with the striking actors.

David Adler's *A Picture Book of Helen Keller* is the best-selling illustrated biography of Helen Keller for young readers. Like the other books I reviewed, this one focuses almost solely on her life before graduating from Radcliffe. The two important adult episodes Adler includes are her visits to blind soldiers during World War II and her work for the American Foundation for the Blind. The book ignores her phenomenal and productive life work as a writer and social activist. On the last page of the book, Adler sums up her life work: "Helen Keller couldn't see or hear, but for more than 80 years, she had always been busy. She read and wrote books. She learned how to swim and even how to ride a bicycle. She did many things well. But most of all, Helen Keller brought hope and love to millions of handicapped [sic] people."

**This demeaning view of Helen Keller celebrates her in a way that keeps her in her place. She never gets to be an adult; rather she is framed as a grown-up child who overcame her disability.**

Adler has space to note that Helen Keller learned to swim and ride a bicycle, but not to state that she helped found the American Civil Liberties Union or take on the medical establishment to change health care for infants. The inadequacy of the information in these books for children is staggering. Her life of hard work is reduced to the phrase "she had always been busy."

Children could also learn from Helen Keller's compassion and recommitment to pacifism after her visit to Hiroshima and Nagasaki in 1948. Deeply moved by the people she met and what they described to her, she wrote that the experience "scorched a deep scar" in her soul and that she was more than ever determined to fight against "the demons of atomic warfare … and for peace."

## What's Wrong with This Story?

"So long as I confine my activities to social service and the blind, they compliment me extravagantly, calling me 'arch priestess of the sightless,' 'wonder woman,' and 'a modern miracle,'" Helen wrote to her friend Robert LaFollette, an early pacifist who ran for president as a third-party Progressive candidate in 1924. "But when it comes to a discussion of poverty, and I maintain that it is the result of wrong economics—that the industrial system under which we live is at the root of much of the physical deafness and blindness in the world—that is a different matter!"

While she was alive, Helen Keller fought against the media's tendency to put her on a pedestal as a "model" sweet, good-natured person with a disability who overcame adversity. The American Foundation for the Blind depended on her as spokesperson, but some of its leaders were horrified by her activism. As Robert Irwin, the executive director of the foundation, wrote to one of the trustees, "Helen Keller's habit of playing around with Communists and near-Communists has long been a source of embarrassment to her conservative friends. Please advise!"

In the years since her death, her lifelong work as a social justice activist has continued to be swept under the rug. As her biographer Dorothy Herrmann concludes:

> Missing from her curriculum vitae are her militant socialism and the fact that she once had to be protected by six policemen from an admiring crowd of 2,000 people in New York after delivering a fiery speech protesting America's entry into World War I. The war, she told her audience, to thunderous applause, was a capitalist ploy to further enslave

the workers. As in her lifetime, Helen Keller's public image remains one of an angelic, sexless, deaf-blind woman who is smelling a rose as she holds a braille book open on her lap.

But why is her activism so consistently left out of her life stories? Stories such as this are perpetuated to fill a perceived need. The mythical Helen Keller creates a politically conservative moral lesson, one that stresses the ability of the individual to overcome personal adversity in a fair world. The lesson we are meant to learn seems to be: "Society is fine the way it is. Look at Helen Keller! Even though she was deaf and blind, she worked hard—with a smile on her face—and overcame her disabilities. She even met kings, queens, and presidents, and is remembered for helping other people with disabilities. So what do you have to complain about in this great nation of ours?"

This demeaning view of Helen Keller celebrates her in a way that keeps her in her place. She never gets to be an adult; rather she is framed as a grown-up child who overcame her disability. Like other people with disabilities, Helen Keller deserves to be known for herself and not defined by her blindness or her deafness. She saw herself as a free and self-reliant person—as she wrote, "a human being with a mind of my own."

It's time to move beyond the distorted and dangerous Helen Keller myth, repeated in picture book after picture book. It's time to stop lying to children and go beyond Keller's childhood drama and share the remarkable story of her adult life and work. What finer lesson could children learn than the rewards of the kind of engaged life that Helen Keller lived as she worked with others toward a vision of a more just world? ◆

---

*Ruth Shagoury teaches new and veteran teachers at Lewis & Clark College in Portland, Oregon. She collaborates with teachers who serve largely immigrant populations as they investigate student-based approaches to literacy.*

## Resources on Helen Keller

**Helen Keller: Rebellious Spirit** by Laurie Lawlor (Holiday House, 2001). A biography for adolescents with excellent photographs that document Keller's life.

**Helen Keller: A Life** by Dorothy Herrman (University of Chicago Press, 1989). A fine biography that covers her adult life as well as her famous childhood.

**Midstream: My Later Life** by Helen Keller (Doubleday, 1929). Helen Keller's fascinating autobiography as an adult gives readers a taste of her writing voice, her passionate beliefs, and her social convictions.

# Why I'm Not Thankful for Thanksgiving

◆ MICHAEL DORRIS

Native Americans have more than one thing not to be thankful about on Thanksgiving. Pilgrim Day, and its antecedent feast Halloween, represent the annual twin peaks of Indian stereotyping. From early October through the end of November, "cute little Indians" abound on greeting cards, advertising posters, in costumes, and school projects. Like stock characters from a vaudeville repertoire, they dutifully march out of the folk-cultural attic (and right down Madison Avenue!) ughing and wah-wah-wahing, smeared with lipstick and rouged; decked out in an assortment of "Indian suits" composed of everything from old clothes to fringed paper bags, little trick-or-treaters and school pageant extras mindlessly sport and cavort.

Considering that virtually none of the standard fare surrounding either Halloween or Thanksgiving contains an ounce of authenticity, historical accuracy, or cross-cultural perception, why is it so apparently ingrained? Is it necessary to the North American psyche to perpetually exploit and debase its victims in order to justify its history? And do Native Americans have to reconcile themselves to forever putting up with such exhibitions of puerile ethnocentrism?

## It's Never Uncomplicated

Being a parent is never uncomplicated. One is compelled, through one's children, to re-experience vicariously the unfolding complexities of growing up, of coping with the uncomprehended expectations of an apparently intransigent and unaffectable world, of carving a niche of personality and point of view amidst the abundance of pressures and demands which seem to explode from all directions. Most people spend a good part of their lives in search of the ephemeral ideal often termed "identity," but never is the quest more arduous and more precarious—and more crucial—than in the so-called "formative years."

One would like, of course, to spare offspring some of the pains and frustrations necessarily involved in maturation and self-realization, without depriving them of the fulfillments, discoveries, and excite-

DIANA CRAFT

ments, which are also part of the process. In many arenas, little or no parental control is—or should be—possible. Learning, particularly about self, is a struggle, but with security, support, and love it has extraordinary and marvelously unique possibilities. As parents, our lot is often to watch and worry and cheer and commiserate, curbing throughout our impulse to intervene. The world of children interacting with children is in large part off-limits.

> **Learning, particularly about self, is a struggle, but with security, support, and love it has extraordinary and marvelously unique possibilities.**

Passivity ends, however, with relation to those adult-manufactured and therefore wholly gratuitous problems with which our children are often confronted. We naturally rise against the greed of panderers of debilitating junk foods; we reject dangerous toys, however cleverly advertised; and we make strict laws to protect against reckless motorists. We dutifully strap our children into seatbelts, keep toxic substances out of reach, and keep a wary eye for the dangerous stranger.

With so many blatant dangers to counter, perhaps it is unavoidable that some of the more subtle and insidious perils to child welfare

are often permitted to pass. The deficiencies of our own attitudes and training may be allowed to shower upon our children, thus insuring their continuation, unchallenged, into yet another generation. Much of what we impart is unconscious, and we can only strive to heighten our own awareness and thereby circumvent a repetition ad infinitum of the "sins of the fathers" (and mothers).

And of course, we all make the effort to do this, to one degree or another. It is therefore especially intolerable when we observe other adults witlessly, maliciously, and occasionally innocently, burdening our children with their own unexamined mental junk. Each of us has undoubtedly amassed a whole repertoire of examples of such negative influences, ranked in hierarchy of infamy according to our own values and perspectives. Even with the inauguration of certain broad controls, Saturday morning cartoon audiences are still too often invited to witness and approve violence, cruelty, racism, sexism, ageism, and a plethora of other endemic social vices.

Attitudes pertinent to "racial" or "sex-role" identity are among the most potentially hazardous, for these can easily be internalized—particularly by the "minority" child. Such internalized attitudes profoundly affect self-concept, behavior, aspiration, and confidence. They can inhibit a child before he or she has learned to define personal talents, limits, or objectives, and tend to regularly become self-fulfilling prophesies. Young people who are informed that they are going to be underachievers do underachieve with painful regularity.

## Indian Fakelore

The progeny of each oppressed group are saddled with their own specialized set of debilitating—and to parents, infuriating—stereotypes. As the father of three Native American children, aged ten, six, and three, I am particularly attuned (but not resigned) to that huge store of folk Americana presuming to have to do with "Indian lore." From the "One little, two little . . . " messages of nursery school, to the ersatz pageantry of boy scout/campfire girl mumbo jumbo, precious, ridiculous, and irritating "Indians" are forever popping up.

Consider for a moment the underlying meanings of some of the supposedly innocuous linguistic stand-bys: "Indian givers" take back what they have sneakily bestowed in much the same way that "Indian summer" deceives the gullible flower bud. Unruly children are termed "wild Indians" and a local bank is named "Indian Head" (would you open an account at a "Jew's hand," "Negro ear" or "Italian toe" branch?). Ordinary citizens rarely walk "Indian file" when about their business, yet countless athletic teams, when seeking emblems of savagery and bloodthirstiness, see fit to title themselves "warriors," "braves," "redskins," and the like.

On another level, children wearing "Indian suits," playing "cowboys and Indians," (or, in the case of organizations like the Y-Indian Guides, Y-Indian Maidens and Y-Indian Princesses, simply "Indians"), or scratching their fingers with pocket knives (the better to cement a friendship) are encouraged to shriek, ululate, speak in staccato and ungrammatical utterances (or, conversely, in sickeningly flowery metaphor)—thus presumably emulating "Indians." With depressing predictability, my children have been variously invited to "dress up and dance," portray Squanto (Pocahontas is waiting in the wings: my daughter is only 3), and "tell a myth."

Not surprisingly, they have at times evidenced some unwillingness to identify, and thus cast their lot, with the "Indians" that bombard them on every front. My younger son has lately taken to commenting "Look at the Indians!" when he comes across Ricardo Montalban, Jeff Chandler, or the improbable Joey Bishop in a vintage TV western. Society is teaching him that "Indians" exist only in an ethnographic frieze, decorative and slightly titillatingly menacing. They invariably wear feathers, never crack a smile (though an occasional leer is permissible under certain conditions), and think about little besides the good old days. Quite naturally, it does not occur to my son that he and these curious and exotic creatures are expected to present a common front— until one of his first grade classmates, garbed in the favorite costume of Halloween (ah, the permutations of burlap!) or smarting from an ecology commercial, asks him how to shoot a bow, skin a hamster, or endure a scrape without a tear. The society image is at the same time too demanding and too limiting a model.

## What Does One Do?

As a parent, what does one do? All efficacy is lost if one is perceived and categorized by school officials as a hypersensitive crank, reacting with horror to every "I-is-for-Indian" picture book. To be effective, one must appear to be super-reasonable, drawing sympathetic teachers and vice-principals into an alliance of the enlightened to beat back the attacks of the flat-earthers. In such a pose, one may find oneself engaged in an apparently persuasive discussion with a school librarian regarding a book titled something like *Vicious Red Men of the Plains* ("Why, it's set here for 20 years and nobody ever noticed that it portrayed all Indi ... uh, Native Americans, as homicidal maniacs!") while at the same time

> **With depressing predictability, my children have been variously invited to "dress up and dance," portray Squanto (Pocahontas is waiting in the wings; my daughter is only 3), and "tell a myth."**

observing in silence a poster on the wall about "Contributions of the Indians" (heavy on corn and canoes, short on astronomy and medicine).

Priorities must be set. One might elect to let the infrequent coloring book page pass uncontested in favor of mounting the battlements against the visitation of a traveling Indianophile group proposing a "playlet" on "Indians of New Hampshire." These possibly well-intentioned theatricals, routinely headed by someone called "Princess Snowflake" or "Chief Bob," are among the more objectionable "learning aids" and should be avoided at all costs. It must somehow be communicated to educators that no information about native peoples is truly preferable to a reiteration of the same old stereotypes, particularly in the early grades.

### "The Indians Had Never Seen Such a Feast!"

A year ago my older son brought home a program printed by his school; on the second page was an illustration of the "First Thanksgiving," with a caption which read in part: "They served pumpkins and turkeys and corn and squash. The Indians had never seen such a feast!"

On the contrary! *The Pilgrims* had literally never seen "such a feast," since all foods mentioned are exclusively indigenous to the Americas and had been provided, or so legend has it, by the local tribe.

Thanksgiving could be a time for appreciating Native American peoples as they were and as they are, not as either the Pilgrims or their descendant bureaucrats might wish them to be.

If there was really a Plymouth Thanksgiving dinner, with Native Americans in attendance as either guests or hosts, then the event was rare indeed. Pilgrims generally considered Indians to be devils in disguise, and treated them as such.

And if those hypothetical Indians participating in that hypothetical feast thought that all was well and were thankful in the expectation of a peaceful future, they were sadly mistaken. In the ensuing months and years, they would die from European diseases, suffer the theft of their lands and property and the near-eradication of their religion and their language, and be driven to the brink of extinction.

Thanksgiving, like much of American history, is complex, multifaceted, and will not bear too close a scrutiny without revealing a less-than-heroic aspect. Knowing the truth about Thanksgiving, both its proud and its shameful motivations and history, might well benefit contemporary children. But the glib retelling of an ethnocentric and self-serving falsehood does not do anyone any good.

Parents' major responsibility, of course, resides in the home. From the earliest possible age, children must be made aware that many people are wrong-headed about not only Native Americans, but about cultural pluralism in general.

Children must be encouraged to articulate any questions they might have about "other" people. And "minority" children must be given ways in which to insulate themselves from real or implied insults, epithets, slights, or stereotypes. "Survival humor" must be developed and positive models must, consciously and unconsciously, be available and obvious. Sadly, children must learn not to trust uncritically.

**Knowing the truth about Thanksgiving, both its proud and its shameful motivations and history, might well benefit contemporary children. But the glib retelling of an ethnocentric and self-serving falsehood does not do anyone any good.**

Protecting children from racism is every bit as important as insuring that they avoid playing with electrical sockets. Poison is poison, and ingrained oppressive cultural attitudes are at least as hard to antidote, once implanted, as are imbibed cleaning fluids.

No one gains by allowing an inequitable and discriminatory status quo to persist. It's worth being a pain in the neck about.

In preparing this essay on stereotyping and Native American children, I did not concern myself with overt or intentional racism. Native American young people, particularly in certain geographical areas, are often prey to racial epithets and slurs—and to physical abuse—just by being who they are. No amount of "consciousness-raising" will solve this problem; it must be put down with force and determination.◆

---

*The late Michael Dorris was an author of award-winning novels for adults and children. He was of Modoc heritage. This essay originally appeared in the* Bulletin of the Council on Interracial Books for Children, *Vol. 9, No. 7.*

# *Mulan's* Mixed Messages
## *Disney's film drags Chinese civilization through the mud*

◆ CHYNG-FENG SUN

Disney's animated film, *Mulan*, which is based on a popular Chinese legend, has a number of positive points. The artistic supervisor for character design was a Taiwanese man, Chen-Yi Chang, and in the character of Mulan he has created an authentic Chinese beauty. Thankfully, Mulan does not repeat the stereotypes that characterize the physical depiction of Chinese people in children's classics such as *The Five Chinese Brothers*, in which the brothers are all slant-eyed and pigtailed, and all look alike. Furthermore, the character of Mulan is neither seductive nor voluptuous; she is probably the only Disney heroine who is emotionally and physically strong and does not wait around for Prince Charming to save her.

In order to put Mulan on a pedestal, however, Disney stomps on the people and culture around her. The China of *Mulan* is the most oppressive, rigid, and sexist culture in the world of Disney's animated children's movies. The movie perpetuates myths about gender roles in China—myths created by Western media, through Western eyes.

Disney also rewrites the traditional Chinese legend. According to the original story, Mulan is working on a weaving machine, worried because the army has drafted her aged father to go to war. She does not have an older brother and so decides to fulfill her filial duty and take her father's place. She buys a horse, leaves home with her parents' consent, and joins the army.

Mulan stays in the army for 12 years. When she returns, the emperor promotes her 12 levels to a high official position. But Mulan would rather go home to her parents. Her military excellence earns her the deep respect and friendship of her colleagues and they accompany her home. It is only when Mulan arrives home and changes back to her women's clothes that colleagues are astonished to discover her true identity.

### Disney's Version

Disney begins the movie very differently. Contrary to the legend, Mulan is not portrayed as a productive woman who has her own place and job within her home and society. Instead, she is pressured to marry, de-

© 1999 DISNEY ENTERPRISES INC.

spite her unwillingness. She goes to a matchmaker's interview—something that is unheard of in China, since matchmaking is usually done in a much more discreet manner between families. In order to impress the matchmaker, Mulan needs to show beauty, obedience, and quietness. However, she is criticized for being too skinny—not good for bearing sons—and speaking her mind too much.

**To anyone familiar with Chinese culture and the true legend, it is painful to see this beloved Chinese woman warrior falling flat on the snow, begging for forgiveness.**

The matchmaker's interview is a clear message: A woman's only value is to get married and bear sons. Furthermore, according to Disney, all Chinese women and men seem to embrace this value system.

Needless to say, Mulan suffers blatant sexism. It comes from her family (even her beloved father says to her, "It's time that you know yours [your place]"); from a government official ("Hold your tongue in men's presence"); from her colleagues in the army (they sing of "the women worth fighting for" and dismiss the possibility of a woman who "speaks her mind"); and even from the strangers she meets on the streets.

But the most dramatic depiction of China's oppressiveness rests on a plot twist invented by Disney.

In the middle of the film, Mulan's smart strategy wins a battle and saves Captain Shang's life. But she was injured in the battle, and her identity is soon discovered. According to the "law" presented in the movie, Mulan must be executed immediately. But because Mulan had saved Shang's life, he spares her and instead expels her from the army. She is left injured and alone on a snow-covered mountain.

The movie's message: One moment Mulan is a hero, the next she is worthless merely because she is a woman. The plot twist hammers home the message of China as an oppressive, cruel, and sexist society. To anyone familiar with Chinese culture and the true legend, it is painful to see this beloved Chinese woman warrior falling flat on the snow, begging for forgiveness.

To be fair, it can be argued that at the end of Disney's movie, Mulan's value is affirmed when she wins the final war as a "woman." Yet in the scenes preceding, Mulan is ignored and despised when, wearing women's clothes, she runs to warn colleagues and people about the enemy. Her companion, a little dragon, reminds her, "People don't listen—you are a girl again, remember?"

## Disney's Bias

Unfortunately, Disney's depiction of Chinese culture is not an aberration. In Western movies and literature, non-white cultures are often seen as "barbaric" because of their oppression of women. It may not be surprising that the three Disney movies with the most sexist cultures are *Pocahontas* (Native American), *Aladdin* (Arab), and *Mulan* (Chinese).

Disney uses a double standard. In *Sleeping Beauty*, its adaptation of the Germanic fairy tale, the princess is bestowed to a prince at birth. Even though this marriage is just as forced as the marriages of Pocahontas, Jasmine, and Mulan, it is portrayed as romantic rather than oppressive.

In general, Disney is a master at producing happy endings, which fulfill the main characters' wishes. That's why the Little Mermaid does not transform into sea foam, as Hans Christian Andersen sentenced, but instead is saved by her prince, marries him, and is blessed by her father.

But, unlike other Disney characters, Mulan's story does not come full circle. In Disney's movie, Mulan sets out to defy a sexist society but ends up settling down with it. As the movie has repeatedly driven home, Mulan has been discriminated against not because she is uniquely Mulan, but because she is a woman. Disney makes Mulan a hero at the end, but this token gesture does not diminish or redeem Disney's depiction of China's sexism toward all women.

**Disney makes Mulan a hero at the end, but this token gesture does not diminish or redeem Disney's depiction of China's sexism toward all women.**

At the movie's end, Mulan returns home and the world has not changed for her. Her mother and grandmother are more impressed by Shang showing up at the front door than by Mulan's saving the country. "Sign me up for the next war," Granny says.

Disney's message is hard to miss. Since there is no liberation for women in the oppressive Chinese society, the practical Granny makes an important point: If going to war brings a man, it must be worthwhile joining. ◆

*Chyng Feng Sun is a clinical associate professor of media studies at McGhee Division at the School of Continuing and Professional Studies at New York University. She is a children's book author in Chinese and English and a filmmaker. Her documentary films include* Mickey Mouse Monopoly: Disney, Childhood, and Corporate Power *(2001),* Beyond Good and Evil: Media, Children and Violent Times *(2003), and* The Price of Pleasure: Pornography, Sexuality, and Relationships *(2008). She would like to thank Rhonda Berkower, Linda Mizell, and Lolly Robinson for their editorial suggestions.*

# A Barbie-Doll Pocahontas

◆ CORNEL PEWEWARDY

Disney's Pocahontas has a Barbie-doll figure, an exotic model's glamour, and an instant attraction to a distinctively Nordic John Smith.

Yet historians agree that Pocahontas and John Smith had no romantic contact. In short, Disney has abandoned historical accuracy in favor of creating a marketable New Age Pocahontas who can embody dreams for wholeness and harmony.

This New Age Pocahontas is in line with shifts in stereotypes about Native Americans. For half a century or more, the dominant image of Indians was that of "savages," of John Wayne leading the U.S. Cavalry against the Indians.

Today the dominant stereotype has shifted to that of the noble savage, which portrays Indians as part of a once-great but now dying culture that could talk to the trees (like Grandmother Willow) and the animals (like Meeko and Flit that protected nature). Such contradictory views of Indians, from terrifying and evil to gentle and good, stem from a Eurocentric ambivalence toward an entire race of people that they attempted to exterminate.

*Pocahontas* is rooted in the "Indian princess" stereotype, which is typically expressed through characters who are maidenly, demure, and deeply committed to some white man. As writer Gail Guthrie Valaskakis notes:

> The dominant image of the Indian princess appeared in the 1920s. She is a shapely maiden with a name like Winona, Minnehaha, Iona—or even Hiawatha. She sits posed on a rock or in a canoe, seemingly suspended, on a mountain-rimmed, moonlit lake, wearing a tight-fitting red tunic and headband with one feather; and she has the perfect face of a white female.

Disney's Pocahontas is a 1990s version of the red-tunic lady. She combines the sexually alluring qualities of innocence and availability. But perhaps the most obvious manifestations of the racism in Pocahontas is in the movie's use of terms such as "savages," "heathens," "pagans," "devils," and "primitive." These terms reflect something wild and inferior, and their use implies a value judgment of white superiority. By

© 1999 DISNEY ENTERPRISES INC.

negatively describing Native lifestyle and basing the movie on a "we-they" format, there is a subtle justification of the subjugation of Indian tribes by so-called "advanced" cultures in the name of progress. The movie makes little reference to the European greed, deceit, racism, and genocide that were integral to the historical contacts between the Indians and Jamestown settlers.◆

**Such contradictory views of Indians, from terrifying and evil to gentle and good, stem from a Eurocentric ambivalence toward an entire race of people that they attempted to exterminate.**

*Cornel Pewewardy, of Comanche and Kiowa heritage, is an associate professor of Native American Studies at Portland State University, in Portland, Oregon.*

# Fiction Posing as Truth

*A Critical Review of Ann Rinaldi's*
My Heart Is on the Ground:
The Diary of Nannie Little
Rose, a Sioux Girl

◆ DEBBIE REESE ET AL.

**Authors' note:** *In March 1999, Debbie Reese (Nambe) saw* My Heart Is On the Ground: The Diary of Nannie Little Rose, a Sioux Girl *in a local bookstore. She picked it up, put it down in distaste, but then decided it couldn't be ignored. Reading through the book, she was outraged and called Beverly Slapin of Oyate and read excerpts to her. Beverly did not look forward to reading it herself. A day later and equally outraged, Beverly called it the "worst book she had ever read." Both women began talking about this book to colleagues.*

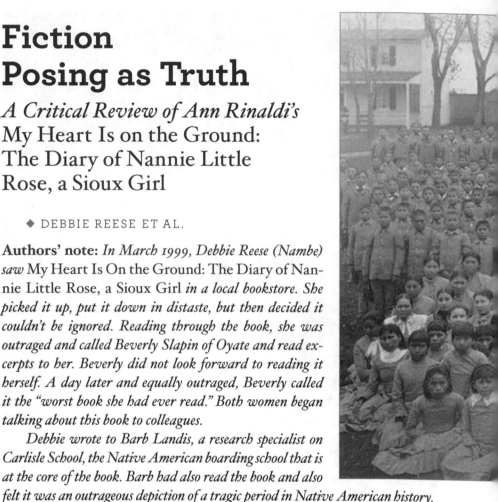

*Debbie wrote to Barb Landis, a research specialist on Carlisle School, the Native American boarding school that is at the core of the book. Barb had also read the book and also felt it was an outrageous depiction of a tragic period in Native American history.*

*We are fully aware we have used the word "outraged" three times in this piece so far, but there is no other word that captures the intensity of emotion we all feel about this book. A series of internet and telephone discussions followed, and the circle grew to the nine women who are listed alphabetically below.*

My Heart Is on the Ground: The Diary of Nannie Little Rose, a Sioux Girl is a book published by Scholastic as part of its "Dear America" series of historical fiction diaries. Immensely popular, the series is prominent both in bookstores and in the book order forms that are a regular feature of elementary school life. Because the books are published by the widely respected Scholastic, many parents and teachers don't think twice about buying them. Rinaldi's story (written for children ages 9–12) takes place in 1880 and tells of Nannie Little Rose, a Lakota child sent to the government-run boarding school for Native Americans in Carlisle, Pa. In the author's note, Rinaldi writes that she visited the Indian burial ground at the school

**Native American student body assembled on the Carlisle Indian School Grounds, 1885.**

and saw the "dozens of white headstones bearing the names of Native American children from all tribes who had died while at the school. The names, with the tribes inscribed underneath, were so lyrical that they leapt out at me and took on instant personalities. Although many of these children attended Carlisle at dates later than that of my story, I used some of their names for classmates of Nannie Little Rose.. ..I am sure that in whatever Happy Hunting Ground they now reside, they will forgive this artistic license, and even smile upon it." We doubt it. In writing this

**Rinaldi has done a tremendous disservice to the memories of the dead children whose names she used, to their families, to Native children today, and to any child who reads and believes this book to be an accurate or authentic story.**

story, Rinaldi has done a tremendous disservice to the memories of the dead children whose names she used, to their families, to Native children today, and to any child who reads and believes this book to be an accurate or authentic story about boarding school life. She has cast the government boarding school in a positive light as though it were a good thing, when it is not regarded as such by Native Americans, historians, educators, or sociologists.

What is the true history of Carlisle? It was founded in 1879 by Captain Richard Henry Pratt, whose main philosophy was "Kill the Indian, save the man." Under his administration, the school was set up to break spirits, to destroy traditional extended families and cultures, to obliterate memories and languages, and especially to make the children deny their Indianness, inside and out.

During the period in which *My Heart Is On the Ground* takes place, Native people were confined to reservations and not allowed to leave without permission of the government-appointed Indian agent assigned to their reservations. Many parents were coerced into sending their children to these early schools. Many children were kidnapped and sent far away to schools where they were kept for years on end. Children died at the school, and died running away from the school, and they were beaten for speaking their Native languages. Physical and emotional abuse is well documented in boarding schools in the United States as well as Canada.

## Appropriation

Appropriation of our lives and literatures is nothing new. Our bodies and bones continue to be displayed in U.S. and Canadian museums. For the last hundred years, many of our traditional stories have been turned into books for children without permission and with little, if any, respect given to their origins or sacred content. Now, Rinaldi has taken appropriation one step further. That she would take the names of real Native children from gravestones and make up experiences to go with them is the coldest kind of appropriation. These were children who died lonely and alone, without their parents to comfort them. They were buried without proper ceremony in this lonely and sad place. Native people who visit the cemetery today express a profound sense of sadness. Rinaldi chose to name this book by appropriating a Cheyenne proverb: "A nation is not conquered until the hearts of its women are on the ground. Then it is done, no matter how brave its warriors nor how strong their weapons." In its original form, this statement is about the strength and courage of Indian women. In its original form, the phrase suggests total defeat, the conquering of a nation, the death of a way of life. Throughout this book, the child protagonist, Nannie Little Rose, uses the phrase "my heart is on the ground" whenever she happens to feel sad or upset. This is a trivialization of the belief system of a people.

NATIONAL ARCHIVES AT COLLEGE PARK, MD | ARC 593347 (LI: 111-SC-85687)

**Chiricahua Apaches as they appeared upon arrival at the Carlisle Indian School, 1886.**

## Lack of Historical Accuracy

Throughout the book, Rinaldi uses the voice of Nannie Little Rose to teach readers about Native ways. It is an artificial device and Rinaldi's presentation of Native culture is fraught with factual errors. A basic criterion of historical fiction is that facts about people who actually lived must be accurate. Here are just a few of the errors:

◆ Sitting Bull was Hunkpapa Lakota, not "of Cheyenne nation" (Dec. 13 entry).

◆ American Horse was not a "chief of the Red Cloud Sioux." He was a cousin to Red Cloud (Dec. 21 entry).

◆ Wealth is not measured by the number of poles in a tipi (Jan. 30 entry).

◆ The whites did not "give" (Dec. 12 entry) the Black Hills to the Lakota people. By treaty, the Lakota were able to retain a small portion of what had been their land for millennia.

◆ When Spotted Tail visited Carlisle in 1880 and found his children unhappy, in military uniform, and drilling with rifles, he insisted that they return with him to Rosebud. In Rinaldi's rendition of this episode, Nannie writes (p. 121) that the children did not want to go with Spotted Tail, and that he even had to drag one of the children into the wagon. But according to historical accounts, the scene was just the opposite. When Spotted Tail visited Carlisle, he learned how miserable and homesick the children were and took all his children to the train with him. Pratt guarded the rest of the children, as there were indications that a general stampede for the train might take place. Some children managed to steal away and hide on the train, but, at Harrisburg, the train was searched and a young Oglala girl was found and dragged screaming back to captivity.

◆ In the historical note, Rinaldi says graduates of the school were able to earn a living away from the reservation. There is no evidence of this. The National Archives document that less than 10 percent of the students graduated, and more students ran away than graduated: 758 of the 10,000 students graduated, and 1,758 of the 10,000 students ran away.

## Lack of Cultural Authenticity

Again, there are numerous examples of this, but here are a few.

◆ A Lakota child in 1880 would not refer to herself as "Sioux." It is a French corruption of an enemy name used by the Ojibwe. She would have referred to herself by her band (Sicangu) or location (Spotted Tail Agency).

◆ A Lakota child would refer to Sitting Bull by his Lakota name, Tatanka Iyotanka.

◆ If a Lakota child had been encouraged to write in a diary that would be read by the white teachers and/or matrons, she would not have made fun of them in the pages of the diary (Dec. 13 entry: "…there is Woman-Who-Screams-A-Lot. She is bad to the eye. Fat and ugly.")

◆ Nannie's entry about Sun Dance, the most sacred ceremony of Lakota people, is exoticized and reflects a lack of understanding of Sun Dance, which is a thank-offering for the good of the community.

◆ Lakota children of that time period did not engage in the same grieving rituals as adults. (See Feb. 4 entry about a burial.) Moreover, what Nannie describes is not a Lakota grieving ritual.

◆ Rinaldi's interpretation of Lakota belief is oversimplified and distorted. (April 30 entry: "A war club has a spirit. A prairie dog has two spirits. Birds, insects, and reptiles have spirits.")

NATIONAL ARCHIVES AT COLLEGE PARK, MD | ARC 593352 (LI: 111-SC-85688)

**Chiricahua Apaches photographed sometime after indoctrination to the Carlisle Indian School, 1886.**

## Stereotypes

A basic criterion of good children's literature is that it be free of stereotypes. However, they abound in children's books about Native Americans and are usually found in descriptive passages about Native characters. A few authors like Rinaldi take this one step further, by placing stereotypical language and images in an Indian child protagonist's own words. Here are two examples:

- On Dec. 2, Nannie writes, "Worst bad part is Missus Camp Bell see I am frightened. With my people this is not good. We must be brave."

- Later, "Our men are very brave and honorable. Our women are noble."

## Final Comments

Nowhere in this book do we find the screaming children, thrown onto horse-drawn wagons, being taken away from their homes. Nowhere to be found are the desperately lonely children, heartbroken, sobbing into the night. Nowhere to be found are the terrified children, stripped naked and beaten, for trying to communicate with each other and not understanding what was expected of them. Nowhere to be found are the unrelenting daily humiliations, in word and deed, from the teachers, matrons, and staff. Nowhere to be found are the desperate runaways, lost, frozen in the snow. And nowhere to be found is the spirit of resistance.

But there was resistance among the Indian students, resistance that was deep, subtle, and long-lasting. Aside from running away, this resistance took many forms: physical, spiritual, and intellectual. Children destroyed property and set fires. They refused to speak English. They subverted teachers' and matrons' orders whenever they could. In *My Heart Is on the Ground,* the only resistance is Charles Whiteshield's "war dance," which is presented as a shameful thing. Resistance and the courage it represents receive no attention in this book. However, in books written by Indian authors (Francis LaFlesche's *The Middle Five* and Basil H. Johnston's *Indian School Days*), this resistance is a central part of their stories.

To those who would argue that "it is possible" that a Native child might have had Nannie Little Rose's experiences, the overwhelming body of evidence, written and oral, suggests otherwise. The premise of this book—that a Native child would, within a period of 10 months, move from someone who reads and writes limited English and has a totally Indian worldview to someone who is totally fluent and eloquent in a foreign language and has been totally assimilated into a foreign culture, and is better off for the experience—is highly unlikely. Brainwashing did not come readily. Brainwashing took time. Given the marketing and distribution forces behind *My Heart Is on the Ground*, we know it will probably be more widely read than any other book about the boarding school experience. This book only adds to the body of misinformation about Native American life and struggle in the United States and Canada. This one book epitomizes the utter lack of sensitivity and respect that characterizes the vast majority of children's books about Native Americans. Non-Native readers of *My Heart Is on the Ground* will continue to be validated in whatever feelings of superiority they may have; Native children will continue to be humiliated.

In the author's note, Rinaldi says, "I am sure that in whatever Happy Hunting Ground they now reside, they will forgive this artistic license, and even smile upon it" (p. 196). That these children might smile upon Rinaldi from their "Happy Hunting Ground" is the epitome of white fantasy: that Indian people will forgive and even smile upon white people, no matter the atrocities past and present. ◆

---

*Marlene R. Atleo (ʔeh ʔeh naa tuu kwiss, Ahousaht First Nation, Nuu-chah-nulth) is grandmother to Tyson, Tara, Alex, Kwin, Kira, and Krista, who are foremost in her mind as she works. She is an associate professor of Adult and Post Secondary Education at the University of Manitoba in Winnipeg, Canada. Her writings focus on changing resources and the implications of same for families and educational systems.*

*Naomi Caldwell (Ramapough Lenape), PhD, is a mother, great aunt, past president of the American Indian Library Association (AILA), and co-founder of the AILA American Indian Youth Book Awards. She is currently a practicing adult learning librarian conducting research and writing in New Zealand.*

*Barbara Landis is a public historian who maintains Carlisle Indian School research web pages at www.carlisleindianschool.org, dedicated to "getting the names to the nations." She is the mother of three grown children and grandmother to five small children.*

*Jean Mendoza is a mother and grandmother. She holds a PhD in early childhood education. Her articles include "Examining Multicultural Picture Books for the Early Childhood Classroom: Possibilities and Pitfalls" (with Debbie Reese) published in* Early Childhood Research & Practice. *She has been teaching children for more than 20 years.*

*Deborah Miranda (Ohlone-Coastanoan Esselen/Chumash) is a poet, mother, grand-mother, and associate professor of English at Washington and Lee University in Lexington, Va. Her article, "A String of Textbooks: Artifacts of Composition Pedagogy in Indian Boarding Schools," appeared in the* Journal of Teaching Writing *(Vol. 16.2, Fall 2000). She is the author of two poetry collections,* Indian Cartography *and* The Zen of La Llorona.

*Debbie Reese (Nambe) is a mother and assistant professor in American Indian studies at the University of Illinois studying representations of American Indians in children's and young adult literature. Her articles include "Mom, Look! It's George and He's a TV Indian!" published in* Horn Book Magazine, *and she publishes the internet resource American Indians in Children's Literature, located at: http://americanindiansinchildrensliterature.net.*

*LaVera Rose (Lakota) is a mother and grandmother, library director at Oglala Lakota College on the Pine Ridge Indian Reservation in South Dakota, and author of* Grandchildren of the Lakota *and* Meet the Lakota People/Oyate Kin.

*Beverly Slapin is a mother and co-founder and former executive director of Oyate. She is the co-editor, with Doris Seale (Santee/Cree/Abenaki), of* Through Indian Eyes: The Native Experience in Books for Children *and* A Broken Flute: The Native Experience in Books for Children. *She is also co-author of* How to Tell the Difference: A Guide to Evaluating Children's Books for Anti-Indian Bias.

*Cynthia Smith (Creek) is a reviewer of Native-themed children's books.*

*Note: This review was adapted from a much longer article that can be read at the Oyate website (www.oyate.org). That article includes material about personal names in Native cultures; details about Lucy Pretty Eagle, colonialism, and authorial perspective; extensive notes addressing other errors in the book; and extended quotes from survivors of boarding schools that could not be included here due to space limitations.

# 'Save the Muslim Girl!'

*Does popular young adult fiction about Muslim girls build understanding or reinforce stereotypes?*

◆ ÖZLEM SENSOY AND ELIZABETH MARSHALL

Young adult titles that focus on the lives of Muslim girls in the Middle East, written predominantly by white women, have appeared in increasing numbers since Sept. 11, 2001. A short list includes Deborah Ellis' trilogy *The Breadwinner*, *Parvana's Journey*, and *Mud City*; Suzanne Fisher Staples' *Under the Persimmon Tree*; and, more recently, Kim Antieau's *Broken Moon*. These titles received high praise and starred reviews from publications like *The Horn Book Magazine* and *Publishers Weekly*. Each features a young heroine trapped in a violent Middle East from which she must escape or save herself, her family, and other innocents in the region. Authors portray Muslim girls overwhelmingly as characters haunted by a sad past, on the cusp of a (usually arranged) marriage, or impoverished and wishing for the freedoms that are often assigned to the West, such as education, safety, and prosperity.

Young adult literature about the Middle East cannot be separated from the post-9/11 context in which these books are marketed and increasingly published. Deborah Ellis' *The Breadwinner,* for instance, was originally published in 2000, but Groundwood Books rushed to rerelease a paperback reprint of it in the United States after 9/11 (Roback & Britton, 2001). Since that time it has been translated into 17 languages and has become an international best-seller (Atkinson, 2003); in 2004 it sold an estimated 15,000 copies a month in the United States (Baker & Atkinson, 2004). "Save the Muslim girl" stories emerge alongside a preoccupation with Islam in mainstream news media and a surge in U.S. and Canadian military, political, and economic activities in the Middle East and West Asia. The texts are framed and packaged to sell in a marketplace at a particular moment when military interventions are centered on Afghanistan and other predominantly Muslim countries.

As many teachers have found, these stories offer an enticing way for students to engage with current events, language arts, and social studies curricula. However, given that these books are written for and marketed primarily to a Western audience, what ideas do they teach young adult readers about Muslim girls, Islam, and the Middle East? In what follows, we detail three lessons that dominate the "save the Muslim girl" stories.

Our interest here is not to defend any particular doctrine (fun-

damentalist Christian, Islamic, or other). Rather, in this article we identify how these books reproduce—and offer opportunities to challenge—longstanding ideas commonly associated with Islam: backwardness, oppression, and cultural decay. We believe that these novels can best be used to teach about the common Western stereotypes that are universalized in these books rather than to teach about Afghanistan, Pakistan, or Islamic cultures.

## Learning a Stereotype Lesson #1: Muslim Girls Are Veiled, Nameless, and Silent

Young adult books about the Muslim girl usually feature a veiled adolescent on the cover. Her face is cropped and concealed, usually by her own hands or her veil. Much of her face is covered, including, most significantly, her mouth. Images serve as a shorthand vocabulary. Consider

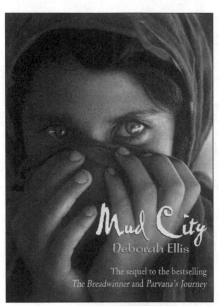

Cover reprinted with permission of Oxford University Press
Photograph © 2003 Steve McCurry/Magnum Photos

how iconic images—a white or black cowboy hat, a scientist wearing a white lab coat, a princess—set up a stock plot. The repeated images of veiled girls reinforce familiar, mainstream ideas about the confined existence of Muslim women and girls. This is the Muslim girl story we expect to read.

These kinds of images have a long history in the West. Steve McCurry's famous 1985 photo of 13-year-old Sharbat Gula on the cover of *National Geographic* provides the most well-known example. When we show the photo of the famous green-eyed Afghan girl in our education courses and ask students to write what they know about her, every student recognizes her image, yet few if any know her name, where she comes from, or that her photograph was "captured" in a refugee camp by a white U.S. journalist. Interestingly, the 2004 Oxford edition of Deborah Ellis's *Mud City* reproduces a photo of Sharbat Gula on its front cover, taken from the same series of photographs McCurry captured in the mid-1980s (see left). The cover of Antieau's *Broken Moon* has a virtually identical image: a close shot of a young girl with a veil covering her mouth, and her hands cupping her lower face (see next page). What ideas about Muslim or Middle Eastern girls—specifically Afghani girls—are we as audience invited to imagine?

Just about every book in this genre features such an image on its cover. These are familiar metaphors for how the Muslim girl's life will be presented within the novel. The way the girls' mouths are covered reinforces existing ideas about their silence and suggests that we in the West (conceptualized as "free" and "liberated") need to help unveil and "give" them voice. The images also invite ideas about girlhood innocence and vulnerability, and invite Western readers to protect, save, and speak for these oppressed girls.

But, is it not true that Muslim girls are oppressed and voiceless? We would argue that all women experience gender discrimination in different ways and with different consequences. The experiences of a U.S. woman (for example) will vary greatly if she is heterosexual or a lesbian, living in an urban center or a rural area.

Imagine this rural lesbian is black, or black and Muslim, or black, Muslim, and a non-native English speaker. In this way, her experiences are determined not simply by her gender, but also by her racial, ethnic, and sexual identity. What strikes us about the books that we review here is that they are written by white Western women who author, orga-

nize, and interpret stories about Middle Eastern girl-
hoods for Western consumption. This raises questions about the politics of storytelling. For instance,
how do (white) Western women decide for "global"
women what their issues and oppressions are? Who
tells whose story and in what ways?

Richard Dyer reminds us that while we may
believe that stereotypes are derived from a limited
truth about particular people, we actually get our
ideas about people from stereotypic images. So it
isn't the kernel of truth that results in stereotypes.
Stereotypes are created and reinforced by the repeated appearance of particular images and the exclusion of others. Thus, the repeated circulation of
the image of the veiled, sad Muslim girl reinforces
the stereotype that all Muslim girls are oppressed.

Cover reprinted with permission of Margaret K. McElderry Books
Photographs © 2006 Michael Frost (girl), © 2006 Getty Images (desert)

Stereotypes are particularly powerful in the case
of groups with which one has little or no personal relationship. Thus,
for young people who get most of their ideas about "others" from textbooks or from media, we need to ask what ideas are learned when they
"see" a very limited image of Muslim girls.

## Learning a Stereotype Lesson #2: Veiled = Oppressed

Gendered violence in Middle Eastern countries, or the threat of it,
organizes many of the books' plots. With few exceptions, the "good"
civilized men in the girl's family are taken from her. In *Under the Persimmon Tree,* a brother and father are forced to join the Taliban as fighters,
while in *The Breadwinner,* the Taliban places the father in jail because
he was educated in England. *Parvana's Journey* opens with the father's
funeral, and a deceased dad also figures in *Broken Moon.* This absence
leaves the heroine vulnerable to the roving, indiscriminate, uncivilized
"bad" men who will beat her for going out without a male escort (*The
Breadwinner* and *Broken Moon*), confine her to the house (*The Breadwinner*), or beat her to preserve the honor of the community (*Broken Moon*).

In this context of an absent/immobilized parent, the girl is placed
at the center of the plot, further emphasizing the danger and vulnerability of her existence. Parvana in *The Breadwinner* and *Parvana's Journey,* Nadira in *Broken Moon,* and Najmah in *Under the Persimmon Tree*
each cut their hair and disguise themselves as boys. This cross-dress-
ing draws heavily on Western ideas that girls should be unfettered by
the requirement to cover themselves, and authors present this type of
transformation as the only humane alternative to wearing a burqa and

the only way to travel safely outside the domestic sphere.

The veil or burqa, which has exclusively functioned as the shorthand marker of women's oppression, is a much more complicated thing. To give you a sense of the range of meaning of the veil, consider for instance that in Turkey—a predominantly Muslim country—the veil (or "religious dress") is outlawed in public spaces as a means to underline the government's commitments to Kemalism, a "modern," secularist stance. In response and as a sign of resistance, some women, especially young university students and those in urban areas, consider the veil to be a marker of protest against government regulation of their bodies and the artificial division of "modern" vs. "faithful." Similar acts of resistance are taken up by feminists in Egypt who wear the veil as a conscious act of resistance against Western imperialism. As another example, before 9/11, the Revolutionary Association of the Women of Afghanistan (RAWA) documented the Taliban's crimes against girls and women by hiding video cameras under their burqas and transformed the burqa from simply a marker of oppression to a tool of resistance.

It is problematic to wholly and simplistically equate women's oppression with the burqa, just as it would be problematic to claim that once Western women stop using makeup to cover their faces, it will mean an end to domestic violence in the United States and Canada. Although veiling has different meanings in different contexts, it exclusively carries a negative connotation in the "save the Muslim girl" texts. For example, in *The Breadwinner*, the reader is educated about the burqa through the main character, Parvana:

> "How do women in burqas manage to walk along the streets?" Parvana asked her father. "How do they see where they are going?" "They fall down a lot," her father replied.

Nusrat, the American aid worker in Staples' *Under the Persimmon Tree*, describes the burqa similarly: "In the cool autumn air, Nusrat forgets how suffocating the folds of the burqa's synthetic fabric can be in hot weather, and how peering through the crocheted latticework eyepiece can feel like looking through the bars of a prison."

In contrast to these confined women, the heroines of these novels, like "free" girls in the West, wear pants and experience freedom of movement. The freedoms associated with Western women are further emphasized in these texts by the addition of non-Muslim characters. The French nurse in *Parvana's Journey* (who works in Pakistan for a relief agency) and the American Nusrat in *Under the Persimmon Tree* (who establishes and runs a school for refugees) each choose to come to the Middle East to help. A white woman veterinarian who "wore the clothes of a Westerner" tends to the camels in *Broken Moon*. These "choices" that enable non-Muslim women to move and to work are placed in contrast to the experiences of the girls/women in the story who are at the mercy of violent events and settings in which their mobility (not to mention their way of dress) is strictly regulated and supervised.

There is a compelling character in *The Breadwinner* who offers the potential to represent Afghani women's liberation in more complex ways. This is Mrs. Weera, who leads a women's resistance group. She also convinces Parvana's mother to join her in running a covert school for girls. It is regrettable that Mrs. Weera does not occupy a more central place in the story since, unlike any other adult woman in the "save the Muslim girl" literature, she offers a transformative representation of activism among Muslim women in Afghanistan.

Again, we want to reiterate that we are not arguing that women and girls in the Middle East or predominantly Islamic societies do not experience domestic violence. In fact, we believe that domestic violence is a global epidemic that most countries, including predominantly Christian countries such as Canada and the United States, have neglected to face head on. Rather, we are arguing that the victim narrative that is so often a part of these young adult novels about Middle Eastern women reinforces the idea that the region is inherently violent and that women must be protected by outside forces. These stories serve as de facto legitimization for the U.S.-led incursions in the region as a project of women's emancipation. As Laura Bush argued in her radio address on Nov. 17, 2001: "The brutal oppression of women is a central goal of the terrorists." In this way, the complexities of Afghanistan's history, as well as U.S. interest in the region and ties to violence, escape attention.

That girls in the Middle East are consistently at risk of gendered violence implicitly suggests that girls in the "civilized" West are immune to such threats. The education students with whom we work are very familiar and comfortable with the stereotype that the lives of Muslim women are *inherently* scary, that they cannot work or vote or walk around without the threat of violence. Of course there are Muslim women who live in oppressive or patriarchal regimes (in the Middle East and elsewhere). What we contend is that young adult novels written by white women and marketed and consumed in the West consistently reinforce the idea that Muslim women are *inherently* oppressed, that they are oppressed in ways that Western women are not, and that this oppression is a function of Islam. By positioning "Eastern" women as the women who are truly oppressed, those in the West pass up a rich opportunity to engage in complex questions about oppression, patriarchy, war, families, displacement, and the role of values (imperialist or faith-based) in these relations.

Although some might argue that an author's literary imagination is her own, we suggest that these representations of Muslim girls do not—and cannot—exist independent of a social context. That these "save the Muslim girl" stories continue to be marketed by major publishers, reviewed favorably by literary and educational gatekeepers, and/or achieve best-seller status like *The Breadwinner* suggests an intimate connection to the current ideological climate within which these stories are told, marketed, and consumed.

## Learning a Stereotype Lesson #3: Muslim Girls and Women Want to Be Saved by the West

For many in the West, the plight of Afghanistan is framed exclusively within a post 9/11, U.S.-led "war on terror." Although radical women's organizations like RAWA have condemned brutality against women in Afghanistan for decades, their voices were absent, and are now muted, in a landscape of storytelling that is dominated by white Western women representing them. In an open letter to *Ms.* magazine, for instance, a U.S.-based supporter of RAWA notes that U.S.-centric women's organizations such as the Feminist Majority fail to give "credit to the independent Afghan women who stayed in Afghanistan and Pakistan throughout the 23-year (and counting) crisis in Afghanistan and provided relief, education, resistance, and hope to the women and men of their country."

Novels like *Broken Moon* play on popular scripts in which the West saves the people of the "East." These stories cannot be seen as simply works of fiction. They ultimately influence real-world experiences of girls in the Middle East and (most relevant to us) of Muslim and non-Muslim girls in our schools in the West.

Deborah Ellis and Suzanne Fisher Staples gain legitimacy as authors because they have visited, lived, and/or spoken to real girls and women in the Middle East. The *Breadwinner* trilogy and *Under the Persimmon Tree* each include a map and an author's note that touches on the "tumultuous" history of Afghanistan and a glossary. The history offered in the end matter and in the texts themselves glosses over the history of colonization in the region. The authors dilute what is an extremely complex history that has led up to the current violence in the Middle East, particularly the role of U.S. foreign policy and military interventions that contributed to the rise of the Taliban.

The authors fail to capture the complexities of U.S. involvement and intervention in favor of stereotypical lessons about educating and saving Muslim girls. As Sonali Kolhatkar, vice president of the Afghan Women's Mission, and Mariam Rawi, a member of RAWA, argue: "Feminists and other humanitarians should learn from history. This isn't the first

time the welfare of women has been trotted out as a pretext for imperialist military aggression." On one level these texts are part of a larger
public pedagogy in which the United States and its allies are framed as
fighting a good fight in Afghanistan and other regions of the Middle
East. Readers are encouraged to continue to empathize with the lead
character and the ideas that are associated with her: saving wounded
children rather than critiquing U.S. policy, "pulling oneself up by one's
bootstraps" rather than organizing together, fighting against all odds—
ideas firmly rooted in mainstream U.S. ideals of exceptionalism and
Western values of individuality.

## Teaching a More Complicated Truth

We support teachers using books like *The Breadwinner* with the pedagogical goals of critical examination. We are not advocating for the one
"right" Muslim girl story, nor do we suggest that teachers avoid using
these books in classrooms (for we recognize that in many cases, decisions about what books teachers have access to are made by economic
constraints at the school and district levels). We would, however, like to
offer suggestions for the kinds of questions teachers could ask in order
to use these resources in ways that are critically minded:

◆ How are Muslim girls visually depicted on the cover? You might
ask students to generate a list of adjectives that describe the girl. The
curriculum *Scarves of Many Colors* is a terrific resource for exploring
the relationship between graphics and students' ideas about people.
Consider questions of accuracy, context, and motivation. For example:
How accurate are the details in the image? When and how will this image be "made sense of"? Who produced this image and why?

◆ Which parts of the novel are you absolutely certain are true? How do
you know? Where did you learn this information? Students can try to
pinpoint the resources they rely upon to get their "facts."

◆ Who is the author of this story? How do authors legitimize themselves as experts? What might be their motivations? Who are they
speaking to and for?

◆ How is the book marketed and what does it intend to teach Western
readers? Students might examine the description on the back of the
book, the author's note, the map, the glossary, and book reviews to make
observations about what kinds of readers are being targeted.

◆ How does Afghanistan (or Pakistan) fit into the region? In the
author's note, Deborah Ellis points out that Afghanistan has been at

war for decades. Often we study one country at a time. A more critical approach would investigate the relationships among countries. Students could explore the historical and current relationships (economic, political, cultural) between Afghanistan and other nation-states such as the former Soviet Union, Pakistan, Iran, and China.

◆ Whose story is missing? Students can create visual representations of the social locations (e.g., the race, class, gender, education) of each of the characters. Given these details, whose story is this? Whose stories are not here, and where might we go to learn about their stories?

Although these examples of young adult fictions do not offer much in the way of transformative education about the Middle East, they do offer the potential to educate us about our own assumptions and our pedagogical purposes when we teach the "oppressed Muslim girl" stories. It is in this capacity that we hope educators will take up these novels. ◆

---

*Özlem Sensoy teaches in the faculty of education at Simon Fraser University in Canada.*

*Elizabeth Marshall, a former elementary school teacher, teaches courses on children's and young adult literature at Simon Fraser University.*

## References

Antieau, K., *Broken Moon*. New York: Margaret K. McElderry Books, 2007.

Bigelow, B., Childs, S., Diamond, N., Dickerson, D., and Haaken, J., *Scarves of Many Colors: Muslim Women and the Veil*. Washington, D.C.: Teaching for Change, 2000.

Dyer, R., *The Matter of Images: Essays on Representation*. New York: Routledge, 1993.

Ellis, D., *The Breadwinner*. Toronto: Groundwood Books, 2000.

Ellis, D., *Parvana's Journey*. Toronto: Groundwood Books, 2002.

Ellis, D., *Mud City*. Toronto: Groundwood Books, 2003.

Kolhatkar, S. and Rawi, M., "Why Is a Leading Feminist Organization Lending Its Name to Support Escalation in Afghanistan?" July 8, 2009: www.alternet.org/world/141165.

Miller, E., "An Open Letter to the Editors of *Ms.* Magazine." *Off Our Backs*. September/March 2002: 59-61.

Sensoy, Ö., "Ickity Ackity Open Sesame: Learning About the Middle East in Images." *Rethinking Curricular Knowledge on Global Societies*. Ed. Binaya Subedi. Charlotte, N.C.: Information Age Publishing, 2009: 39-55.

Staples, S.F., *Under the Persimmon Tree*. New York: Simon & Schuster, 2005.

# Marketing American Girlhood

◆ ELIZABETH MARSHALL

Felicity's tilt-top tea table and chairs: $98.00; Addy's trunk: $159.00; Molly's vanity table: $60.00; girls learning about consumption and brand loyalty by the age of 10: priceless.

American Girl, makers of high quality dolls, historical fictions, films, and other products for girls, has cornered the market on how to sell American girlhood to the public. Its popularity came to my attention during my university teaching. I regularly teach an introductory children's literature course for preservice teachers. With few exceptions, most of the young women in my class enthusiastically remember reading the historical American Girl books and playing with the dolls. After several semesters of hearing about the merits of American Girl from my students, I decided it was time to investigate this cultural phenomenon.

KATHERINE STREETER

I remember two dolls from my girlhood, Barbie and Crissy, who had hair that you could adjust in length by twisting a knob on her back. These dolls did not fare well; they experienced numerous multilevel falls from bedroom windows and hairdressing appointments during which my sister and I melted each doll's lovely locks on hot light bulbs. One of Barbie's feet had been half-gnawed off by a mouse in our attic. Thus, I came to the American Girl materials with a certain distance and ambivalence about dolls.

Nevertheless, I signed up to receive the American Girl catalogs

**Let's just say I don't anticipate a Black Panther American Girl doll to turn up any time soon.**

and read the historical fictions. I learned that they are expensive: the Samantha Parkington doll, book, and accessories, for instance, cost $105.00. I made a trek to the American Girl Place, a three-story shop in Chicago. American Girl Place transports the visitor to another world where one can shop for dolls, accessories, books, or child-size versions of American Girl doll clothes; stop by the hair salon to get an American Girl doll a new "do"; make a reservation at the cafe where adults, girls, and their dolls (sometimes dressed in the same outfits) enjoy brunch, lunch, afternoon tea, or dinner; pose for a picture at the photo studio; or watch a movie in the theater.

A brief history of American Girl reveals a winning coming-of-age story. American Girl, LLC, was founded by Pleasant Rowland, a former Wisconsin schoolteacher who, according to the company's website, "wanted to give girls an understanding of America's past and a sense of pride in the traditions they share with girls of yesterday." American Girl produces a variety of products, including books, dolls, movies, a magazine, a catalog, and a website. American Girl published its first direct-mail catalog for girls aged 7 through 12 in 1986. Since that time, they have sold 132 million American Girl books, and 18 million American Girl dolls. Their magazine *American Girl* has a circulation of 500,000 and the website americangirl.com attracts at least 56 million visits per year. American Girl dolls were originally marketed as "anti-Barbie." Ironically, in 1998 Pleasant Rowland sold American Girl for $700 million to Mattel, the company that manufactures Barbie.

American Girl is perhaps best known for the historical American Girl doll collection. The usual suspects in this collection include Molly, Samantha, Felicity, Kit, Kirsten, Addy, Josefina, Kaya, and Julie. At first glance, the American Girl historical collection offers strong and plucky girls who counter images and/or storylines of girlhood offered by Disney, Bratz, or Barbie. However, any potential "girl-power" lessons are short-circuited in these books through the use of historical fiction to deliver traditional lessons about what girls can and should do. While the stories take place in key historical moments, such as the Civil War, and World War II, the girls rarely participate in historical events in any substantial way. *Meet Molly* is set in WWII and her father, a doctor, serves in the U.S. military. Molly's concerns center on what to be for Halloween and how to deal with a bothersome brother. The historical fictions encourage a limited independence and emphasize conventional "good-girl" behaviors. Girls might go on an adventure or two, but these are usually within the bounds of family relationships (e.g., playing tricks on brothers) rather than as social actors in a larger world. In addition, the visuals on the covers of the American Girl cata-

KATHERINE STREETER

log undercut the lessons about empowerment that the books offer. For example, on the front cover of the October 2006 catalog, two upper-class white girls sit quietly in front of a fireplace holding their dolls. The girls are placed inside rather than outside and are stationary, watching rather than doing.

The American Girl historical girl collection also purports to be multicultural and includes African American (Addy), Latina (Josefina), and Native American (Kaya) characters. However, this inclusion is superficial and represents the ways

**A persuasive curriculum of consumerism dominated the young women's recollections of these materials rather than any educational or historical aspects.**

in which "difference," like "girl power," has become a commodity that American Girl markets to its consumers. American Girl hires an advisory panel of "insiders" or cultural experts when creating characters such as Addy, Kaya, and Josefina; however, the histories that the corporation ultimately settles on invite critique. For instance, Kaya's story takes place in 1764 before Lewis and Clark arrive in 1805 and before the Nez Perce are forced to move to disease-ridden Fort Leavenworth in 1877. In a review of the Kaya series, Beverly Slapin (2007) writes that, "The series oversimplifies and sanitizes Nimíipuu history, and by doing so, makes history more palatable to the contemporary sensibilities of the young non-Native girl readers for whom this series was conceptualized." The glossary of Nez Perce and Spanish words included in the Kaya and Josefina books further highlight the point that these books are mainly intended to educate readers unfamiliar with these "other" cultures.

Josefina's story takes place on a *rancho* near Santa Fe, New Mexico, in 1824 before the Mexican-American War. The nonfictional "Looking Back: America in 1824" at the end of Meet Josefina dilutes this colonial history by limiting discussion to two sentences about the Mexican-American War and pointing out that when it ended in 1848, America "claimed most of the land that is now the southwestern United States" (Tripp, 1997, p. 83). The author of this history then moves on to describe the benefits of this war. "Although Josefina would never have imagined it when she was 9 years old, she would one day be an American—and the cultures and traditions of the New Mexican settlers and their Pueblo neighbors would become part of America, too" (p. 83). It is important to note that this loss of sovereignty was especially significant for New Mexican women, who had many more rights as Mexicans than they had as Americans—like the right to own their own property. The creators at American Girl favor a whitewashed version of this history, and Josefina's narrative reads as a melting pot story in which difference is assimilated into a larger American girlhood identity. Like *Meet Josefina*, each of the historical fictions takes place in the past and in this way allows issues such as racism, colonization, and war to be presented as things that America has overcome.

Each book includes a textbook-like "Peek at the Past" or "Looking Back" section at the end of each girl's story that adds historical context. This background material parallels standard textbook fare. Given that American Girl claims to provide girls with a sense of history, it is striking that these brief narratives focus on general American history rather than on the history of girls or even women in the United States. The representation of American girlhood in these materials avoids any

KATHERINE STREETER

lessons about social activism and refuses to teach girls about how to organize or how to fight ongoing gender and/or racial discrimination. Real-life examples could have been included, such as the story of 11-year-old Harriet Hanson, who led a strike in Lowell, Mass., in 1936 against unfair and harsh working conditions for mill girls. American Girl chooses to market a less controversial story about girlhood in The Great Depression in which Kit Kittredge sacrifices her room for one in the attic so that her family can take boarders into their house for extra money. For the year 1944, American Girl focuses on a white privileged girl rather than choosing to tell a story about the experiences of a Japanese American girl interned in a camp. Let's just say I don't anticipate a Black Panther American Girl doll to turn up any time soon.

**American Girl is invested in marketing a particular version of American girlhood that plays on the good intentions of parents, grandparents, and educators.**

Some might argue that American Girl is not as bad as other materials on the market, or as offensive as Barbie or Bratz dolls. This argument misses the key features of what makes this phenomenon so insidious: how corporations play on the feminist and/or educative aspirations of parents, teachers, girls, and young women and turn these toward consumption. American Girl is less about strong girls, diversity, or history than about marketing girlhood, about hooking girls, their parents and grandparents into buying the American Girl products and experience.

On this point, it is interesting to hear from young women who played with these materials as children. For instance, when I spoke with my undergraduate students about what appealed to them about American Girl, they talked mostly about shopping. These young women talked not about any specific history but about looking through and buying things from the catalog. One student said that one of the reasons that she loved playing with American Girl dolls was because, "It came with all these cool things." Another student agreed, "It came with everything. The little glasses and little necklaces." Two other young women remembered really wanting Addy because "she came with different stuff." The eight students that I spoke with associate the pleasure of American Girl with the "stuff" and "cool things" that came with each doll. A persuasive curriculum of consumerism dominated the young women's recollections of these materials rather than any educational or historical aspects.

These responses demonstrate how savvy American Girl is about product placement in their historical fictions. As one of my students told me: "I would read something in the book and they [the author] would be talking about the bedroom and I'd get out the catalog and I could look at all the stuff and see what I could get to recreate what was going on in the story." The books function as advertisements for other American Girl paraphernalia. For instance, in *Changes for Kaya: A Story of Courage*, Kaya receives a beautiful saddle "at the giveaway after Swan Circling's burial" (Shaw, 2002, p. 56). In the catalog and website, the saddle sells for $18.00. Kaya's horse "Steps High" comes with a "fringed hide blanket" and young readers can buy this combination for $75.00. Similarly, in *Meet Molly*, Molly "goes Hawaiian" for Halloween and dresses as a hula dancer (Tripp, 1986, p. 27). The book includes a stereotypical illustration of a young, brown-skinned, presumably Hawaiian woman with a flower lei and a grass skirt. You can buy this costume for your doll for $28.00.

Additionally, at the end of the novels that I read, I found a pullout postcard that encouraged me to sign up for an American Girl catalog. One of the cards reads: "While the books are the heart of The American Girls Collection®, they are only the beginning. The stories in the collection come to life when you act them out with the beautiful American Girl dolls and their exquisite clothes and accessories." When you receive the catalogue, you quickly see how the books tie into a larger cross-promotional strategy. The accessories that accompany each doll are in bold. For instance, in the October 2006 catalog: "Samantha arrives in a **dress** with stockings, **shoes**, a **hair bow** and a *Meet Saman-tha* paperback book. Her accessories set includes a **locket, hat, purse, hankie,** and pretend Indian head **penny**." It is no wonder that young women remember the accessories rather than the history.

The American Girl materials are complex. The storylines offer faux-empowerment and reductive historical narratives that are often difficult to unpack. This complexity as well as the range of materials (website, dolls, books, catalogs, magazines) marketed to girls by Ameri-can Girl invites a critical stance. American Girl materials, like other popular texts produced for and/or consumed by children, warrant our attention and cannot be dismissed as innocent girlhood materi-als. Rather, American Girl is invested in marketing a particular ver-sion of American girlhood that plays on the good intentions of parents, grandparents, and educators. American Girl challenges us to critically examine the cultural lessons about gender and history contained in this unofficial yet salient curriculum, and tests us to find ways to get our students thinking critically about the tactics corporations use to school and gender young consumers under the guise of education.

*Elizabeth Marshall is a former elementary school teacher. She currently works as an assistant professor at Simon Fraser University in British Columbia, where she teaches courses on children's and young adult literature. She wishes to thank her students for sharing their expertise.*

## References

American Girl Corp. (2010). Fast Facts. Retrieved Oct. 14, 2010 from http://www.americangirl.com/corp/corporate.php?section=about&id=6

American Girl Corp. (2006). *American Girl: Follow your inner star.* October. Middleton, WI: Pleasant Company Publications.

American Girl Corp. (2007). *Welcome to Pleasant Company.* Retrieved April 11, 2008 from http://www.americangirl.com/corp/html/customers.html

Shaw, J. (2002). Changes for Kaya: A story of courage. Middleton, WI: Pleas-ant Company Publications.

Slapin, B. (2007). "American Girls Collection: Kaya." . Retrieved April 11, 2008 from http://americanindiansinchildrensliterature.blogspot.com/2007/04/american-girls-collection-kaya-broken.html

Tripp, V. (1986, 1989, 2000). *Meet Molly.* Middleton, WI: Pleasant Company Publications.

Tripp, V. (1997, 2000). *Meet Josefina.* Middleton, WI: Pleasant Company Publications.

Tripp, V. (2000). *Meet Kit.* Middleton, WI: Pleasant Company Publications.

# Part 3:
# Examine Race, Class, Gender, Sexuality, and Social Histories in Popular Culture and Media

KATHERINE STREETER

# Girls, Worms, and Body Image

*A teacher deals with gender stereotypes among her second and third graders*

◆ KATE LYMAN

"I need to lose weight," Kayla was saying. Another 2nd-grade girl chimed in: "So do I. I'm way too fat." My students' conversation shocked me. Distracted from my hallway responsibility of monitoring the noise level at the water fountains, I listened in more closely. Linda, a 3rd-grade girl who is thin to the point of looking unhealthy, grabbed a piece of paper from Kayla. "I'm the one who needs this."

"No, I need it!" insisted Rhonda.

The hotly contested paper turned out to contain the name of an exercise video that my 2nd- and 3rd-grade class had seen in gym class. The gym teacher later assured me that the student teacher had stressed that the exercises were for health and fitness, not weight loss. However, the girls were convinced that the video would help them lose weight and were frantic to get hold of it.

Issues of women and body image are certainly not new to me. I thought back to when I was a teenager struggling to make my body match the proportions of the models in *Seventeen* magazine. I had learned that the average model was 5'9"and 110 pounds. I was the ideal 5'9", but even on a close-to-starvation diet of 900 calories a day I could not get my weight down to 110 pounds.

But that was in the 1960s. Hadn't girls liberated themselves from such regimens, I asked myself? And even back in the 1960s, it wasn't until high school that I remembered my classmates living on coffee and oranges. Seven-and 8-year-olds ate all the cake and candy and potato chips that they could get their hands on.

I wondered how I could enlighten my 7- and 8-year-old girls who were so concerned about their body image. What follows are ways— sometimes successful, sometimes not—in which I struggled with the issue throughout my teaching last year. At the time of the incident with the gym video, I had been teaching a unit on women's history, and the class had shown an interest in learning about women's struggle to get the vote. I realized the unit needed to take a new turn. It was time to move on to the gender issues they faced as girls and women today.

## Facts and Stereotypes

I decided to start by learning more about the students' knowledge and perceptions about gender. I divided the students into two groups and asked the girls to decide on 10 facts about boys/men and the boys to do the same in regard to girls/women. Before the activity, I tried to clarify the difference between opinions and facts, but the lists of "facts" revealed the futility of my attempts:

**Facts About Boys/Men**
(written by the girls)
1. Boys are selfish.
2. Boys are different from girls because of their body parts.
3. Men make their wives take care of the children and house.
4. Dads make the moms do the shopping.
5. Men get paid more than women.
6. Men get women just for their looks.
7. Men are mean and lazy and jealous.
8. Men are picky eaters and like their dinners when they get home.
9. Men and boys are bossy.

**Facts About Girls/Women** (written by the boys)
1. They always complain.
2. They are too loud and picky.
3. They are sensitive.
4. Girls and women are better bakers than boys and men.
5. They are bossy.
6. Girls are always talking about boys and men.
7. Girls and women aren't as smart as boys and men.
8. Girls are more jealous than boys.
9. Girls and women spend a long time getting ready to look pretty.

We discussed the "facts" as a group and tried to come to an agreement about which statements were indeed facts and which were stereotypes, generalizations, or opinions. The girls protested vehemently to the idea that boys and men were smarter than girls and women. They insisted, in fact, that the opposite was true.

Many students were reluctant to concede the veracity of some of the other statements. One student, Yer, for instance, argued, "I know for a fact that women are better bakers than men!" Anna countered that not only was her dad a good cook, but he also helped with the shopping and didn't insist on his dinner on time.

The other students saw Anna's dad as a single exception to the rule, but were willing to add the qualifier "most" to the statements about men and household tasks.

It occurred to me that a short story, "X," would be a good vehicle for further discussions on gender stereotypes. In "X," written by Lois Gould (in *Stories for Free Children*), a couple agrees to let their baby be part of a scientific experiment in which no one is allowed to know the baby's gender except the parents and the baby him/herself.

At first, students responded to the dilemmas posed by X's situation with their own gender blinders. In the story, X's relatives cannot figure out what kind of presents to buy X: "a tiny football helmet" or "a pink-flowered romper suit." The students in my class were equally confounded.

"Maybe they could buy an outfit that was split down the middle, half blue and half pink," said one student. Another suggested that X "could wear a baseball top and pink lacy bottoms."

I asked them to look around the room at each other's clothes. To a child, they were wearing unisex outfits—mainly jeans and t-shirts. But it still didn't occur to them that there might be baby clothes that would be suitable for either a boy or girl.

After my frustrating attempts to define fact vs. stereotypes about

gender and my less-than-successful attempts at discussion around the story "X," I again thought back
to my childhood. A photo taken of me at about my
students' ages shows me in a lacy dress, cuffed white
socks, and patent leather Mary Jane shoes, my hair
tightly braided and tied in ribbons. I am sitting on
a bench in my yard, surrounded by my dolls. My head is turned to the
side and I am smiling shyly. What would I have said about men's and
women's roles? Would the story of X have made any sense to me? I'm not
sure how that 1950s girl would have fit into the gender discussion, but I
do remember that under the neat, frilly dress was a girl whose heroes
were TV cowboys, a girl who daydreamed about being a boy so she, too,
could have adventures on horseback.

> **The girls protested vehemently the idea that boys and men were smarter than girls and women.**

I was trapped in the much more rigid gender expectations of the
1950s, and yet I wondered if my girls in their jeans and sweats really
had that many more options than I had had. The girls in my class were
right. Most women do have the major responsibility for taking care of
the children and house. Most men do still get higher pay in their jobs.
And the stereotypes still abound.

I was stuck in this examination of gender roles. Stuck in the classroom and stuck with my own personal history. I did not know where I
was going with the unit.

## A Saving Rain

But then, just as lesson plans were failing me as often as not, nature co-
operated with a heavy rain that forced hundreds of worms up from the
soil onto the playground. At recess the boys picked the worms up and
dangled them at the girls while the girls ran screaming. Kayla, Stephanie, and Melissa, who will take on any drama, were leading the group
with their screaming. Linda, Mandy, and other more shy, usually passive girls were joining in, following their lead.

Kayla came running up to me. "Help, help, Tony's got a bunch of
worms and he's chasing me with them. The worms are going to bite me!"

Reasoning was useless. Boys and girls were too engrossed in their
drama. I picked up a worm and demonstrated that it did no harm, but
my attempts to educate the girls failed. The chasing and screaming continued. I was successful at stopping Tony from coming into the school
with worms in his shoes and pockets, but the screaming continued into
the halls and music class.

I felt defeated. Times had not changed. This playground scene
could have occurred in my elementary school in the 1950s. I decided
that before I moved on to more subtle aspects of gender stereotyping, I

needed to deal with girls and worms.

Then, after recess, Stephanie and Kayla took a brave step forward. They came back to the classroom with rubber gloves that they had gotten from the "lunch lady" so that they could touch the worms. I suggested to the class that we could collect worms for our classroom, but that the rubber gloves were not necessary.

I put Kayla in charge of the terrarium and gave Stephanie the spoon. A group of 10 or 12 girls followed them outside to collect worms for the classroom.

"Can't boys help get the worms? Only girls?" asked David dejectedly.

I assured him that he could help, and several other boys joined the project, but the ringleaders were still the girls. They quickly got over their squeamishness.

"I'm not scared of worms anymore!" Anna proudly announced. Soon we had about two dozen large, fat earthworms and several cups of dirt. The worm center was so noisily enthusiastic that I could barely hear the principal's announcement over the intercom. I think it had something to do with keeping the halls clean by not tracking the mud in from the playground.

The girls had conquered their fears of worms, but I still heard conversations—and, even worse, insults—about body image. One girl told another student that he should think about going to Jenny Craig.

## Toys and Media

I decided to lead a critique on two sources of stereotypical images of women: toys and the media. I wanted to give the students an opportunity to analyze images of women that they see every day, to have some understanding how those images influence their self-concepts.

I began with a lesson focused on a Barbie doll. Most girls in my class said that they owned Barbies, but none remembered to bring one in, so I borrowed one from another classroom. I started with an open-ended question: "Tell me what you notice about Barbie."

I was somewhat nervous because there was a university student visiting my classroom and I had little confidence in what my probing would bring about. Quickly, however, the observations poured out. Kayla, who is of stocky build herself, as is her mom, was quick to point out that Barbie has a very skinny waist.

"But she has big boobs," added Stephanie. I asked Stephanie if she knew a respectful way to refer to that part of a woman's body and she nodded. "Breasts," she corrected. "She has huge breasts."

"Barbie has tiny feet," someone said. "They are made for high heels."

"She has a cute, turned-up nose."

"She has a very long, skinny neck."

"She has very skinny arms and legs."

Students agreed that Barbie looked very different from the women they knew— their moms, grandmas, and teachers. The students didn't bring up Barbie's ethnicity, so I asked them to look around the circle and see how else she was different from many of them. They looked around at each other, more than half with dark or various shades of brown faces, and only one blonde-haired child among them.

> **I decided that before I moved on to more subtle aspects of gender stereotyping, I needed to deal with girls and worms.**

"She's white!" yelled out Shantee. "She has yellow hair and blue eyes."

"My mom will only let my sister play with black Barbies," added Steven.

"Do the black Barbies look like real-life African American girls?" I asked.

"No, they have hair like white people," concluded Shantee. "Only it's colored black."

I asked them why the toy manufacturers might make a doll for girls to play with that looked so different from real girls and women. The consensus was that girls want to look like her so that men would like them better. The only dissenting voice was Kayla, who said that her mom's partner liked his women big.

Other comments were that women wanted to look beautiful, like Barbie, all skinny and pretty, with hair down to their waist. To further probe why that might be, I moved to the part of my lesson dealing with women in advertisements.

I hoped my students could grasp the concept that advertisers create an illusion that their product will transform a woman into a younger, prettier, more appealing self. I also wanted my students to practice looking at advertisements more critically—to analyze the hidden messages and to begin to see how women are objectified and minimized. I didn't expect them to understand all these concepts; I saw the lesson as an introduction.

I had torn out dozens of ads from women's magazines, general magazines such as *Ebony*, and other sources, showing women using products from cigarettes to weight-loss formulas to cosmetics. We discussed several ads as a group. I asked my students to look at how the woman was shown, what product the advertiser was trying to sell, and what the advertiser was telling women about what would happen if they bought the product. Then I sent them on their own to choose one of the ads and write about it. After they typed and edited their writing, they made the ads and script into posters that I hung in the hall.

Stephanie chose a cigarette ad with the message "A Taste for the Elegant" and the picture of a thin, sophisticated woman in a white pantsuit and high heels. Her commentary read: "'A taste for the elegant' is what it says on my poster, but it can't be a taste for the elegant because cigarettes don't taste good. Cigarettes are bad for your lungs."

Anna wrote that her ad for a perfume product was saying that "Women have to be skinny and have a dress with no sleeves and if she uses this perfume then she gets a man."

Kayla wrote: "I think she's trying to get people to get the Oil of Olay to look young when they look just fine the way they are. I mean they don't have to listen to a woman that wants people to look young. That's stupid. The people look fine the way they are!!"

Rhonda interpreted the message in a shampoo ad as "You should be cute and be skinny. The ad says that you should use Redken Shampoo, and wear a lot of makeup, and wear cute clothes so you can look like a Barbie doll."

Nathan saw some humor in his ad about a weight-loss product: "It is telling women that they have to be skinny, wear lipstick, and wear high heels. And from the picture of what she used to look like, I think she looks so different [now] that she should get a new [driver's] license."

Afterward, I thought of many things I should have done differently with the lesson. More background on advertising. More time for discussion and sharing. Perhaps a follow-up action product. The visiting university student, however, was impressed that elementary students could handle such a complex topic so well.

Maybe I was on the right track.

## An Old-Fashioned Day

But just to make sure, I wanted to provide an opportunity for the class to experience gender discrimination firsthand, in an exaggerated yet playful setting. For the last day of our unit, I decided to have a role play of an old-fashioned school day, with an emphasis on how girls and boys were treated differently.

I sent home interview sheets in which kids questioned their parents on what school was like when they went to school, including how boys and girls were treated differently. The students shared their findings (one student noted, "My mom got hit with a PADDLE!"). My student teacher shared some old books and a slate that her grandfather had saved. Students read a book, *Early Schools*, and, using information from it, wrote first-person accounts about a day in an old-fashioned school.

Not concerned with strict historical accuracy (also knowing that schools varied regionally), we planned the morning based on the parent interviews, the book on early schools, and our own experiences. We sent home a note preparing the families for this experiment. Girls were to come dressed in dresses (not above the knees) and boys in slacks and shirts with collars. We pushed back the tables, moved the chairs into rows and set up an "old-fashioned" schedule of handwriting, spelling bees, rote math, and textbook science. We used a variety of discipline techniques: Children got sent to the corner, they had to write 100 sentences, they had to wear the dunce cap—anything short of physical punishment.

**I thought that if I exaggerated the effect of gender discrimination, maybe then they would be better able to recognize the more subtle forms that they encountered within and outside of themselves.**

We also incorporated differential treatment for boys and girls in everything we did, from having a boys' line and a girls' line, to calling on the boys more often than the girls, to chastising the girls more for messy handwriting. The experiment went on for two-and-a-half hours, with the participation of the gym teacher and principal. The latter came in sporting a white wig and a paddle.

After gym class, we gathered back in our circle to discuss how the kids felt about the morning. I was especially interested to hear if they noticed the differential gender treatment, which was not as obvious as the differences in the setup of the room, work, and punishments. Not only did they notice the bias, but the girls were indignant, while the boys were gleeful.

"You were paying more attention to the boys!" was the first comment. "Boys were called on more and they were getting all the answers." My students noted that there were different rules for boys than for girls. A boy had been allowed to whistle. A girl had been reprimanded for the same behavior.

"I didn't like how you said, 'That's not ladylike,'" said Stephanie.

"I liked how you didn't make us do it over when we smudged our handwriting," noted Henry.

"Yeah, you tore mine up and made me start over," said Melissa. "And I hate wearing dresses," added Rhonda.

Girls were upset about how they had to play with Hula-Hoops while the boys played dodgeball in gym and how in science, boys did hands-on experimentation with worms while girls filled out glossary definitions from their science book.

"I know why you did this," said Anna, her face lighting up with a sudden realization. "You wanted us to know what prejudice feels like!"

Well, Anna was close. I thought that if I exaggerated the effect of gender discrimination, maybe then they would be better able to recognize the more subtle forms that they encountered within and outside of themselves. Certainly, my experience growing up had made me sensitive to gender stereotyping. But, at the same time, the cynical side of me knew that experiences with gender discussions, worms, and media critiquing paled in the light of Barbies, television, and Jenny Craig.

As I was packing up to go home after a long day, one especially exhausting due to our old-fashioned school experiment, Stephanie and Rhonda ran through the classroom to cut through the back door. As they stepped out to head for home, I heard Stephanie ask Rhonda, "So if I come over to your house, will you still be on your diet?"

"Oh, no," answered Rhonda flippantly. "I don't do that on the weekend." ◆

---

*Kate Lyman has taught kindergarten through 3rd grade in Madison, Wisconsin, for 34 years. Together with her class and students at the University of Wisconsin—Madison, she has tackled a variety of social justice issues.*

# Math and Media

*Students use math to track media bias*

◆ BOB PETERSON

Math, like language, is an essential tool to analyze and address social problems. This is particularly true when helping students critique the mass media for bias. Below are several teaching ideas that can be used in classrooms while integrating math into language arts and social studies.

## Photo Fairness

Fairness and Accuracy in Reporting (FAIR), a media watchdog group based in New York, looked at the front-page photos for one month in three major dailies, the *New York Times, USA Today,* and the *Washington Post,* and found that women were dramatically slighted.

MICHAEL DUFFY

A number of years ago, FAIR found that in the *Washington Post,* only 13 percent of the front-page photo subjects were women. In the *New York Times,* the percentage was 11 percent. *USA Today* featured more women (30 percent), but while 55 percent of white men seen on *USA Today*'s front page were representatives of government or business, not a single woman was in those categories.

People of color in the three papers seemed to fit neat stereotypes. Thirty percent of all men of color in front-page photos were athletes; another 14 percent were criminals. All the women of color on the *Washington Post* front page were victims—of fire, poverty, or homes destroyed by drugs.

Students can monitor newspapers or magazines in a similar fashion, keeping records in journals and making visual displays on bulletin boards. Math skills of simple computation, averages, percent, and graphing can be utilized. Students could take action against any inequities they might discover by writing to the newspaper and using their findings to teach younger children about the bias they detected.

## Resources

**www.medialit.org**
The Center for Media Literacy has an extensive catalog of critical media materials including curricula promoting general analysis of advertising and others with a special emphasis on alcohol and tobacco ads.

**www.adbusters.org**
Adbusters is a global network of culture jammers and creatives working to change the way information flows, the way corporations wield power, and the way meaning is produced in our society.

**www.media-awareness.ca/english/index.cfm**
The Media Awareness Network provides resources and support for people interested in media and digital literacy.

**www.evc.org**
The Educational Video Center is a nonprofit youth media organization dedicated to teaching documentary video to develop the artistic, critical literacy, and career skills of young people, while nurturing their idealism and commitment to social change.

**www.projectcensored.org**
Project Censored publishes an annual list of unreported and underreported stories.

## Researching Bias in Newspapers

Discovering whose perspective is printed in newspapers is easy, and fun to tabulate. Using different color highlighters, have students mark every time certain people are quoted in the paper. Then analyze results by gender, race, government vs. nongovernment officials, celebrity status, and other categories of your choosing. For example, how often do newspapers quote grassroots activists opposed to governmental policies, especially on the federal level?

Students can do the same with entire stories. They can outline in one color all those stories about violence and crime, for example, and use another color to outline stories about people working for justice and peace. Similarly, one can highlight how many times people of color are featured in stories of crime or drug addiction, and how many times they are portrayed positively.

A FAIR study of 2,850 articles in the *Washington Post* and the *New York Times* found that 78 percent of the stories were primarily based on the words of government officials. Another FAIR study found that only 13 percent of those quoted in front-page stories in the *Post* were women, and women were responsible for only 6 percent of the quotes on the front page of the *Times*. ◆

---

*Bob Peterson teaches at La Escuela Fratney in Milwaukee and is an editor of* Rethinking Schools *magazine. Material for the above was taken from* Extra!, *a publication of FAIR, Vol. 4, No. 7.*

# Human Beings Are Not Mascots

◆ BARBARA MUNSON

A 35-foot metal Chief Wahoo sign was removed from the roof of the Cleveland Indians stadium in 1994.

ASSOCIATED PRESS PHOTO | MARK DUNCAN

" Indian" logos and nicknames create, support, and maintain stereotypes of a race of people. When such cultural abuse is supported by one or many of society's institutions, it constitutes institutional racism.

These logos—along with other abuses and stereotypes—separate, marginalize, confuse, intimidate, and harm Native American children and create barriers to their learning throughout their school experiences. In addition, the logos teach non-Indian children that it's alright to participate in culturally abusive behavior.

As long as such logos remain, both Native American and non-Indian children are learning to tolerate racism in schools. The following are some common questions and statements that I have encountered in trying to educate others about the "Indian" logo issue.

> As long as such logos remain, both Native American and non-Indian children are learning to tolerate racism in schools.

### "We have always been proud of our 'Indians.'"

People are proud of their school athletic teams even in communities

**Native people are saying that they don't feel honored by this symbolism. We experience it as no less than a mockery of our cultures.**

where the team's name and symbolism do not stereotype a race of people. In developing athletic traditions, schools have borrowed from Native American cultures the sacred objects, ceremonial traditions, and components of traditional dress that were most obvious—without understanding their deep meaning or appropriate use. Such school traditions are replete with inaccurate depictions of Indian people, and promote and maintain stereotypes. Schools have taken the trappings of Native cultures onto the playing field where young people have played at being "Indian." Over time, and with practice, generations of children have come to believe that the pretended "Indian" identity is more than what it is.

### "We are honoring Indians; you should feel honored."

Native people are saying that they don't feel honored by this symbolism. We experience it as no less than a mockery of our cultures. We see objects sacred to us—such as the drum, eagle feathers, face painting, and traditional dress—being used, not in sacred ceremony, or in any cultural setting, but in another culture's game.

Why must some schools insist on using symbols of a race of people? Other schools are happy with logos that offend no human being. Why do some schools insist on categorizing Indian people along with animals and objects?

### "Why is the term 'Indian' as a mascot name offensive?"

The term "Indian" was given to indigenous people on this continent by an explorer who was looking for India, a man who was lost and who subsequently exploited the indigenous people. "Indian" is not the name we prefer to be called. We are known by the names of our Nations— Oneida (Onyota'a:ka), Ho-Chunk, Stockbridge-Munsee, Menominee (Omaeqnomenew), Chippewa (Anishinabe), Potawatomi, etc.

### "Why is an attractive depiction of an Indian warrior just as offensive as an ugly caricature?"

Both depictions are stereotypes. Both firmly place Indian people in the past. The logos keep us marginalized. Depictions of mighty warriors of the past emphasize a tragic part of our history; they ignore the strength and beauty of our cultures during times of peace. Many Indian cultures view life as a spiritual journey filled with lessons to be learned from every experience and from every living being. Many cultures put high value on peace, right action, and sharing.

Indian men are not limited to the role of warrior; in many of our cultures a good man is learned, gentle, patient, wise, and deeply spiritual. The depictions of Indian "braves," "warriors," and "chiefs" also ignore the roles of women and children. Although there are patrilineal Native cultures, many Indian nations are both matrilineal and child centered.

**Most Indian adults have lived through the pain of prejudice and harassment in schools when they were growing up, and they don't want their children to experience more of the same.**

### "We never intended the logo to cause harm."

It may be true that no harm was intended when the logos were adopted. But we Indian people are saying that the logos are harmful to our cultures, and especially to our children, in the present. When someone says you are hurting them by your action, if you persist, then the harm becomes intentional.

### "Aren't you proud of your warriors?"

Yes, we are proud of the warriors who fought to protect our cultures and preserve our lands. We don't want them demeaned by being "honored" in a sports activity on a playing field.

### "This is not an important issue."

If it is not important, then why are school boards willing to tie up their time and risk potential lawsuits rather than simply change the logos?

I, as an Indian person, have never said it is unimportant. Most Indian adults have lived through the pain of prejudice and harassment in schools when they were growing up, and they don't want their children to experience more of the same. This issue speaks to our children being able to form a positive Indian identity and to develop appropriate levels of self-esteem.

In addition, it has legal ramifications in regard to pupil harassment and equal access to education. If it's not important to people of differing ethnic and racial backgrounds within the community, then change the logos. They are hurting the community's Native American population.

### "What if we drop derogatory comments and clip art, and adopt pieces of 'real' Indian ceremony, like pow-wows and sacred songs?"

Though well intended, these solutions are culturally naive. To make a parody of such ceremonial gatherings for the purpose of cheering on the team at homecoming would multiply exponentially the offensiveness. Bringing Native religions onto the playing field through songs of tribute to the "Great Spirit" or Mother Earth would increase the mockery of Native religions even more than the current use of drums and feathers.

**"This logo issue is just about political correctness."**
Using the term "political correctness" to describe the attempts of concerned Native American parents, educators, and leaders to remove stereotypes from the public schools trivializes a survival issue. A history of systematic genocide has decimated more than 95 percent of the indigenous population of the Americas. Today, the average life expectancy of Native American males in some communities is age 45. The teen suicide rate among Native people is several times higher than the national average. Stereotypes, ignorance, silent inaction, and even naive innocence damage and destroy individual lives and whole cultures. Racism kills.

**"Why don't community members understand the need to change? Isn't it a simple matter of respect?"**
On one level, yes. But respecting a culture different from the one you were raised in requires some effort. Even if a person lives in a different culture, insight and understanding of that culture will require interaction, listening, observing, and a willingness to learn.

The Native American population, in most school districts that display "Indian" logos, is proportionally very small. When one of us confronts the logo issue, that person, his or her children and other family members, and anyone else in the district who is Native American become targets of insults and threats; we are shunned and further marginalized. We appreciate the courage, support, and sometimes the sacrifice, of all who stand with us by speaking out against the continued use of "Indian" logos.

When you advocate for the removal of these logos, you are strengthening the spirit of tolerance and justice in your community; you are modeling for all our children thoughtfulness, courage, and respect for self and others. ◆

---

*Barbara Munson, Oneida, is active in educating school and community groups about the insensitivity in using stereotypes as school mascots and logos. This is excerpted from an article that appeared at www.nativeweb.org.*

# Race: Some Teachable—and Uncomfortable—Moments

◆ HEIDI TOLENTINO

"**Y**ou can never know what it's like to be black," Carlen said sharply. The class went silent. It was the fourth week of school and my juniors had just begun Sue Monk Kidd's *The Secret Life of Bees*. The novel is set in South Carolina in the mid-1960s. Something intrigued me about the perspective and the interracial relationships during such social upheaval. I chose this book because I love the characters, but also because it opens the door to discussions of racial justice—both historically and today.

Growing up the only Asian American student in my community, I promised myself that I would never walk away from issues of race in a classroom setting. Thus, for my 11th-grade American Literature class, I choose multicultural literature that explores how race plays out in characters' lives, which I hope will in turn trigger discussions about how race plays out in our lives. One of my aims is to help students—especially my predominantly white students—recognize that life in our society confronts us with choices about whether and how we will act to counter racism. Too often, "racism" is reduced to how people treat one another on an interpersonal level. But I wanted them

DAVID McLIMANS

**I knew what it felt like to be one of the only students of color in a classroom and to have to wait for other students to make comments that were stereotypical and painful.**

**We examined the tricks used in the test to keep African Americans from voting.**

to think in broader terms about this country's history of legislated racism and the lingering patterns of inequality produced by that history. Some of this curriculum I can map out in advance in lesson plans, but part of this work is improvisational, and I know I need to be alert to the unpredictable, and sometimes uncomfortable, ways that students respond to this teaching.

As part of Portland's annual "curriculum camp," I worked with a group of high school teachers to create a unit around *The Secret Life of Bees* as a stepping-stone for teaching about the human effects of institutionalized racism. I began the unit in my 11th-grade language arts class at Portland's Cleveland High School, an urban school, but one that is more than 75 percent European American. My students and I were early in the unit and just beginning our exploration of the impact of segregation in the lives of characters in the novel.

I opened our reading of *The Secret Life of Bees* by examining the dichotomy between the lives of whites and blacks in the South during the 1960s. I used Spike Lee's documentary *4 Little Girls*, to help students gain insight into the chasm between the two communities. The film focuses on the bombing of the 16th Street Church in Birmingham, Alabama, by white supremacists. This African American church was the center of civil rights activity there at the time of the bombing; the congregation was focused on helping black citizens gain the right to vote. Four young girls were murdered and Spike Lee focuses both on the repercussions of their deaths and how members of the community honored their lives through continuing civil rights activism. I chose this film to begin our unit because it is a powerful look at the blatant and violent racism that existed in 1965 and the struggle of African Americans and their white allies to fight for equal rights through their push to register African American voters. This was our starting point.

Shortly after watching the film, I initiated a discussion on a scene from *The Secret Life of Bees* in which Rosaline, one of the book's African American characters, is arrested while on her way to register to vote. We reflected on what we'd learned about work for voting rights, and I brought out copies of the Louisiana voting rights test given to African Americans who tried to register.

We examined the tricks used in the test to keep African Americans from voting. I set the scene for them: "Imagine the fear that must have come with walking through that door, seeing the men with rifles standing a few feet behind you, and being handed a test, given 10 minutes to finish, and realizing that there was no way for you to pass." The students were appalled and kept pointing out new questions for us to examine and to try to decode them, and finally concluded that there was no way to decode trick questions. They couldn't take their eyes off the document.

As students put the tests away, I noticed Evan watching the clock from his desk, and I walked over and joked, "Stop counting down the minutes until you can run from the classroom." He shushed me and told me he was timing Jessie to see if she could finish the test in 10 minutes. She wrote frantically as she sat hunched over the paper. Without glancing up she said, "I want to know what it was like."

Suddenly, from across the room I heard: "You can never know what it's like. You will never understand." I turned quickly to see the fury on the face of one of my African American students as she glared at Jessie. Jessie looked up from the test, her pencil poised over the paper, and stared across the room.

The State of Louisiana

Literacy Test (This test is to be given to anyone who cannot prove a fifth grade education.)

Do what you are told to do in each statement, nothing more, nothing less. Be careful as one wrong answer denotes failure of the test. You have 10 minutes to complete the test.

1. Draw a line around the number or letter of this sentence.

2. Draw a line under the last word in this line.

3. Cross out the longest word in this line.

4. Draw a line around the shortest word in this line.

5. Circle the first, first letter of the alphabet in this line.

6. In the space below draw three circles, one inside (engulfed by) the other.

7. Above the letter X make a small cross.

8. Draw a line through the letter below that comes earliest in the alphabet.

   Z V S B D M K I T P H C

9. Draw a line through the two letters below that come last in the alphabet.

   Z V B D M K T P H S Y C

10. In the first circle below write the last letter of the first word beginning with "L".

11. Cross out the number necessary, when making the number below one million.

   10000000000

12. Draw a line from circle 2 to circle 5 that will pass below circle 2 and above circle 4.

13. In the line below cross out each number that is more than 20 but less than 30.

   31  16  48  29  53  47  22  37  98  26  20  25

I knew I had to make a choice quickly and either cut off discussion or open the door all the way. I decided to let it swing wide open. I said: "Talking about issues of race is so difficult. It's painful. Most adults don't want to touch it and will silence others when they do. But I've found that at our school students will discuss it, and I want to give you room to do so. You need to know that when you say something in this class, you have to be ready to explain yourself and have an open discussion about it as a class."

I motioned to the student who had confronted Jessie and said, "Carlen, tell us what you meant." I sat down at a student desk and the room went completely silent. The students sat rigidly at their desks, and the tension in the room was palpable.

Carlen took a deep breath, leaned forward, and said pointedly to Jessie who was seated directly across from her, "You can never know what it's like to be black." Her face became more serious with each word, her tone angry. "I also don't understand why white people always

**When I encourage students to think about race in an almost all-white classroom, do I do it on the backs of my students of color? Do I force them to carry a load that is too heavy just to help white students begin to deal with their own issues of race?**

say, 'I want to know what you're feeling and know what it feels like.' You don't want to know what it feels like to walk down the street and have white women clutch their purses. You don't want to know what it's like to be different every single day. You can't want to know because it's horrible."

Jessie pushed her blonde hair back from her face and came right back at her and said: "But should I just remain ignorant then? Don't you think it's important for me to try and understand so that things can change? Race is a huge issue in 2006 and things haven't changed and I think we have to learn to change things." Her voice shook just the slightest bit, but she looked determined. No one made a sound.

"But there is nothing you can do to understand it. You are white and you will always be white and you won't ever know what it's like to be me." Carlen never shouted, but the intensity of her words filled the room.

"But don't I have to try? Shouldn't I try?" Jessie's voice sounded desperate.

"But, why? What will it change?" Carlen sat back in her seat and I felt 34 pairs of eyes turn my way.

The girls looked at each other for a moment, and I stepped toward them. I told them how much I appreciated their honesty and that I wanted them to feel that they could always stop our discussions to be honest about what they were feeling and thinking. I explained that we were not going to end this conversation for good—we would come back to it over and over so they should reflect on today and think about what they'd heard, felt, and thought. In retrospect, I wish I had stopped the class and had them journal about what occurred so that they could gain some perspective in the moment. But, if I had, the following discussion may never have happened.

### The 'N' Word

I breathed a sigh of relief as we returned to the book and Rosaline, who was on her way to register to vote. Before we began to read, I explained that in the next section and in sections to come, the N-word would be used, and I wanted them to understand my policy around that word. I explained that because of its painful history, I ask students not to say the word when we read aloud. Instead, I have them say N. I also explained that we would naturally never use that word in the classroom at any time or toward anyone. Just as a student continued our read-aloud, I noticed a hand out of the corner of my eye. In my gut, I knew that something was coming. I'd known the student for two years and I knew his penchant for creating chaos, but I asked anyway. "Joe, do you have a question about the book?"

"No, but I have a question about the N-word. Why can black people use it and white people can't?"

Voices exploded from every corner of the room. "Are you a complete idiot for bringing that up now?" "Why are you trying to start something?" "What is wrong with you?"

I silenced the class and, with an inner grimace, thanked Joe for asking such a difficult question. What I really wanted to say was, "We don't have time for that question now. Just don't use the N-word." But I knew that this was

14. Draw a line under the first letter after "h" and draw a line through the second letter after "j".

a b c d e  f g h i j k l m n o p q

15. In the space below, write the word "noise" backwards and place a dot over what would be its second letter should it have been written forward.

16. Draw a triangle with a blackened circle that overlaps only its left corner.

17. Look at the line of numbers below, and place on the blank, the number that should come next.

2  4  8  16  ____

18. Look at the line of numbers below, and place on the blank, the number that should come next.

3  6  9  ____  15

19. Draw in the space below, a square with a triangle in it, and within that same triangle draw a circle with a black dot in it.

20. Spell backwards, forwards.

21. Print the word vote upside down, but in the correct order.

22. Place a cross over the tenth letter in this line, a line under the first space in this sentence, and circle around the last the in the second line of this sentence.

23. Draw a figure that is square in shape. Divide it in half by drawing a straight line from its northeast corner to its southwest corner, and then divide it once more by drawing a broken line from the middle of its western side to the middle of its eastern side.

a pivotal point in my year and if I wanted to push kids, I had to push myself. I asked the students to close their books.

Internally I was shaking. *What was I going to say? How did I let it get this far? Why wasn't I prepared for this?* I had five seconds to come up with something.

I explained to students that words that are historically used against a community in hate are often taken back by that community and turned around and used as words of power. I told them about my 6th-grade experience when I told my parents that we played "smear the queer" at school that day and how my parents almost jumped out of their chairs trying to cover my mouth. They explained why that word was never to be used again in our house because it was derogatory and disrespectful. I never forgot that, so when a friend of mine used "queer" years later when talking about her own community, I was taken aback. I asked her about its use and she explained how the gay and lesbian community had taken it back and used it as a word of power. I told kids that the N-word had an even more horrific past and so much pain connected to it and we had to be careful when dealing with it.

Joe was not appeased. He peered out at me from behind his glasses, "But why can't white people use it?"

**I have to be willing to deal with the unexpected if I want to truly be an anti-racist teacher.**

I explained that even within the African American community, there was a split about whether or not to use the N-word and that the debate was heated and might always be that way. I noticed some students raising their hands, waving them around, and I had to make another split-second decision. I knew that they wanted to put their two cents in about the topic, and I was usually open to hearing what everyone had to say, but this was different. We had already had an intense blowup and two of my African American students looked uncomfortable and were not making eye contact with anyone.

I knew what it felt like to be one of the only students of color in a classroom and to have to wait for other students to make comments that were stereotypical and painful. I knew the feeling in the pit of my stomach as I waited for the comment and knew everyone was looking at me and waiting for my reaction. So I continued: "But if you are not a member of that community and have never had that word used against you in hate, you don't get to be part of the debate." The hands slowly lowered. "The African American community can discuss its use and debate its power, but we won't use that word here and I hope you won't use it anywhere."

The class was silent for a few moments. No one spoke or moved and they seemed to ponder what I was saying. In solidarity with my African American students, I had shut down a discussion that most of the class wanted to have, and I wasn't sure that I had made the right choice; I followed my instincts and they were the only thing that I had in that moment. There were only a few minutes left in class, and I reminded them that this would not be our last discussion and that they should continue to bring up these important questions. I reiterated their reading homework and the bell rang.

## Second Thoughts

Before Carlen left the room, Jessie walked over to her and said: "I'm sorry, Carlen. I hope you know that I wasn't trying to make you angry. I just really wanted to know what it felt like." Carlen simply nodded.

I asked Carlen to stay after class so that I could talk to her because she looked upset. After the students filed out, Carlen and I sat down and she began to cry. "I hate this. I hate having to deal with this. Why does it happen over and over?" I hugged her and we sat there for a moment. "Why do I always have to defend people of color? Why do I always have to explain?" I wanted to comfort Carlen, but my internal struggles were so heavy from such an intense class and the fear that I had done and said everything wrong, that I was at a loss for the right words.

I told Carlen, "I'm so proud of you for how openly you spoke and how willing you were to go to that place."

"But it didn't help. It never helps."

"I think it helped more than you will ever know. You got people thinking. But you didn't get to say everything, and I think you need to write about it. I want you to go home and write down everything that comes to mind about today. Reflect on it and get as angry as you need to. We'll meet tomorrow and talk about it again."

Carlen nodded and seemed to relax a bit. I sent her to the library to write and I went to my desk and put my head down. I was over-

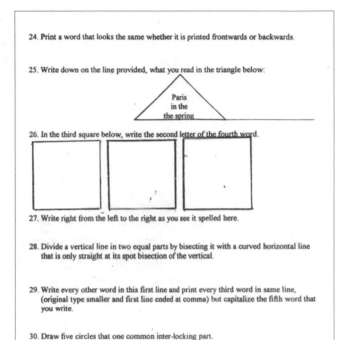

whelmed both emotionally and physically. I took a moment to email Carlen's mom because I wanted her to know what to expect when Carlen came home. I needed someone to talk to, and I needed some help in processing the day.

I found our school campus monitor, Joann. She had been my ally for the past three years. Like me, she had grown up mixed-race (African American and European American) and was also the only person of color in her community. We had spent hours talking about issues of race and how to work with students around those issues. Outside of school, she worked with African American writers in the community and African American at-risk youth and had amazing insight into how to confront difficult topics.

So I asked her: "When I encourage students to think about race in an almost all-white classroom, do I do it on the backs of my students of color? Do I force them to carry a load that is too heavy just to help white students begin to deal with their own issues of race? It was too heavy for me, so am I just doing the same thing to them?"

She reminded me that many, perhaps most, teachers feel so much discomfort confronting issues of race that they try to avoid it in their classes. I was talking about race in a way that not everyone was willing to take on and that it was always going to be uncomfortable—for students and for me. But hadn't we said that we worked with kids because of what we both experienced in our youth? Students of color were forced to carry the load of racism every day because racism is entangled in every aspect of their lives. As educators we have to find ways to be their allies and be sensitive to how our work in the classroom affects them.

## Carlen's Story

The next day, Carlen returned with a letter that she wrote to the class. I asked her if I could read it aloud and she agreed. The following is an edited version of what she wrote:

> Yesterday in class was very intense for everyone because of the subject matter and no matter how many times you can say you were comfortable sitting there, it is a fact that no one was. I don't regret anything I said yesterday because I meant every word. When Jessie said that she wanted to take the test to get a feel for what it was like, my first reaction was to give her the benefit of the doubt and to think of it as just a statement. That was only half of my brain saying to keep my mouth shut.... the impulse part of me always speaks up and I commented back as everyone knows. But I shouldn't have forgotten that Ms. T. makes everything a discussion.
>
> Although I am not the only person of color in the classroom, I always have something to say... and yesterday I did. Honestly, I was about to cry because I am tired of having to talk about racism and tired of having to feel this way once again because I always get offended. It hurts to have to think about the people out there that don't think you deserve to be in a classroom with them or to even be alive. It makes me feel like as a black person I am stripped of my rights, confidence, value, and self-image every time I have to open a book or see a movie about slavery or racism.
>
> After class and the discussion was over, Ms. T. and I talked. I was really upset and I hate to admit it, but I cried. It didn't upset me that Jessie made that statement or that it became a big deal. I was upset because I will never be able to explain to anyone who isn't a person of color what it is really like. I can't just walk in a store and not be watched or followed. I can't make people feel safe around me when they assume that I want to steal something of theirs. I don't get automatic respect from white people; I have to try even harder because someone always has a stereotype. I make jokes all the time, but it's only because I wish it made me feel better about who I am and the race I am. I'm not saying I am ashamed and I have never wanted to be white. I just wish I didn't have to be so different or so judged. But everything having to do

with the subject just makes me want to leave the room, but I can't let my people down by not getting through it.

Hopefully yesterday taught everyone something. But I also realize it only makes me stronger every day. I hope you all don't hate me and I hope you understand where I am coming from and who I am as a person. But, to end it with four encouraging words...peace and love, everyone.

## Carlen

Students were silent after I finished reading. They applauded Carlen and thanked her for her writing. I talked to them about the idea of sympathy vs. empathy—that it is not possible for us to *feel* what people in other times or circumstances felt, but that it's crucial that we attempt to *understand* how the conditions in people's lives affect them. And from this empathy we can consider ways that we can work to make the world a more just place for everyone.

Looking back, I wish that I had stopped myself before handing students my conclusions, and instead asked them to write a reflection about what had happened the day before. It could have been something that they wrote to me or something that they wrote to Carlen or to Jessie, which I would read and give to them later. I missed an opportunity to use their writing as a means for them to reflect on crucial issues. I want students to gain insight because *they* come to realizations, not because I tell them. This writing might not have elicited realizations, but it would have given them an opportunity to express what they felt and wondered, which could have led to a valuable discussion.

## Jessie

After class I stopped Jessie as she was leaving and commended her for what she had said the day before. I told her that I knew how strong Carlen's anger must have felt, yet she did not back down. I was so impressed by her courage. She told me that she wished she hadn't started the conflict and that she hadn't meant anything by it, but she really wanted to explain what had motivated her. She gave me a thoughtful look before she left but didn't say any more.

My own role in prompting the blowup in class continued to gnaw at me. Hadn't I put Jessie in that situation? Hadn't I asked her, and the entire class, to "imagine the fear" of people who took the voting test? Hadn't Jessie simply done what I'd asked of all my students? Wasn't this attempt at historical imagination a crucial component of social justice teaching?

Perhaps. And yet Jessie's attempt to imagine the impact of racism in people's lives felt presumptuous to Carlen—like Jessie was proposing to understand something that her white privilege would never permit her truly to grasp.

But what about Jessie? How did the exchange affect her? Jessie and I didn't talk at length about the incident until the last day of school when I shared a draft of this article with her. Jessie explained that she felt "cornered" that day and had felt unable to express what she truly meant or felt. I think that she was politely telling me that I hadn't helped open a space for her to speak. I'd allowed the conversation to happen, but hadn't made it safe enough for her to express her intent or her confusion. She told me that she wished that she had been brave enough to speak her piece and help the class understand that she wasn't trying to "be black," but rather hoped to understand the severity of the situation so that she could better understand the extent to which institutionalized racism affects an individual's daily life.

Jessie and Carlen's responses were both legitimate; how does my teaching honor each of these? This is an issue I'm still pondering.

## Lessons Learned

I learned many things from this experience both about my teaching and about myself. I realized that I hadn't appreciated how uncomfortable it can be to teach about race, even though I considered myself an anti-racist teacher. It's one thing to map out lesson plans on a novel about the Civil Rights Movement, but students' reactions cannot be "scripted" in the same way that a lesson plan can be. Anti-racist teaching requires a willingness to go where students' responses take us. I have to be willing to go deeper than just interactions between characters in a book.

I realized that I have to keep myself from being bound by my own calendar and recognize when students are engaged. I have to remember that learning comes in the cracks when we are open and willing to deal with the uncomfortable conversations, the unpredictable questions, and the spontaneous outbursts. I can choose books, films, and other resources that create opportunities to discuss racism, but that is not enough without being open to allowing the tough conversations to happen. I have to be willing to make mistakes and not have all of the answers and let my students learn without me always leading them there. I have to be willing to deal with the unexpected if I want to truly be an anti-racist teacher. ◆

*Heidi Tolentino taught English for seven years at Cleveland High School in Portland, Oregon. After the birth of her daughter, she transitioned into the counseling office at Cleveland High School where she now works.*

# Seventh Graders and Sexism

*A new teacher helps her students analyze media stereotypes*

◆ LISA ESPINOSA

I began teaching three years ago in a predominantly Mexican neighborhood on the South Side of Chicago. As a daughter of Mexican immigrants, I feel a strong connection to this community. Teaching, for me, is an opportunity to help my students think critically about society's inequities.

I feel strongly about the injustices that our male-dominated society has created, especially for women of color. Part of my commitment to this issue has to do with my own struggles growing up with the strict gender roles in my family.

Early on, I realized there was a double standard in many families in my community. The expectations and responsibilities were different for boys and girls. Boys were expected to be independent and strong, to grow up to be heads of families, to be leaders. In preparation for this, they were encouraged, both explicitly and implicitly, to express their thoughts and ideas. Girls, on the other hand, were taught to cook, do chores, be nice, and not defy authority. We were strictly monitored and warned against having inappropriate encounters with boys.

I don't want to make it seem worse than it was. Girls were also encouraged to do well in school, and

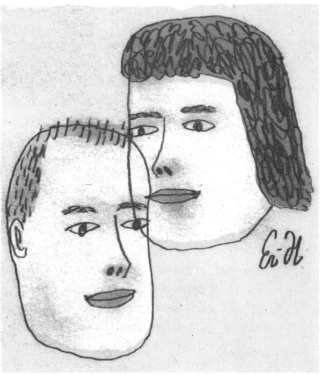

ERIC HANSON

**I had become worried when, in answer to a question about their future hopes and dreams, several girls had responded "to find a guy to take care of me" or "to get married," whereas nearly all the boys had mentioned either an educational or professional goal.**

our parents wanted us to have a better life than they had. But the expectations were clearly different for us than they were for boys.

Perhaps not surprisingly, many of the girls I grew up with became teenage mothers while still in high school. I became pregnant when I was 18, during my first year in college. Even though it was difficult, I continued my education. It took me eight years to graduate, and by the time I did, I had four children.

Along the way, influential professors and works by authors such as Paulo Freire, Ronald Takaki, Gloria Anzaldúa, and bell hooks helped me become more politicized and broaden my understanding of issues of social justice, especially sexism. I read a lot about feminism and was frustrated to realize that men still earned more than women, that men still held most leadership roles, and that many women were still victimized by the men in their lives. I also realized that racism and classism intensified this problem for minority women.

When I became a teacher, I understood that I alone couldn't solve these problems in my classroom, but I felt it was my responsibility to address and discuss these issues with my students.

## Why Learn About Gender?

Problems that arose in the beginning of this school year in my 7th-grade class prompted me to focus specifically on gender and sexism sooner than I had anticipated. Rivalries among girls seemed to be constantly erupting, girls accused boys of touching them inappropriately, and students used the terms "gay" or "faggot" frequently when boys engaged in any activity that deviated from accepted male behavior.

I had also become worried when, in answer to a question about their future hopes and dreams, several girls had responded "to find a guy to take care of me" or "to get married," whereas nearly all the boys had mentioned either an educational or professional goal. Although I tried to deal with these issues and incidents as they came up, I felt that exploring issues of gender in a more sustained way might be useful.

I planned a language arts gender unit for my homeroom class. My homeroom students are the students with whom I spend most of the day and with whom I establish the strongest connections. (I also teach science to the three 7th-grade classes in my school.) One of my first goals was for my students to understand that sexism is still a problem, since many of them, I found, thought gender equality had been achieved. I planned for them to reflect on some common gender biases and to critically analyze the media's role in reaffirming these stereotypes. I wanted them to gain a deeper understanding of feminism and move beyond the common notion that feminists are a bunch of angry, bitter women who hate men. Finally, I hoped that both my boys and girls would incorporate the ideas and ideals of gender equity in their lives.

To facilitate this, I tried to help them make connections. For example, I wanted my female students to begin questioning why most of them continued to let the boys do most of the talking in class discussions, why many of them tied so much of their identity to their appearance, and why there was so much jealousy and competition among the girls instead of a sense of unity. I wanted my male students to explore this as well, and to begin asking themselves why many of them felt threatened to show emotions such as caring and empathy, why many of them used such homophobic language, and to reflect on how they related to the girls in our class both verbally and physically. In addition, I wanted both the boys and girls to challenge their expectations of what they could strive for in life.

We started the unit by reading *An Island Like You* by Judith Ortiz Cofer. I also used the Spanish version, titled *Una Isla Como Tu*. The stories in the collection deal with issues like body image, peer pressure, and gender expectations—told from the perspective of Latino teens.

## Examining Stereotypes

Although the stories had already helped provoke some discussions about gender issues in class, we had not explicitly discussed how and where we learn gender stereotypes. In order to facilitate such a conversation I did an activity originally developed by Paul Kivel of the Oakland Men's Project in Oakland, California.

I began by putting up two pieces of poster board, one with "Act Like a Man" and the other with "Be Ladylike" as headings. I then asked my students to brainstorm words and phrases they associated with these labels. Beforehand, I had gone over some ground rules, explaining to my students that although I wanted them to feel safe to share their ideas, I also expected them to do so in a respectful way.

At first, it was a slow process getting my students to participate. Many students seemed afraid of what reaction their peers might have to what they might say. Eventually, though, we had a lively class. Although it was tempting to interject, at this point I tried to just facilitate the discussion. As usual, the boys did most of the talking initially and I had to explicitly invite the girls to share their ideas.

In the end, both posters were full of the students' ideas. Under "Be Ladylike" were words and phrases such as "be nice," "helpful," "have catfights," "gossip," "shop," "wear makeup," "talk on the phone," "like guys," "cry," and "do housework." On the "Act Like A Man" poster were "don't cry," "like sports," "mature," "violent," "responsible," "serious," "tough," "work hard," "fix cars," among others.

I asked students to compare the two lists and to think about where these ideas come from. Although at first no one said anything, two of my most vocal boys soon spoke up.

"Because it's the truth," Rolando said.

"That's how it is," Fabian added.

Several other boys laughed at their comments. The girls once again retreated and fell into silence. Whenever this happened I encouraged them to contribute—something I feel they both appreciated and dreaded because many were more comfortable letting the boys do the talking.

Finally, Rita said, "From our families?"

Elena followed with "From TV?" I noted, as I often had, that the girls offered their suggestions in the form of a question as opposed to the confident answers the boys tended to offer. At these times I often interjected and pointed out to my students the difference in amount and type of participation between the boys and girls and how this was connected to girls having their opinions devalued.

Other students joined in with suggestions: music videos, *telenovelas* (soap operas), commercials, songs, magazines, and billboards.

I then asked students to think about what happens when boys or girls defy these gender roles. Some of the boys, referring to the "Act Like a Man" poster, said "they're a sissy," "a wimp," "a fag."

"Boys aren't supposed to cry," someone said.

"So are boys never supposed to feel sad?" I asked them. "Are girls just more emotional?" Reminding them of what we had learned in our science class about the human body, I asked them if there was some physiological reason that prevented boys from crying. If not, then when—and why—did boys start believing that it was wrong to show certain emotions?

By this point, many students pointed out that boys are told early on that they shouldn't cry like a girl—and being called a girl seemed to be the ultimate insult. "Why is being called a girl so horrible?" I asked, reminding them that when I talk to a group of boys and girls and refer to them all as guys (something I'm trying to stop doing), no one seems to mind. The students pondered these ideas but still seemed pretty skeptical. Although somewhat frustrated, I realized that at this early stage in our unit, students had done very little, if any, critical thinking about gender stereotypes. Still, it was a beginning, and it allowed us to visibly explore their gender biases, even if they didn't yet identify them as stereotypes.

## Finding Resources

In planning this unit I understood that I was going to have to provide a lot of background knowledge, which unfortunately was not in any of our textbooks. One of the challenges of teaching outside the prescribed curriculum has been finding and adapting resources to suit my class. This is made harder because, of the 31 students in my room, five are beginning English learners. My room is not a designated bilingual classroom but because I am the only fluent Spanish-speaking teacher, I tend to get most, if not all, of the students with the greatest language needs. Although I realize that these students might be better served in my room, I am not a trained bilingual teacher. Still I do the best I can, and I am learning along the way.

> I noted, as I often had, that the girls offered their suggestions in the form of a question as opposed to the confident answers the boys tended to offer.

For this unit and other lessons, I incorporate a variety of methods, including gathering materials in Spanish, getting Spanish versions of the novels we are reading, translating resources, and pairing students with peer helpers. A bilingual resource teacher also comes in on a semi-regular basis.

The resources I gathered for the gender study included the introductory essay from *Feminism Is for Everyone,* by bell hooks; the short story "Girl," by Jamaica Kincaid; essays from *My Sisters' Voices,* edited by Iris Jacob; and a news article titled "Latinos Redefine What It Means to be Manly." Unfortunately, I found that there is not a lot written specifically for teenagers about this subject, and for a lot of the readings I had to provide extensive support. For example, several of the readings had challenging words so I used those as the vocabulary words of the week. There was also a lot of figurative language that had to be explained to the students in simpler terms. Because of this, we did most of the readings in class. When I assigned readings as homework I often accompanied them with questions that would help them get through the text and pick out the important ideas in the readings. And I supplemented the readings with several videos that deal with gender issues, including *The Fairer Sex, What a Girl Wants, Bannat Chicago,* and *Tough Guise.*

Because I felt that my students needed to read about other teenage boys or young men who were trying to do something to change sexist behavior, I tried to incorporate these into our unit. However, these proved to be the hardest to find. The closest I came to finding something like this was a publication by Men Can Stop Rape called *REP.* This magazine targets 13- to 18-year-old-boys and includes articles about making tough choices, communicating with girls, and dating respectfully and responsibly. It also features several ads with young men saying things such as "Our strength is not for hurting, so when other guys dissed girls, we said that's not right" and "My strength is not for hurting, so when I wasn't sure how she felt, I asked." This magazine helped generate lively discussions around dating and relationships, something that many of my students, whether ready or not, are dealing with.

## Free Writing

In the beginning of our unit, I was often discouraged at what I interpreted as lack of interest or inner reflection from my students. Our discussions hardly included the type of deep critical thinking I had hoped would help them make connections to their own behavior and attitudes. It was out of frustration that I began incorporating free writing at the end of our lessons. These, I explained to my students, were not formal essays to be edited and graded (although we also did those), but rather a time for them to share freely what they were feeling or thinking about a particular topic.

It was through this writing that I saw the most evidence that the students were reflecting on what we were doing in class. On many occasions, students expressed things they hadn't felt comfortable sharing aloud. For example, we watched the video *What a Girl Wants*, a documentary in which teenage girls are interviewed about the effects that depictions of women in music videos and movies have on their self-esteem.

Afterward, I had students write about their reactions. Elena agreed with the girls in the video who'd said that media images influence the way they feel about themselves.

"When girls see models or Britney Spears or Christina Aguilera," she wrote, "[and] how nice and pretty they are and they have big breasts but they are skinny...it makes girls want to have breast surgery."

Jose wrote specifically about the pressure that many girls in the video expressed of having to look perfect to get boys' attention: "I thought that is not fair for girls. A girl has to get the same rights like boys. What a girl wants is respect. A girl shouldn't be treated bad or called names by someone."

Elena wrote, "This video made me think about how unfair a woman is treated. She is seen as lower than a guy." Claudia, after writing about what she liked about the video, added that seeing the images of women "made me feel bad, because people always say I'm ugly and these people are boys in this classroom, in school, or in the street."

Some boys felt defensive and added that not all boys disrespect girls. Cezar, for example, wrote: "I also think that there are a lot of guys that still do look for personality [in a girl]. I'd personally look for both looks and personality. But all the stuff the girls talked about was mostly right."

One of the most surprising pieces of writing came from a more formal narrative the students had to do. The school requires monthly compositions from each class and I try to incorporate them into our current focus. When the narrative composition came up, I asked my students to write a story that had to do with any of the issues we had discussed so far in our gender unit. We brainstormed a list together and came up with, among other topics, body image, gender roles, homophobia, and standards of beauty. I told them the composition could be fictionalized.

**When they see an item on the news about a kid getting harassed because of his or her sexual orientation, they bring it up in class so we can discuss it.**

Rolando was one of the first to show me a draft of his writing. I was surprised because he had been one of the boys who seemed most resistant to the ideas we were talking about. He especially had difficulty accepting the idea that boys could express themselves in a variety of ways and was very prone to angry outbursts in class. On more than one occasion I had confrontations with him about his behavior or language.

As I read though his draft, with some trepidation, I was surprised to read that it was about a boy who was being harassed for being gay. His story described a fictionalized situation in which he and a group of friends begin to suspect that one of their friends is gay. After some teasing they finally ask him if he is gay. After he admits that he is, the boys laugh and Rolando writes, "I thought if I step up [and defend him] they will think I'm gay and they probably will laugh, and I looked down and left."

Rolando continues describing how he decides to go to his friend's house and finds him with a gun pointed to his head ready to kill himself because of the despair he feels from the rejection of his friends. Rolando writes, "Don't worry: a lot of people are gay. He started to put the gun down and he got on his knees and start to cry. I said 'It will be alright, OK.'"

Although I realize that his story still contained some stereotypes and was overly dramatic, it was very encouraging to see Rolando even attempting to address these issues.

Another telling piece came from Mari, one of my most reflective students, which she titled "A Part of My Life." Mari's story, like Rolando's, was fictionalized, yet written in the first person. The protagonist was a 12-year-old girl who is very "mature physically and emotionally" and looks like a girl who is 16. Mari writes about this girl's ambivalent feelings toward being harassed by men on the street and boys in school. "While I kept walking many guys kept looking at me. In some ways I felt bad, but in others I like to get their attention (all women like that)." She continues: "I'm a girl and this is why I get harassed like this. Some people tell me that if I don't take care of myself, I might be raped. I just hope nothing bad happens to me. Maybe I'm just going to have to cover up a little bit more."

The story, although fictionalized, seemed very autobiographical. Mari was dealing with a lot of the same problems, especially harassment from boys. Several of the girls in the class argued that they should have the freedom to dress however they wanted and that the boys harassing them was something the boys needed to work on. Although I agreed that the boys should be held responsible for their actions I also wanted the girls to reflect on their self-worth and identity and how much of it was tied into their appearance. Mari had never said much about this during class, and it was very encouraging to see her reflecting on these issues, even if it was clear that she still had a lot to sort through. Although I realize these are small victories, they showed a growing awareness on Rolando's and Mari's part, and were signs that what we were doing in class was perhaps making a difference.

## Analyzing Media

One of the final activities we did was making collages that either countered or reaffirmed common gender stereotypes. I decided to do this because I wanted my students to critically analyze many of the popular magazines they liked to read. I hoped they would see how the media perpetuates the gender stereotypes we had been discussing. First, I collected as many old magazines as I could, trying to get at least some targeted to African Americans, Latinos, and other minority groups. Posting a sign in the office asking for magazine donations was helpful in getting all the magazines we needed.

I then arranged my class in groups of four or five. I assigned each group a specific task of either creating a collage that countered gender biases or one that reaffirmed them. For example, group one had to do a collage that countered male gender stereotypes, group two would do a collage that reaffirmed male gender stereotypes, and so on. Each group was given a stack of magazines and a small poster board and then was allowed time to browse through the magazines noting words and images they could use for their collage. A timer was useful in keeping them on track since it was easy for them to get sidetracked by the articles. I also provided a large manila envelope for them to keep their cutouts in order.

Although I pushed them to stay on task, I also encouraged the groups to interact, especially since some might find images that would be useful for the collage another group was doing. It was encouraging to hear the students express frustration at the limited number of images available that countered gender stereotypes. During the activity I would hear students call me excitedly when they found a particularly positive image of a man or woman. There were also frustrating moments, like when I overhead

**One student asked one of the candidates, "What would you do to end sexism in our neighborhood?"**

Fabian say that he was in the "gay group" because he was looking for images of men in nontraditional roles. In the end, we had several collages: some that contained images reinforcing male stereotypes, others that reinforced female stereotypes, and still others that countered stereotypical images of men and women.

It's hard to assess how successful I was in achieving my goals for the class. As I look back, there are things I would have done differently. For example, I would have assigned more formal essays, and there were several readings and activities I never got to. I often wonder how much my lack of experience affected what my students gained from these lessons. Since I was doing many of these activities for the first time, I didn't always anticipate the questions or problems that might arise.

It is frustrating to see that I am still struggling with some of the same problems as before. In particular, many of the girls still don't speak up nearly as often as the boys. On the other hand, my students many times initiate conversations dealing with some of the topics we discussed. For example, when they see an item on the news about a kid getting harassed because of his or her sexual orientation, they bring it up in class so we can discuss it, or we'll critically analyze some of their favorite TV shows—many of which, unfortunately, are very sexist.

One of the clearest signs that the students were reflecting on these issues came several weeks after our unit was over during our elections for class representative. I was glad to hear many of the candidates being asked what they were going to do about sexism in the school and in the community. One student asked one of the candidates, "What would you do to end sexism in our neighborhood?" Before he could answer, another student exclaimed: "It'll never end. It's too hard. It's too much." Several students looked at me hoping for a more optimistic reply. At that moment, I understood that in some ways my student was right: The problem was too big. But I also believed and shared with my class that we could make things better, and that we could start with our classroom. ◆

*Lisa Espinosa teaches 7th grade at Ruiz School in the Pilsen neighborhood of Chicago. She has five beautiful children.*

# Rethinking Agatha Christie

*The strange and offensive history of* Ten Little Indians

◆ SUDIE HOFMANN

A bright yellow flyer hung on the wall of a local high school promoting a school-sponsored play. A bottle of poison and a rope appeared near the title of the play, *Ten Little Indians*. The subtitle read *And Then There Were None*.

I found it surprising that this controversial play was being performed in St. Cloud, Minnesota, a community where indigenous issues—such as the use of American Indian mascots and team nicknames—have been at the forefront of social justice activism for more than a decade.

When I found the flyer, I shared it with the Coalition Against Cultural Genocide (CACG), a local network of community activists with whom I have been active on the mascot issue for many years. We quickly conducted research on the history of the play and decided to present it to the school administration.

An internet search provided us with a cover of the original 1939 Christie book, titled *Ten Little Niggers*. The cover featured a "black" doll or golliwog (originally spelled golliwogg), hanging from a noose. Golliwogs, according to Ferris State University's Jim Crow Museum of Racist Memorabilia website, are "grotesque creatures, with very dark, often jet-black skin, large white-rimmed eyes, red or white clown lips, and wild frizzy hair." They made their appearance in the children's book series by Florence Kate Upton, which was published in England beginning in 1895. In the books, golliwogs, looking much like caricatures of black-faced minstrels, haunted a toy store where they terrorized two Dutch dolls, Peg and Sarah Jane.

I decided to dig deeper into the history of Christie's book and play. The history is complicated and often cloaked in legend and misinformation. The origin of Christie's title is based on a song and chorus written in 1849 by a Philadelphia songwriter, Septimus Winner. His original rhyme, "Old John Brown," contained the refrain "one little, two little, three, little Indians." In 1866, Winner expanded the song and retitled it "Ten Little Indians." This version is replete with refer-

DAVID McLIMANS

ences to American Indians "out upon a spree," "dead drunk," in canoes, living in "wigwams" with "Daddy Injun" and "Mommy Squaw." In 1869, Frank Green and Marc Mason created a minstrel tune, based on the song, for tenor G. W. "Pony" Moore to perform in St. James Hall in Picadilly. Its popularity with young children eventually established it as a nursery rhyme.

The rhyme metamorphosed in England, the United States, and Germany into *Ten Little Niggers*, *Ten Little Indians*, *The End of Ten Little Negroes*, and

**Golliwogs, according to Ferris State University's Jim Crow Museum of Racist Memorabilia website, are "grotesque creatures, with very dark, often jet-black skin, large white-rimmed eyes, red or white clown lips, and wild frizzy hair."**

*And Then There Were None.* The lines of the rhyme vary from decade to decade, and country to country. The 1943 theatrical version of Christie's book, *Ten Little Niggers*, was based on a popular version of the rhyme in England at the time. The play, like the book, is set on Nigger Island, a name given to it because it resembled, "a man's head—a man with Negroid lips," according to Charles Osborne in *The Life and Crimes of Agatha Christie*. The play employs the use of the children's nursery rhyme in which individuals die by different means. A few stanzas include:

> Ten little Nigger boys going out to dine;
> One choked his little self and then there were nine.
> Seven little Nigger boys gathering up sticks; One chopped himself in half and then there were six.
> Two little Nigger boys playing with a gun; One shot the other and then there was one.
> One little Nigger boy left all alone;
> He went and hanged himself and then there were none.

When the book version of *Ten Little Niggers* was published in the United States in 1940 by Dodd Mead, its title was changed to *And Then There Were None,* presumably in an effort to avoid offending African Americans. However, the title changed again to *Ten Little Indians* when Pocket Books published it in 1964. The play has subsequently been produced in some U.S. communities as *Ten Little Injuns* and more recently, playbills have indicated that the Indians referred to in the play are East Indians, as was the case in the local high school production mentioned earlier. Although the Christie title has changed over the last 66 years, its focus has always been about eliminating a specific group of people of color.

The subtitle or alternative title, *And Then There Were None*, presents another aspect of embedded racism, which is that of genocide. Rarely is the connection made from this ideological message of the title of the play to centuries of racism, colonization, and genocide. "And then there were none" has often been the intended goal of many colonial governments as well as that of U.S. government policies.

As I continued my research, I found that the play has problems reaching beyond the title. Some versions of Act III include the line "Nigger in a woodpile," which is a phrase used to cast suspicion on a particular character in the play. It was included in versions of the play published as recently as 2003.

In spring 2003 I began corresponding with the staff at Samuel French Inc. the publishing house holding exclusive U.S. rights for the play. I suggested some changes that could be made in the play, all of which involved the removal of references to people of color. As I suspected, only the Christie estate, managed by Chorion PLC in London, could approve the changes.

**I thought this could be a place to begin the discussion and link it to the issues of xenophobia, racism, and stereotypes in the play.**

I began to contemplate how I could approach the school and initiate a dialogue about the issues this play presents for a school currently experiencing racial tensions. The shifting demographics of the school, which included Somali and Ethiopian students, brought out the worst in some parents and students. Confederate flags appeared on belt buckles and swastikas were created with black markers on upper arms, all carefully out of the sight of teachers. Physical altercations on and near the school campus precipitated the need for several open parent meetings that produced few results.

I thought this could be a place to begin the discussion and link it to the issues of xenophobia, racism, and stereotypes in the play. The school did not return my phone calls and declined my offers of providing videos from the Southern Poverty Law Center's Teaching Tolerance project and making teacher education students available for small-group discussions.

When the CACG reviewed my research, members of the group presented copies to the administration of the area high school and they forwarded them to the members of the student-directed play. Students, in turn, contacted a local newspaper with claims that their free speech rights were being infringed upon by local activists. The wire services picked up the story and the *Wall Street Journal* saw fit to poke fun at our concerns in its "Tony & Tacky" column that week. The column did not include even a fragment of our research or critique.

Eventually, the cast and crew of the show made several slight modifications. They reduced the type size of the title in the playbill and included a disclaimer from the director, pointing out that no attempt was being made to intentionally offend anyone with the production. But they also chose to print every line of the nursery rhyme in the playbill.

Within a month of the controversy at the high school, a local university began promoting its spring student production of *Ten Little Indians*. Once again CACG shared its research with the director of the play. Something very different happened this time. Initially, the director made no commitments to CACG beyond agreeing to study the information provided to her. She shared the information with the cast and crew and subsequently invited members of CACG to one of their meetings. Although there was dissent within the group, they decided, with the permission of Samuel French to delete the "woodpile" line, replace "Ten Little Indians" with "Ten Little Devon Boys" (referencing the fictitious Indian island off the coast of Devon that is the scene of Christie's play), and use nondescript styrofoam figurines on the mantelpiece in place of the American Indian figurines that are tipped over after each murder in the play. (Christie's play includes all the various forms of murder/suicide used in the nursery rhyme and the famous dramatic effect of statuettes tipping over was restaged in this manner.)

## And Then There Were Some Changes

In August 2004 I received a copy of the 2004 edition of *And Then There Were None* from Samuel French. A letter accompanying the play detailed the changes, which likely came about due to activism and public pressure. The play is now officially licensed as *And Then There Were None* and the Act III reference to a "nigger in the woodpile" has been changed to "guilty party." The fictitious Indian Island has been changed to Soldier Island. The opening paragraph of the play states that, "a cluster of statuettes—ten little soldier boys—sits on the mantelpiece of a weird country house on an island off the coast of Devon. A nursery rhyme embossed above them tells how each little boy met his death, until there was none." I immediately contacted Samuel French upon receiving the letter and inquired about the reasons for the changes. Their only response was that the "Christie Estate chooses to make these changes at this time." Nonetheless, after nearly seven decades, the play no longer uses images of people of color as a "creative" staging approach.

A review of the 2004 book version of *Ten Little Indians*, now published by St. Martin's Griffin as *And Then There Were None*, reveals that editorial revision is still needed. Page 57 includes the statement "natives don't mind dying." Anti-Semitism is also expressed on pages 5, 6, and 124, when a Mr. Morris is referred to as "little Jew" and "Jewboy" with "thick Semitic lips."

Schools might attempt to produce the play under the former title, blow off the dust from the "Indian" statuettes stored in a school closet, and use the original nursery rhyme. It would not be difficult to anticipate this happening, given the considerable resistance to changing American Indian school mascots and nicknames in local communities. But this would violate agreements with Samuel French.

## Helping Schools Understand the Changes

Given the enormous popularity of *And Then There Were None* in U.S. high schools and universities, it is likely that schools will need effective ways to educate students about the reasons for the changes that have been made in the play. Below are some possible discussion points for generating critical thinking about the controversies surrounding this play.

◆ Discuss the problematic nature of *Ten Little Indians* after considering issues of race, xenophobia, privilege, and power.

◆ Study definitions of genocide and talk about current issues of race in the community or possible racial tensions in the school.

◆ Practice owning up to the racism inherent in many "classic" works.

◆ Address the violence throughout the play and consider whether issues of suicide, depression, guns, and murder are appropriate for school-sponsored events.

Educational communities owe it to themselves to genuinely address the stated goals of diversity within the school. Presenting community concerns regarding racism by using counterproductive communication techniques, such as rolling one's eyes or dismissing the voices of people of color by trivializing their perceptions and analyses, provides a powerful racist lesson in the hidden curriculum.

De-emphasizing approaches that shame or blame students can help minimize defensiveness and help them to make better choices for school productions. Informed problem-solving, using input from local communities of color, might just be one of the most important learning experiences in a student's career. ◆

---

*Sudie Hofmann teaches at St. Cloud State University in Minnesota.*

**Resources**

**The Golliwog Caricature** by David Pilgrim (2002) available at the website of Ferris State University, Jim Crow Museum of Racist Memorabilia.

**The Life and Crimes of Agatha Christie** by Charles Osborne (Contemporary Books, 1982).

# School Days:
# Hail, Hail Rock 'n' Roll!

◆ RICK MITCHELL

I am usually impressed when teachers tell me that they've always known they wanted to be teachers, and that they've never had another job. I am one of those who took a more circuitous route to this profession. In fact, I might have been voted "least likely to become a teacher" among the class of 1970 by the administration of Katella High School in Orange County, California, which suggested that I unceremoniously depart midway through my senior year.

In college, I thought I found my calling as a journalist. Instead, I became a professional rock critic, which is sort of like being a journalist except that you never have to grow up. Perhaps no career besides that of professional athlete or musician affords such an opportunity for supposedly mature individuals to extend their adolescent passions so deep into adulthood. For 20-odd years, through countless mainstream newspapers and alternative magazines, seedy dives, and concert halls, I soldiered on with my appointed duty, until I finally outgrew the mysterious joy and pride I once had found in telling people that music they enjoyed actually sucked. Only then, in a desperate epiphany cleverly disguised as altruism, did I decide that education was my true calling. I now teach English, history, and philosophy at a private international school in Houston.

So how does my past life as an opinionated and erudite pop culture snob influence what I do in the present as a kind and caring adult who is routinely interrupted and ignored by teenagers?

Well, I still listen to a lot of music, new and old, for my own enjoyment. The fact that I am far more conversant in hip-hop than the average middle-aged white guy gives me a semi-secret code for relating to certain students who otherwise might be difficult to reach. I also try to stay current with trends in rock, R&B, jazz, various regional styles, and music from around the world. As a result, a few of my more musically astute students seem to think I'm pretty cool for an old fart and ask to borrow obscure stuff from my collection, or want to know my opinion of their favorite new CDs.

Most of my students, on the other hand, couldn't care less what music I listen to on my own time. What is relevant to them, and to the purposes of this article, is the music we listen to together in class. I

J. D. KING

regularly incorporate music into lesson plans for all three of the subjects I teach, from thematic connections between song lyrics and poetry in English, to the epistemological implications of aesthetics as a philosophical area of knowledge. I also give an eight-week series of guest lectures on the history of jazz for the advanced music classes.

**We must study these contradictions so that we will not be fooled by those who would insist that Americans have always been the good guys. Or, for that matter, the bad guys.**

What I want to focus on here, however, is the integral role music plays in the curriculum for my 9th-grade U.S. history class. Although I sometimes have to remind students that listening to music in class is not an invitation to start the party before the bell rings, the music lessons are treated as special events by most students, and, like historically based films, they serve to augment and enliven the lecture/discussion cycle that necessarily takes up the bulk of the class periods.

## Race in U.S. Music

One of the central themes of my history course is that the United States is a nation of great contradictions. The history of American music provides an excellent means for illuminating perhaps the most basic contradiction of all in U.S. society, that of race. How could the author of the Declaration of Independence, which declares that "all men are created equal" and possess an "inalienable right to life, liberty, and the pursuit of happiness," have been a slave owner? How could the founding fathers be inspired by the example of limited government set by the Iroquois Nations yet engage in a policy of genocide when indigenous tribes interfered with westward expansion?

Music in the United States—jazz, rock, rap, R&B, gospel, country—has been the most alive and innovative musical tradition in the world for at least the last century. All these forms come out of the gumbo pot of African, European, and Native American sources that characterizes the musical heritage of both North and South America. Yet, in the United States, black artists typically have done the lion's share of the innovating, while white artists (and white-owned record labels) have reaped the lion's share of the financial rewards. Furthermore, our cultural elites still overwhelmingly look to Europe to validate "high" culture, when what makes us unique is the unprecedented cultural crossbreeding that has taken place here. Compare the corporate and government support for "classical" forms such as the symphony, opera, and ballet to what's afforded to jazz, which should be considered the classical expression of American vernacular music. It is impossible to seriously study the history of 20th-century U.S. music, from ragtime to rap, without also studying the history of racism.

Yet American music is also the story of gradual and sometimes spectacular triumphs over racism and class discrimination, of self-taught geniuses and bootstrap capitalists who neither asked for nor received public subsidies, and whose musical creations, for better and worse, have captured the imagination of the world for the past half-century. As trumpeter/educator Wynton Marsalis frequently has commented, jazz music can be seen as the ultimate artistic expression of U.S. democracy, in its emphasis on individual expression within a cohesive group context.

My 9th-grade U.S. history course syllabus begins with the European conquest of the Americas and the disastrous consequences that followed for the Native American population and enslaved Africans. During the first week of class, as the class is doing homework assignments from the text about European conquest and colonization, I devote the better part of two 50-minute periods to demonstrating how Native American, African, and European elements came together and evolved into all the myriad forms of American music. I use recordings that reflect the traditional roots of the music, while explaining that all musical forms evolve over time and that 20th-century recordings inevitably have introduced modernizing influences.

Because of time constraints, I generally explain what elements I want students to listen for in a given piece and then play an excerpt that illustrates the point I am trying to make. I often fade the music down to talk over it, then fade it back up to let the music reinforce what I've just said. The DJ in me would, of course, prefer to play each track in its entirety—and sometimes students will implore me to let the music play—but excerpts are usually better suited to 50-minute periods and short adolescent attention spans.

**In the United States, black artists typically have done the lion's share of the innovating, while white artists (and white-owned record labels) have reaped the lion's share of the financial rewards.**

I begin in South America with an example of Inca music from Peru, pointing out the distinctive handmade instrumentation and piping melodies. Next I play some West and Central African drumming, focusing on the complex polyrhythms not commonly found in European or Native American music. This is followed by examples of Spanish and Portuguese guitar music, during which I refer to the earlier North African influence on Spanish flamenco. I then show how these distinct elements were fused to create Afro-Cuban salsa, Colombian cumbia and Brazilian samba.

For example, the music of Totó la Momposina, a wonderfully folkloric female singer from Colombia, consciously combines Native American flutes with Afro-Latin percussion and Spanish guitar. When her full band brings in the horns, it becomes a contemporary cumbia orchestra. As I point out to students, this sort of pervasive intercultural exchange characterizes not only the music of the Americas, but virtually all aspects of culture as well—our food, language, religion, and social customs. It is, effectively, what defines us as Americans.

I launch the North American segment of the lesson by explaining some of the ways in which the practices of British slave owners in North America differed from the Spanish, French, and Portuguese in Latin America and the Caribbean. Most notably, the British banned hand drums and other African instruments, so that slaves were forced to invent their own instruments or adapt those of the Europeans to their purposes. The polyrhythmic hand clapping in black churches and the bottleneck slide guitar favored by Delta blues singers are examples of such improvised African retentions. (The exception to this was New Orleans, essentially a Caribbean city until the early 1800s, which is why New Orleans plays such an important role in the birth of blues and jazz.)

I first play recordings of West African griot music, in which singer-songwriter historians travel from village to village, singing praises to the various clans. I then play examples of traditional Celtic music from Ireland and Scotland, noting the similarities between West African griots and Celtic bards. Both functioned as oral historians as well as musicians, and both made their livings by bestowing praise upon wealthy clan chieftains. (Rappers who give "shout-outs" to fellow rappers and their record label execs are thus perpetuating an old African tradition.) Next, I show how the West African griot tradition survived in North America in the archetype of the itinerant Delta bluesman, and how Irish and Scottish music mated with African American blues in the backhills of the Appalachians to produce country and bluegrass music. Then I briefly fast-forward to the mating of "black" blues, gospel, and R&B with "white" country and bluegrass that gave birth to rock 'n' roll. The first rockers, I tell my students, were the slave musicians who took the master's instruments back to the slave quarters and put them to their own purposes, whether praising the Lord or getting the party started. Elvis Presley's first record featured a bluegrass cover on one side and a blues tune on the other. Both sides came out sounding like what we now call rockabilly.

Students are invited to ponder the ironic contradiction. Because of slavery, African and European musical concepts met and made love on unfamiliar ground. The heritage spawned by this act of cultural miscegenation is contemporary U.S. music, in all of its artistic glory and commercial crassness.

It has conquered the world in a way that U.S. military and political might never will. That such a terrible and dehumanizing institution as slavery could create the conditions that allowed the brilliance and beauty of great black artists such as Louis Armstrong, Duke Ellington, Otis Redding, and Aretha Franklin to flourish is one of the tragic ironies of modern Western civilization. U.S. history is full of such contradictions. As historians, and as citizens in a nominally democratic society, we must study these contradictions so that we will not be fooled by those who would insist that Americans have always been the good guys. Or, for that matter, the bad guys.

There are, of course, no recordings to document how American music evolved from the 17th century through the 19th century. But from the invention of the phonograph in the early 20th century, popular musical recordings have charted what average people were thinking and feeling, how they talked, how they sang, and how they danced. For history teachers not to take advantage of these historical artifacts, especially in light of the technological advancements that have vastly improved the sound quality of old recordings, is comparable to leaving the photographs out of a textbook.

## From Harlem Renaissance to 'Hippie Day'

**Musical recordings offer vivid evidence of what was taking place in previous decades and centuries and can bring history alive in ways that books, photos, and even films cannot.**

I come back to music throughout our study of the 20th-century United States. When we read about the Harlem Renaissance in the 1920s, I play classic recordings by blues and jazz greats such as Bessie Smith, Fletcher Henderson, Armstrong, and Ellington to demonstrate the cultural sensibility that produced the poetry of Langston Hughes and Zora Neale Hurston. In 2000, Rhino Records released an excellent four-disc set called *Rhapsodies in Black: Music and Words from the Harlem Renaissance*, featuring poetry readings by well-known African American actors, musicians, and celebrities spliced with original recordings from the era by the artists mentioned above and many others. For students to hear rappers such as Ice-T and Chuck D, and actors such as Debbie Allen and the late Gregory Hines, reading African American poetry helps to make the connection between the historical context and their own lives. It also helps make the music—which was, of course, the funkiest party music of its time—come more fully alive.

When we discuss the Great Depression and the New Deal, the class watches the movie *The Grapes of Wrath* (one of the few films I show in its entirety) over two-and-a-half class periods. This is followed by a half-period lesson on the tradition of white, working-class protest music, from Woody Guthrie's *Dust Bowl Ballads* through Bob Dylan's early political protest songs, Bruce Springsteen's *The Ghost of Tom Joad* and Rage Against the Machine's rock/rap cover of Springsteen's title track, which echoes Tom Joad's last lines from the movie: *"Wherever there's somebody fighting for a place to stand/Or a decent job or a helpin' hand/Wherever somebody's struggling to be free/Look in their eyes, Ma, you'll see me."*

In this case, I don't announce what I am about to play before I play it. I'd rather have students make the connection on their own. There is always a nod of recognition when the buzzsaw electric guitar kicks in—"Ah, Rage," some guy will mutter—and then another nod when students realize that they are listening to the same song they just heard sung by Springsteen in a stripped-down acoustic arrangement, and that the lyrics are taken from the movie we have just watched. Again, hearing a contemporary band that they claim as music of their own generation, or at least not far removed, helps students to make the connection between the historical context of the Depression and their own lives.

When we come to the 1950s I devote two class periods to retracing the musical and cultural conditions that gave rise to rock 'n' roll. In the first, I cover the parallel development of black music (gospel, blues, swing, rhythm and blues) and white hillbilly music (country, western swing, bluegrass) from the 1920s through the 1940s. I then show how these styles were crossbred in the early 1950s by black artists such as Fats Domino and Chuck Berry and white artists such as Bill Haley. For example, Chuck Berry's "Mabellene," an early rock classic, has the same beat as Bob Wills and the Texas Playboys' "Ida Red," a traditional western swing tune from two decades earlier. Yes, Chuck Berry, like many black artists of his generation, was influenced by country music as well as blues. On the other hand, Bill Haley's "Rock Around the Clock," one of the first rock 'n' roll records by a white artist, takes its musical cues from Joe Turner's "Shake, Rattle and Roll," a jump blues tune sung by a much older black artist with roots in the swing era.

Rock 'n' roll existed in form before Elvis Presley, but the moment of pop culture conception arrived with Presley's first single for Sun Records in Memphis, which, as I alluded to earlier, covered Bill Monroe's "Blue Moon of Kentucky," a bluegrass tune, on one side and Arthur "Big Boy" Crudup's "That's Alright, Mama," a blues tune, on the other. It's no coincidence that Presley's next single was a cover of Roy Brown's "Good Rockin' Tonight," one of the first R&B hits to use the term "rock" (a frequent euphemism for sex) in the title.

In the next day's lesson, we examine the relationship between rock 'n' roll and the postwar emergence of a popular mass culture focused on youth. We watch excerpts from Presley's movies—the big dance number from "Jailhouse Rock" is always a winner—and listen to his huge hits from the late 1950s, as well those of other teen idols from the period including Jerry Lee Lewis, Little Richard, Buddy Holly, and Frankie Lyman. We also listen to Otis Blackwell, an obscure black musician whose original recordings of "Don't Be Cruel" and "All Shook Up" were "borrowed" by Presley, almost note for note. (Hear for yourself on Blackwell's only CD release, *All Shook Up*, reissued on the Shanachie label in 1995.)

The music lesson should naturally lead to a discussion of the impact popular youth culture has had on U.S. life in the past 50 years, and how musical integration opened the door to legal integration. Once large numbers of average white kids started listening to popular black music and attending concerts featuring white and black acts sharing the same stage, it became increasingly difficult for local authorities to keep audiences racially separated. Rock 'n' roll promoters such as Cleveland disc jockey Alan Freed began to insist that their concerts be integrated. It is widely assumed by rock historians that Freed's conviction in the payola scandal of the late 1950s was due, at least in part, to his courageous stand against segregation.

Undoubtedly, the most anticipated music lesson I give all year is Hippie Day, which has become a spring tradition at my school. On the day after the big essay exam that covers the Civil Rights Movement and Vietnam, the principal gives the entire freshman class permission to come to school dressed in 1960s fashions instead of the usual uniforms. Some of them, especially the girls, really get into it. For a child of the 1960s such as myself, it is a wondrous sight to behold, all the more so because so many of my students are not born in the United States and have grown up in Europe, Latin America, the Middle East, or Asia. Of course, I bring in old college photos of myself with shoulder-length hair and a bushy moustache, which are always good for a few gasps and a lot of laughs, since most of the hair is long gone. At lunch, we hold a "sit-in" on the quad, featuring performances by student and faculty musicians. (Last year, our faculty band, the Blinding Foreheads, performed a five-song set that culminated with a sing-along on "Ohio," Neil Young's incendiary response to the Kent State massacre.)

**Once large numbers of average white kids started listening to popular black music and attending concerts featuring white and black acts sharing the same stage, it became increasingly difficult for local authorities to keep audiences racially separated.**

During my history class periods, I play classic rock and R&B records while explaining the evolution of 1960s protest music from the folk music revival through folk rock and into acid rock, and from civil rights-era soul to Black Power funk. Feel free to substitute your own favorites, but I start with Dylan ("The Times They Are A-Changin'," "Subterranean Homesick Blues") and Peter, Paul, and Mary ("Blowin' in the Wind") and move forward through the Byrds ("Mr. Tambourine Man"), Simon and Garfunkel ("The Sounds of Silence"), Donovan ("Sunshine Superman," "Mellow Yellow"), Buffalo Springfield ("For What It's Worth"), the Doors ("Break on Through"), Jefferson Airplane ("White Rabbit"), the Beatles ("All You Need Is Love"), Jimi Hendrix ("Are You Experienced," "All Along the Watchtower"), Aretha Franklin ("A Change Is Gonna Come"), James Brown ("Say It Loud: I'm Black and I'm Proud"), Sly and the Family Stone ("Everyday People"), and Edwin Starr ("War").

Explaining the drug references in some of these songs is always a bit dicey, since I do not want to be accused of promoting drug use, and that's exactly what these songs do. But my students seem to be sophisticated enough to appreciate that while much of the music was great, and much of the politics admirable, the 1960s counterculture bequeathed a mixed legacy to subsequent generations.

It's too simple to blame today's crack babies on the Beatles' use of LSD and to blame the AIDS epidemic on "free love." But it's also too simple to say there is no connection at all. It's another of those contradictions that serve to make the United States the complex society that it is, and another reason why we should be suspicious of those who try to make complex issues seem simpler than they really are, like those who thought drugs would be a shortcut to nirvana, and those who now brandish the slogan "zero tolerance" as a weapon of righteousness.

## Cultural History Is Real History

For culture war conservatives, I suppose my music lessons could be considered at best fluff, at worst a subversive challenge to the notion of a classical Eurocentric education. I would agree that they might very well be subversive, but they are not fluff. They are instead the stuff of real history.

Too often, history is taught as a timeline of wars and famous leaders, in which average people are little more than pawns and cannon fodder. Just as thousands of anonymous soldiers died when Napoleon met his Waterloo, from which he emerged unscathed, so too will the war in Iraq be remembered as Bush's war, though he is likely to survive no matter how many historically nameless Iraqi and U.S. citizens do not.

Although major military and political events serve as natural landmarks in any history syllabus, the true and oft-untold history of our world consists of what societies were doing both during and between these cataclysmic chapters. Musical recordings offer vivid evidence of what was taking place in previous decades and centuries and can bring history alive in ways that books, photos, and even films cannot. Of course, it is important to examine how culture reflects and influences political events. But cultural history should not be considered merely a sidebar to military and political history. It is important in its own right, perhaps more important than memorizing the names of past presidents and generals.

In "School Day," his ebullient mid-1950s ode to the newborn child called rock 'n' roll, schoolboy Chuck Berry can't wait for the bell to ring so he can head down to the corner juke joint and rock out. Why wait for the bell, Chuck, when we can learn so much about who we are as a society from listening to your records? Hail, hail rock 'n' roll! ◆

---

*Rick Mitchell is the former popular music critic at the* Houston Chronicle *and the* Oregonian *in Portland. He is the author of two books on music, including* Whiskey River (Take My Mind): The True Story of Texas Honky-Tonk *(University of Texas Press).*

# Deconstructing Barbie

*Math and popular culture*

◆ SWAPNA MUKHOPADHYAY

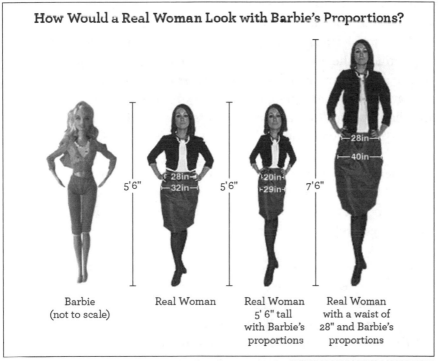

**How Would a Real Woman Look with Barbie's Proportions?**

| Barbie (not to scale) | Real Woman | Real Woman 5' 6" tall with Barbie's proportions | Real Woman with a waist of 28" and Barbie's proportions |

BRITISH BROADCASTING CORPORATION

Math and popular culture are rarely associated, although phrases like "do the math" are commonly heard. Undoubtedly this is a prime example of the unfortunate disconnect between math in school and its real-life applications. Many teachers, however, use mathematics for the analysis of complex real-world issues. Teaching mathematics as a cognitive tool for everyday sensemaking is an approach that addresses the alienation of many students from early grades.

Beyond sensemaking, using mathematics as a tool to interrogate issues of importance to students, their communities, and society in general brings to light the generally hidden cultural, historical, and political nature of mathematics education.

Here's an activity that treats mathematics as a tool for learning about a number of social issues. It begins with inviting a Barbie doll—the popular cultural icon—to the classroom. The activity teaches concepts such as averages and ratios, in a way suitable for middle school students.

## Materials

Besides a few Barbie dolls from my thrift store collection, I also bring tape measures, a ball of string, and calculators as my material props.

## Procedure

The task starts with a probe: What would Barbie look like if she were as big as you? Students, working in small groups, need to figure out first the "average" of the group, so that they can begin to "construct" a real-life Barbie of the same height. After confronting the mathematical notion of average and its contradiction to real life (for example, "Jenny," the "average" in our group, is a blond European American, whereas I am a dark-skinned Indian), the students measure the ratio of the height of the designated person to that of the Barbie doll to find the enlargement ratio or the scaling factor.

Then, with a table I provide, they measure the body parts of the doll and compute its corresponding real-life measurements.

The next part of the task consists of drawing the contour of Jenny-the-average on butcher paper with one color marker, and then superimposing the blown-up Barbie on Jenny's image with a different color. Drawing two human figures—the contour of familiar Jenny and Barbie-as-big-as-Jenny—immediately highlights the unrealistic dimensions of Barbie, which are not so obvious on the doll itself, or even in the computed measures collected in tabular form.

Repeating the exercise with male superhero action figures and the "average" male student makes it clear that the issue is not confined to female representations.

## Discussion

This activity then generates discussion connecting to the impact of representations in popular culture on body image, self-worth, and eating disorders. Other issues raised include the superficially "multicultural" nature of contemporary Barbie and the sweatshop labor that produces the dolls. ◆

---

*Swapna Mukhopadhyay was born and raised in Kolkata (Calcutta). She is a mathematics educator who focuses on issues of critical mathematics education and cultural diversity. For the last few years she has been organizing public lecture series on alternative forms of knowledge construction in mathematics at Portland State University. She is co-editor of* Culturally Responsive Mathematics Education *and* Words and Worlds: Modeling Verbal Descriptions of Situations.

# Unlearning the Myths That Bind Us

*Critiquing fairy tales and cartoons*

◆ LINDA CHRISTENSEN

I was nourished on the milk of U.S. culture: I cleaned the dwarves' house and waited for Prince Charming to bring me life; I played Minnie Mouse to Mickey's flower-bearing adoration, and, later, I swooned in Rhett Butler's arms—my waist as narrow and my bosom every bit as heaving as Scarlett's. But my daddy didn't own a plantation; he owned a rough-and-tumble bar frequented by loggers and fishermen. My waist didn't dip into an hourglass; in fact, according to the novels I read, my thick ankles doomed me to be cast as the peasant woman reaping hay while the heroine swept by with her handsome man in hot pursuit.

© WALT DISNEY ENTERPRISES

Our students suckle the same pap. Our society's culture industry colonizes their minds and teaches them how to act, live, and dream. This indoctrination hits young children especially hard. The "secret education," as Chilean writer Ariel Dorfman dubs it, delivered by children's books and movies, instructs young people to accept the world as it is portrayed in these social blueprints. And often that world depicts the domination of one sex, one race, one class, or one country over a weaker counterpart. After studying cartoons and children's literature, my student Omar wrote, "When we read children's books, we aren't just reading cute little stories, we are discovering the tools with which a young society is manipulated."

**The "secret education," as Chilean writer Ariel Dorfman dubs it, delivered by children's books and movies, instructs young people to accept the world as it is portrayed in these social blueprints.**

Beverly Tatum, who wrote the book *Why Are All the Black Kids Sitting Together in the Cafeteria?*, helps explain how children develop distorted views of people outside of their racial/cultural group:

> The impact of racism begins early. Even in our preschool years, we are exposed to misinformation about people different from ourselves. Many of us grow up in neighborhoods where we had limited opportunities to interact with people different from our own families.... Consequently, most of the early information we receive about "others"—people racially, religiously, or socioeconomically different from ourselves—does not come as a result of firsthand experience. The secondhand information we receive has often been distorted, shaped by cultural stereotypes, and left incomplete.

Cartoon images, in particular the Disney movie *Peter Pan*, were cited by the children in a research study as their No. 1 source of information. At the age of 3, these children had a set of stereotypes in place.

Children's cartoons, movies, and literature are perhaps the most influential genre "read." Young people, unprotected by any intellectual armor, hear or watch these stories again and again, often from the warmth of their mothers' or fathers' laps. The messages, or "secret education," linked with the security of their homes, underscore the power these texts deliver. As Tatum's research suggests, the stereotypes and worldview embedded in the stories become accepted knowledge.

I want my students to question this accepted knowledge and the secret education delivered by cartoons as well as by the canon. Because children's movies and literature are short and visual we can critique them together. We can view many in a brief period of time, so students can begin to see patterns in media portrayals of particular groups and learn to decode the underlying assumptions these movies make. Brazilian educator Paulo Freire wrote that instead of wrestling with words and ideas, too often students "walk on the words." If I want my students to wrestle with the social text of novels, news, or history books, they need the tools to critique media that encourage or legitimate social inequality.

To help students uncover those old values planted by Disney, Mattel, and Nike, and construct more just ones, I begin this "unlearning the myths" unit with two objectives. First, I want students to critique portrayals of hierarchy and inequality in children's movies and cartoons. Then I want to enlist them to imagine a better world, characterized by relationships of respect and equality.

© KING FEATURES SYNDICATE

## Exposing the Myths: How to Read Cartoons

Prior to watching any cartoons, I ask students to read the second chapter of Ariel Dorfman's book *The Empire's Old Clothes: What the Lone Ranger, Babar, and Other Innocent Heroes Do to Our Minds.* Students keep track of their responses in a dialogue journal. I pose the question: Do you agree with Dorfman's position that children receive a "secret education" in the media? Do you remember any incidents from your own childhood that support his allegations?"

**Early in the unit, I show a Popeye cartoon, "Ali Baba and the 40 Thieves," which depicts all Arabs with the same face, same turban, same body—and they are all thieves swinging enormous swords.**

This is difficult for some students. The dialogue journal spurs them to argue, to talk back, and create a conversation with the writer. Dorfman is controversial. He gets under their skin. He wrote:

> Industrially produced fiction has become one of the primary shapers of our emotions and our intellect in the twentieth century. Although these stories are supposed to merely entertain us, they constantly give us a secret education. We are not only taught certain styles of violence, the latest fashions, and sex roles by TV, movies, magazines, and comic strips; we are also taught how to succeed, how to love, how to buy, how to conquer, how to forget the past and suppress the future. We are taught more than anything else, how not to rebel. (p. xxi)

Many students don't want to believe that they have been manipulated by children's media or advertising. No one wants to admit that they've been "handled" by the media. They assure me that they make their own choices and the media has no power over them—as they sit with Fubus, Nikes, Timberlands, or whatever the latest fashion rage might be. And Dorfman analyzes that pose:

> There has also been a tendency to avoid scrutinizing these mass media products too closely, to avoid asking the sort of hard questions that can yield disquieting answers. It is not strange that this should be so. The industry itself has declared time and again with great forcefulness that it is innocent, that no hidden motives or implications are lurking behind the cheerful faces it generates. (p. xxi)

Justine, a senior in my Contemporary Literature and Society class, was bothered by Dorfman's quest "to dissect those dreams, the ones that had nourished my childhood and adolescence, that continued to infect so many of my adult habits." In her dialogue journal she responded:

> Personally, handling the dissection of dreams has been a major cause of depression for me. Not so much dissecting—but how I react to what is found as a result of the operation. It can be overwhelming and discouraging to find out my whole self-image has been formed mostly by others or underneath my worries about what I look like are years (17 of them) of being exposed to TV images of girls and their set roles given to them by TV and the media. It's painful to deal with. The idea of not being completely responsible for how I feel about things today is scary. So why dissect the dreams? Why not stay ignorant about them and happy? The reason for me is that those dreams are not unrelated to my everyday life. They influence how I behave, think, react to things.... My dreams keep me from dealing with an unpleasant reality.

In looking back through this passage and others in her dialogue with Dorfman, Justine displayed discomfort with prying apart her identity and discovering where she received her ideas; yet, she also grudgingly admitted how necessary this process was if she wanted to move beyond where she was at the time. Her discomfort might also have arisen from feeling incapable of changing herself or changing the standards by which she was judged in the larger society. But she knew such questioning was important.

In a later section of her journal, she wrote, "True death equals a generation living by rules and attitudes they never questioned and producing more children who do the same." Justine's reaction may be more articulate than some, but her sentiments were typical of many students. She was beginning to peel back the veneer covering some of the injustice in our society, and she was dismayed by what she discovered.

## Charting Stereotypes

I start by showing students old cartoons because the stereotypes are so blatant. We look at the roles women, men, people of color, and poor people play in the cartoons. I ask students to watch for who plays the lead. Who plays the buffoon? Who plays the servant? I encourage them to look at the race, station in life, body type of each character. What are the characters' motivations? What do they want out of life? What's their mission? If there are people of color in the film, what do they look like? How are they portrayed? What would children learn about this particular group from this film?

**For some students the cartoon unit exposes the wizardry that enters our dreams and desires, but others shrug their shoulders at this.**

How does the film portray overweight people? What about women other than the main character? What jobs do you see them doing? What do they talk about? What are their main concerns? What would young children learn about women's roles in society if they watched this film and believed it? What roles do money, possessions, and power play in the film? Who has it? Who wants it? How important is it to the story? What would children learn about what's important in this society?

As they view each episode, they fill in a chart answering these questions. Students immediately start yelling out the stereotypes because they are so obvious. Early in the unit, I show a Popeye cartoon, "Ali Baba and the 40 Thieves," which depicts all Arabs with the same face, same turban, same body—and they are all thieves swinging enormous swords. At one point in the cartoon, Popeye clips a dog collar on helpless Olive Oyl and drags her through the desert. Later, the 40 thieves come riding through town stealing everything—food, an old man's teeth, numbers off a clock—even the stripe off a barber pole. The newer cartoons—like Mulan, Aladdin, and Pocahontas—are subtler and take more sophistication to see through, but if students warm up on the old ones, they can pierce the surface of the new ones as well.

On first viewing, students sometimes resist critical analysis. After watching a Donald Duck cartoon, for example, Kamaui said, "This is just a dumb little cartoon with some ducks running around in clothes." Then students start to notice patterns—like the absence of female characters in many of the older cartoons. When women do appear, they look like Jessica Rabbit or *Playboy* centerfolds—even in many of the new and improved children's movies.

After filling in a few charts, collectively and on their own, students write about the generalizations children might take away from these tales. From experience, I've discovered that I need to keep my mouth shut for a while. If I'm the one pointing out the stereotypes, it's the kiss of death to the exercise. Besides, students are quick to find the usual stereotypes on their own: "Look, Ursula the sea witch is ugly and smart. Hey, she's kind of dark looking. The young, pretty ones only want to hook their man; the old, pretty ones are mean because they are losing their looks." Kenneth noticed that people of color and poor people are either absent or servants to the rich, white, pretty people. Tyler pointed out that the roles of men are limited as well. Men must be virile and wield power or be old and the object of "good-natured" humor. Students began seeing beyond the charts I'd rigged up for them. They looked at how overweight people were portrayed as buffoons in episode after episode. They noted the absence of mothers, the wickedness of stepparents.

Later in the unit, Mira, a senior, attacked the racism in these Saturday morning rituals. She brought her familiarity with Native American cultures into her analysis:

> Indians in Looney Tunes are also depicted as inferior human beings. These characters are stereotypical to the greatest degree, carrying tomahawks, painting their faces, and sending smoke signals as their only means of communication. They live in tepees and their language reminds the viewer of Neanderthals. We begin to imagine Indians as savages with bows and arrows and long black braids. There's no room in our minds for knowledge of the differences between tribes, like the Cherokee alphabet or Celilo salmon fishing.

## A Black Cinderella?

After viewing a number of cartoons, Kenya scolded parents in an essay, "A black Cinderella? Give Me A Break." She wrote: "Have you ever seen a black person, an Asian, a Hispanic in a cartoon? Did they have a leading role or were they a servant? What do you think this is doing to your child's mind?" She ended her piece, "Women who aren't white begin to feel left out and ugly because they never get to play the princess." Kenya's piece bristled with anger at a society that rarely acknowledges the wit or beauty of women of her race. And she wasn't alone in her feelings. Sabrina wrote, "I'm not taking my kids to see any Walt Disney movies until they have a Black woman playing the leading role." (It is important to note that when I originally wrote this piece Disney had yet to release *The Princess and the Frog*. Although Tiana offers a positive representation of a girl of color in a lead role, the film simultaneously upholds the class bias central to princess scripts.)

Both young women wanted the race of the actors changed, but they

WALT DISNEY CORPORATION (from Ariel Dorfmann and Armand Mattelart's *How to Read Donald Duck*)

didn't challenge the class or underlying gender inequities that also characterize the lives of Cinderella, Ariel, and Snow White.

> **I want students to understand that if the race of the character is the only thing changing, injustices may still remain.**

Kenya's and Sabrina's anger is justified. There should be more women of color who play the leads in these white-on-white wedding cake tales. Of course, there should also be more women of color on the Supreme Court, in Congress, as well as scrubbing up for surgeries. But I want students to understand that if the race of the character is the only thing changing, injustices may still remain.

So I have students read Mary Carter Smith's delightful retelling of Cinderella, "Cindy Ellie, A Modern Fairy Tale" which reads like laughter—bubbly, warm, spilling over with infectious good humor and playful language. In Smith's version, Cindy Ellie, who lived in East Baltimore, was "one purty young Black sister, her skin like black velvet." Her father, "like so many good men, was weak for a pretty face and big legs and big hips." Her stepmother "had a heart as hard as a rock. The milk of human kindness had curdled in her breast. But she did have a pretty face, big legs, and great big hips.... Well, that fool man fell right into that woman's trap."

Cindy Ellic's stepsisters were "two big-footed, ugly gals" who made

Cindy Ellie wait on them hand and foot. When the "good white folks, the good Asian folks, and the good black folks all turned out and voted for a good Black brother, running for mayor" there was cause for celebration, and a chance for Cindy Ellie to meet her Prince Charming, the mayor's son. With the help of her Godma's High John the Conqueror Root, Cindy Ellie looked like an "African Princess." "Her rags turned into a dazzling dress of pink African laces! Her hair was braided into a hundred shining braids, and on the end of each braid were beads of pure gold! . . . Golden bracelets covered her arms clean up to her elbows! On each ear hung five small diamond earrings. On her tiny feet were dainty golden sandals encrusted with dazzling jewels! Cindy Ellie was laid back!"

The students and I love the story. It is well told and incorporates rich details that do exactly what Sabrina, Kenya, and their classmates wanted: It celebrates the beauty, culture, and language of African Americans. It also puts forth the possibility of cross-race alliances for social change.

But, like the original tale, Cindy Ellie's main goal in life is not working to end the plight of the homeless or teaching kids to read. Her goal, like Cinderella's, is to get her man. Both young women are transformed and made beautiful through new clothes, new jewels, new hairstyles. Both have chauffeurs who deliver them to their men. Cindy Ellie and Cinderella are nicer and kinder than their stepsisters, but the prince and Toussant, the mayor's son, don't know that. Both Cinderellas compete for their men against their sisters and the rest of the single women in their cities. They "win" because of their beauty and their fashionable attire. Both of these tales leave young women with two myths: happiness means getting a man, and transformation from wretched conditions can be achieved through consumption—in their case, through new clothes and a new hairstyle.

I am uncomfortable with those messages. I don't want students to believe that change can be bought at the mall, nor do I want them thinking that the pinnacle of a woman's life is an "I do" that supposedly leads them to a "happily ever after." I don't want my female students to see their "sisters" as competition for that scarce and wonderful commodity—men. As Justine wrote earlier in her dialogue journal, it can be overwhelming and discouraging to find that our self-images have been formed by others, but if we don't dissect them, we will continue to be influenced by them.

### Writing as a Vehicle for Change

Toward the end of the unit, students write essays critiquing cartoons. I hope that this exercise will encourage them to look deeper into the issues—to challenge the servant/master relationships or the materialism that makes women appealing to their men. For some students the cartoon unit exposes the wizardry that enters our dreams and desires, but others shrug their shoulders at this. It's OK for some people to be rich and others poor; they just want to see more rich people of color or more rich women. Or better yet, be rich themselves. They accept the inequalities in power and exploitative economic relationships. Their acceptance teaches me how deep the roots of these myths are planted and how much some students, in the absence of visions for a different and better world, need to believe in the fairy tale magic that will transform their lives—whether it's a rich man or winning the lottery.

Many students write strong critiques following the viewing. But venting their frustrations with cartoons—and even sharing it with the class—can seem an important but limited task. Yes, they can write articulate pieces. Yes, they hone their arguments and seek the just-right examples from their viewing. Through critiques and the discussions that follow, they are helping to transform each other—each comment or observation helps expose the engine of society, and they're both excited and dismayed by their discoveries.

But what am I teaching them if the lesson ends there? That it's enough to be critical without taking action? That we can quietly rebel in the privacy of the classroom while we practice our writing skills, but we don't really have to do anything about the problems we uncover, nor do we need to create anything to take the place of what we've expelled? Those are not the lessons I intend to teach. I want to develop their critical consciousness, but I also hope to move them to action.

For some the lesson doesn't end in the classroom. Many who watched cartoons before we start our study say they can no longer enjoy them. Now instead of seeing a bunch of ducks in clothes, they see the racism, sexism, and violence that swim under the surface of the stories.

Pam and Nicole swore they would not let their children watch cartoons. David told the class of coming home one day and finding his nephews absorbed in Looney Tunes. "I turned that TV off and took them down to the park to play. They aren't going to watch that mess while I'm around." Radiance described how she went to buy Christmas presents for her niece and nephew. "Before, I would have just walked into the toy store and bought them what I knew they wanted—Nintendo or Barbie. But this time, I went up the clerk and said, 'I want a toy that isn't sexist or racist.'"

Students have also said that what they now see in cartoons, they also see in advertising, on prime-time TV, on the news, in school. Turning off the cartoons doesn't stop the sexism and racism. They can't escape, and now that they've started analyzing cartoons, they can't stop analyzing the rest of the world. And sometimes they want to stop. Once a student asked me, "Don't you ever get tired of analyzing everything?"

During a class discussion Sabrina said: "I realized these problems weren't just in cartoons. They were in everything—every magazine I picked up, every television show I watched, every billboard I passed by on the street." My goal of honing their ability to read literature and the world through the lens of justice had been accomplished at least in part. But as Justine wrote earlier, at times my students would like to remain "ignorant and happy." Without giving students an outlet for their despair, I was indeed creating what Wayne Au et al. call "factories of cynicism" in my classroom—and it wasn't pretty.

## Taking Action

I look for opportunities for students to act on their knowledge. In Literature and U.S. History class, these occasions have presented themselves in the form of unfair tests and outrageous newspaper articles about Jefferson that provoked spontaneous student activism (Au, et al., 2007). But in my Contemporary Literature and Society class, I discovered that I had to create the possibility for action.

Instead of writing the same classroom essays students had written in years before, I asked students to create projects that would move beyond the classroom walls. Who could they teach about what they learned? I wanted their projects to be real. Who could their analysis touch enough to bring about real change? Students filled the board with potential readers of their work: Parents, peers, teachers, children's book authors, librarians, Disney, video store owners, advertisers.

My only rule was that they had to write a piece using evidence from cartoons or other media. Don't just rant in general, I told them. Use evidence to support your thesis. The examples might come from cartoons, advertisements, novels, your mother or father's advice. You might use lines from TV or movies. You don't have to stick to cartoons—use the world. We discussed possible options:

◆ Focus on one cartoon—critique it, talk about it in depth. Write about *Mulan* or *Peter Pan*. Using the chart, analyze the representation of men, women, people of color, and poor people in that movie.

◆ Focus on the portrayal of one group. Write about how women, men, African Americans, Latinos, Arabs, overweight people, or the poor are depicted and give examples from several cartoons or across time.

◆ Take an issue—like the representation of women—and relate it to your life and/or society at large. (See "Looking Pretty: Waiting for the Prince," page 201.)

One group of playful students wanted to create a pamphlet that could be distributed at PTA meetings throughout the city. That night they went home with assignments they'd given each other—Sarah would watch Saturday morning cartoons; Sandy, Brooke, and Carmel would watch after-school cartoons; and Kristin and Toby were assigned before-school cartoons. They ended up writing a report card for the various programs. They graded each show A through F and wrote a brief summary of their findings:

> DUCK TALES: At first glance the precocious ducks are cute, but look closer and see that the whole show is based on money. All their adventures revolve around finding money. Uncle Scrooge and the gang teach children that money is the only important thing in life.
> **Grade: C-**

> TEENAGE MUTANT NINJA TURTLES: Pizza-eating Ninja Turtles. What's the point? There isn't any. The show is based on fighting the "bad guy" Shredder. Demonstrating no concern for the townspeople, they battle and fight, but never get hurt. This cartoon teaches a false sense of violence to kids: fight and you don't get hurt, or solve problems through fists and swords instead of words.
> **Grade: D**

> POPEYE: This show oozes with horrible messages from passive Olive Oyl to the "hero man" Popeye. This cartoon portrays ethnic groups as stupid. It is political also—teaching children that Americans are the best and conquer all others.
> **Grade: F**

On the back of the pamphlet, they listed some tips for parents to guide them in wise cartoon selection.

Catkin wrote about the sexual stereotyping and adoration of beauty in children's movies. Her article described how she and other teenage women carry these messages with them still:

> Women's roles in fairy tales distort reality—from Jessica Rabbit's six-mile strut in *Who Framed Roger Rabbit?* to Tinker Bell's obsessive vanity in *Peter Pan*. These seemingly innocent stories teach us to look for our faults. As Tinker Bell inspects her tiny body in a mirror only to find that her minute hips are simply too huge, she shows us how to turn the mirror into an enemy.... And this scenario is repeated in girls' locker rooms all over the world.
> Because we can never look like Cinderella, we begin to hate ourselves. The Barbie syndrome starts as we begin a lifelong search

for the perfect body. Crash diets, fat phobias, and an obsession with the materialistic become commonplace. The belief that a product will make us rise above our competition, our friends, turns us into addicts. Our fix is that Calvin Klein push-up bra, Guess jeans, Chanel lipstick, and the latest in suede flats. We don't call it deception; we call it good taste. And soon it feels awkward going to the mailbox without makeup.

Catkin wanted to publish her piece in a magazine for young women so they would begin to question the origin of the standards by which they judge themselves.

Most students wrote articles for local and national newspapers or magazines. Some published in neighborhood papers, some in church newsletters. Lila Johnson's article "Looking Pretty: Waiting for the Prince" and Hasina Deary's "Help Me Syndrome" have both been published nationally.

The writing in these articles was tighter and cleaner than for-the-teacher essays because it had the potential for a real audience beyond the classroom walls. The possibility of publishing their pieces changed the level of students' intensity for the project. Anne, who turned in hastily written drafts last year, said, "Five drafts and I'm not finished yet!"

But more importantly, students saw themselves as actors in the world; they were fueled by the opportunity to convince some parents of the long-lasting effects cartoons impose on their children, or to enlighten their peers about the roots of some of their insecurities. Instead of leaving students full of bile, standing around with their hands on their hips, shaking their heads about how bad the world is, I provided them the opportunity to make a difference. ◆

---

*Linda Christensen is director of the Oregon Writing Project at Lewis & Clark College in Portland, Oregon. During her 30-year career in Portland Public Schools, she taught language arts at Jefferson and Grant high schools and worked as Portland's language arts coordinator. She is the author of* Reading, Writing, and Rising Up: Teaching About Social Justice and the Power of the Written Word *(Rethinking Schools, 2000), where this article first appeared, and* Teaching for Joy and Justice: Re-Imagining the Language Arts Classroom *(Rethinking Schools, 2009).*

## Resources

**Rethinking Our Classrooms: Teaching for Equity and Justice** by Wayne Au, et al. (Rethinking Schools, 2007).

**The Empire's Old Clothes: What the Lone Ranger, Babar, and Other Innocent Heroes Do to Our Minds** by Ariel Dorfman (Duke University Press, 2010).

**"Cindy Ellie, A Modern Fairy Tale"** by Mary Carter Smith in *Talk That Talk: An Anthology of African-American Storytelling,* Linda Goss, ed. (Touchstone, 1989).

**A Pedagogy for Liberation** by Ira Shor and Paulo Freire (Bergin & Garvey, 1987).

**Why Are All the Black Kids Sitting Together in the Cafeteria? And Other Conversations About Race** by Beverly Tatum (Basic Books, 1997).

# Looking Pretty, Waiting for the Prince

◆ LILA JOHNSON

*As a high school senior, Lila Johnson uncovered the "secret education" that cartoons, advertising, and the media slipped into her life. She wrote this article to educate others about the inaccurate visions Disney and company sells children.*

My two brothers and I lived for our daily cartoon fix. We hungered for the vibrant reds, blues, and yellows that raced around our screen for an insane hour or two. When we were away from the tube, we assumed the roles of our favorite characters: Bugs Bunny, that wisecracking, carrot-munching rabbit; Yosemite Sam, rough and tough shoot-'em-down cowboy; and Popeye, the all American spinach-guzzling sailor. We took our adopted identities outside and to school where our neighbors and friends did the same.

Now, as a senior in high school, I see that cartoons are not just lighthearted, wacky fun. Animated material touches on such sensitive issues as roles of men and women in society, and people of color.

Cartoons are often the birthplace of the cultural stereotypes we learn and remember, as I do today: the idea that Indians are savages—tomahawks and moccasins, tepees and war paint—the bad guys who pursued my favorite cowboys, or the belief that Arabs have nothing better to do than to tear across deserts in robes while swinging fierce swords and yelping like alien creatures.

These notions didn't just occur to my brothers and me magically. We saw Indians in our afternoon cartoons and on some of our favorite Disney movies like *Peter Pan*. We witnessed villainous Arabs thieve their way through violent episodes of "Popeye."

What is not seen in relation to people of different cultures can be as harmful as some of the things that are seen. People of color are rarely seen as the heroes of animated presentations. I can think of only one Disney classic where a person of color is the principal and heroic character—*The Jungle Book*. Not an impressive list.

Children search for personal identity. In 1st grade I adored Bonnie Bondell, a girl in my class. She wasn't a cartoon character, but she could have been. She had glossy blonde hair and blue eyes. She had a sparkly smile and a sweet voice. She could have been Cinderella's younger sister or Sleeping Beauty's long lost cousin. For those reasons, I longed to be just like her. I look at old photos of myself now, and have decided that I was pretty cute. I wasn't a traditional cutie, and that's exactly what bothered me then. My father is African American and my mother is German and Irish. Put the two together and I'm the result. Olive complexion, dark curly hair, brown and green eyes. All wrong. At least according to the "Fairy Tale Book of Standards."

The pride that I had in myself as a person with a colorful heritage did not blossom before it was crushed. The pride that I had in myself as a female was following the same path.

Women's roles in cartoons lack the cleverness and depth of their male counterparts. Instead, they are laced with helplessness and ignorance. The women are often in need of rescue—they seem incapable of defending or helping themselves. When they aren't busy being rescued, they spend their time looking pretty, waiting for a prince.

In 1st grade, these illustrations moved me to action. They influenced me to push aside my slacks and rustic bike and turn to dresses and dolls. I had to start practicing perfection if I was going to be happy. Weak, helpless, boring, I struggled to be all of those; then I could call myself a princess, an awkward one, but a princess nonetheless.

At the same time, my brothers swung guns and swords like they were attached to their hands. They tossed aside their piles of books and tubs of clay: Heroes didn't read or create—they fought! So they flexed their wiry muscles and wrestled invisible villains. They dressed, ate, talked, became miniature models of their violent heroes.

Sometimes it was fun, like a game, playing our parts. But we began to feel unhappy when we saw that some things weren't quite right. As I said, I wasn't Bonnie Bondell or Cinderella. My brothers, never destined to be hulks, went to great lengths to grow big, but gallons of milk and daily measurements didn't help. It wasn't a game anymore.

I have some fond memories of those afternoons with my brothers, yet I know that I will also remember them for the messages I swallowed as easily as gumdrops. My newfound awareness has enabled me to better understand those messages I absorbed and the ones I observe daily, whether on billboards, in movies, or in magazines. I see them in a new light. A critical one. I don't have to be a princess to be happy or pretty. I don't need to rely on characters to learn about real people.

I proudly perceive myself as an exuberant, creative, responsible, open-minded individual who will never be reduced to a carbon copy of a fictional being. ◆

---

*Lila Johnson is a former student of Linda Christensen's.*

# Looking for the Girls

*An educator makes some disturbing discoveries
when she watches a day of music videos*

◆ ANDREA BROWN-THIRSTON

DIANA CRAFT

When young people go home and turn on the television, what kinds of things do they see? What is the "curriculum" of music videos that seem to dominate the airwaves? I decided I would watch a full day of music videos to get an idea of the images and messages that a child could potentially see. As an African American woman, I am particularly interested in how the music videos portray African American women; the videos that I watched were a mixture of R&B and hip hop.

**Young black women are present more as ornaments and objects than as human beings. They are often in the background and virtually never have anything to contribute besides big breasts and butts.**

One all-too typical video was "What You Want" by rapper DMX. The song's hook phrase is "What y'all really want from a nigga?" and is sung by R&B singer Sisqo, who was made famous by the "Thong Song." Sisqo sits on the roof of a car that few men, let alone teenage boys, could afford. As the car spins around in a slow, hypnotic, circular motion, the woman on the hood of the car comes into view. She is lying across the car, with her legs spread apart and her head thrown back as if she is on the verge of orgasm. Sisqo continues to ask, "What y'all really want from a nigga?"

Later in the same video, DMX runs through a list of women's names that seemed to have given him some pretty intense sexual memories: Lisa. Nicole. Cynthia. Pam. With every name, a woman flashes on the screen. Each is shown less than 15 seconds and none ever says a word.

In the video "How Many Licks?" by rapper Lil' Kim, one Lil' Kim doll after another travels down the assembly line. Lil' Kim asks, "How many licks?"—referring to how long oral sex would have to last. The video features her as the main character with a swarm of female backup dancers. The camera views them from a wide shot as they dance closer and closer, hands cupped over their crotches, asking, "How many licks does it take till you get to the center of a uhh-uhh?"

Each scene pictures her dressed in different costumes, from a blonde curly wig and a sparkling silver two-piece bikini to a black wig, heavy black makeup, and a patent leather bodysuit. This Lil' Kim doll can be dressed up any way you like her. She is a fantasy. In one part of the song, she brags about the men in prison dreaming about her. In the video, they show her in a prison cell wiggling around on top of the inmate. He begins to move slowly down her body while "TOO HOT FOR TV" covers the sex act in question.

## The Effects

What effect are these images having on the children and youth watching the videos?

One Saturday afternoon I was watching *Teen Summit*, a program on Black Entertainment Television (BET) when the host asked a group of teens if the music videos affect the way they relate to each other. One of the boys blurted out, "Yeah, man. I'm still looking for the girls in DMX's videos"—hence the title of my essay. The others laughed but understood what he meant.

I think he meant that the girls in the videos represent a lifestyle that blends money, power, respect, material wealth, and beautiful women. This lifestyle does not just dominate music videos; much of the "curriculum" in mainstream media focuses on this lifestyle as the essence of the

American dream. However, the music videos that I watched are particularly dangerous because they expose young black men and women to a range of negative images. These videos, then, have a range of potential effects on young black men and women, as well as on the African American community as a whole. In addition, there is the issue of promoting stereotypical images of African Americans among young white men and women—a topic beyond the scope of this essay.

Healthy, respectful, and equal relationships with women are certainly not promoted in the images that I saw. Young black women are present more as ornaments and objects than as human beings. They are often in the background and virtually never have anything to contribute besides big breasts and butts.

Although the artists, lyrics, and story lines were different, the basic message for African American young men was that money can buy you beautiful, sexy, and seductive women. For example, many videos had one similar scene in particular: The camera scans a seemingly endless stream of beautiful women. They are all dancing seductively with their "come-get-me" expressions. Simply put, if you were ballers and shot callers like these male artists, you could have your pick; all these women wanted and longed for them. The reason these women were attracted to the men was not because of their looks, intelligence, or sense of humor. It was because of their money and the things that this money could get them.

Similarly, these music videos may also have negative effects on young black women. The women in the videos become the standard by which beauty and desirability are measured. Black girls may internalize these images and begin to accept the role of sex object. According to these images, the most desirable woman is not the black woman you would see at the bus stop or in the grocery store. The boy on *Teen Summit* was not turned on by a girl in his biology class or one who lived next door; he wanted the ones who are highlighted in the music videos, thereby pushing an image that most black girls will never achieve.

Furthermore, the videos teach young black women to aspire to be the trophies of powerful men. They do not show decent, loving male-female relationships. Instead, they display women who will do anything for the love of money. The women are indeed getting paid for these cameos and many of them find that it is an easy way to make money, which again supports this notion of quick fixes and fast money. The half-naked women are always smiling and laughing in the videos, so they seem to be having a good time, thus making it even more difficult for young people to form a critique of the videos.

Because the dreams promoted in the videos are so materialistic and individualistic, the videos betray the tradition of collectivism that has been the cornerstone of African American struggle. Historically, African Americans have stressed the importance of moving the entire community forward. Yet these videos promote the progress of the individual by any means necessary.

## The American Dream

The American dream was not created by or for African Americans but it is one that many of us fiercely desire. Yet what happens to those whose daily lives are closer to nightmares rather than dreams? Should we continue to allow these images to cloud the minds of millions of African American children who will not be excessively rich actors, athletes, or entertainers? If we do, we must be prepared for the consequences.

Given the racist, classist, and sexist nature of the educational system, the justice system, and society as a whole, the focus on these dreams increases the likelihood that young black people will find alternative ways of achieving these goals, which may be illegal and possibly violent. If we sincerely want our children to have a different set of goals, dreams, and priorities, we must create that environment.

What are the priorities we should be promoting? What are the alternatives to what the mainstream media feed our children? First, I believe that we should encourage children to start being critical rather than passive consumers of the media. Too often, educators ignore the potential impact on students or do not see these issues as "appropriate" curricular content. In other words, adults need to give children opportunities to openly and honestly discuss the images in music videos and media in general.

Second, adults need to be realistic about how powerful and enticing these images are. We cannot simply tell children that the women in these videos are bad or that chasing money is the wrong priority. We have to show them that there are other ways to have their needs met without becoming addicted to consumerism; in addition, we have to challenge young people to think critically about what it means to live the "good life."

Finally, I think that educators, parents, and community members need to understand the influence that we have in our children's lives. Young people do want direction, structure, and advice. If we do not want young people to become lulled into the fantasy world depicted in music videos, we have to demonstrate that our confidence comes from who we are rather than what we have. ◆

*Andrea Brown-Thirston is the chief academic officer at the Chicago International Charter School.*

# Miles of Aisles of Sexism

*Helping students investigate toy stores*

◆ SUDIE HOFMANN

**Y**ou sure wouldn't know our society has experienced almost 40 years of significant changes in the area of gender equity in education after a trip to the mall.

Toy stores are stubbornly resistant to change and remain entrenched in sex-role stereotypes and the unabashed glorification of war. Boys are still blasting, crushing, striking, and pulverizing their way through playtime. And girls are cleaning, diapering, and primping through theirs.

Unfortunately, toy stores continue to support levels of male and female gender bias not unlike what we saw before Title IX was passed in 1972. The aisles of girl toys are designated with pale pink letters and the names of the girl toys arc in oval signs framed in purple or pink. The boys' aisles are marked with green letters or blue frames—even today in

> **The copy usually includes words such as "kitten," "princess," "fairy," "precious," "wish," "dream," and "wonder."**

Toys 'R' Us, one of the nation's leading toy stores. And in many stores, child-sized Dirt Devils and Easy Bake Ovens crowd the girls' department and plastic power tools fill the boys'.

Some say corporations are just giving consumers what they want by providing friends and family with the products that will put smiles on kids' faces at weekend birthday parties. Yes, trendy toys and gadgets reflect societal values, habits, and the quest for stimulation. But let's look at the long-term messages that are sent to kids. Are toys providing innocent fun, or are children being socialized in ways that could ultimately influence career and life choices? Are boys encouraged to demonstrate power and control during playtime by simulating violence and war? I attempted to answer these questions by taking a look around Walmart, Target, Kaybee Toys, and Toys 'R' Us to consider the possible effects of gender-based toys. I came up with several areas of concentration such as gender segregation, career-related toys, militarism, and themes in packaging such as color usage and marketing language. After completing my investigation, I designed an exercise that required my students in a university gender issues course to explore a local toy store and report back to the class.

## Investigating Stores

A visit to several chain toy stores at the Mall of America and suburban shopping centers in the Minneapolis/St. Paul metro area taught me a powerful lesson about how toy manufacturers operate. I began by recording the categories of toys in the girls' and boys' sections. The boys' section was dominated by weaponry. Using Myriam Miedzian's powerful critique included in her 1991 book, *Boys Will Be Boys: Breaking the Link Between Masculinity and Violence*, I observed that boys' toys have become even more "lethal" since 1991. But the language used on the packaging now justifies the use of force or violence in the name of being a "peacekeeper," completing a "mission," or being a "superior defender." The text used on the war toys Miedzian observed was seemingly more honest about being the aggressors. For example, the Rambo 81mm Mortar Thunder-Tube Assault declares the "army will stop at nothing to control the world" and the motto for the Rampage Transformer is "those who conquer act: those who are conquered think." Madison Avenue now encourages violence during playtime in the name of peace and justice.

The colors commonly used on the packaging are black, red, and deep yellow to provide images of flames. Jagged letters suggest lightning, the icon for speed and power.

Words such as "bashing," "kicking," "deadly," and "assault" are standard fare used to promote these children's toys. Toys such as Power Brutes, Battle Arena, and Big Brother (whose box states "Get Ready for the Real Confrontation") can be purchased at just about any discount or toy store.

Kaybee Toys committed more than one-third of one aisle to Power Team Elite, manufactured by Hong Kong-based M&C Toy Centre; featured were about two dozen action figures with guns, scopes, grenades, Humvees, and an A-F Combat Helicopter. These toys offer children a particular perspective: Patriotism and superiority are the ultimate goals, and aggression and training for war are justified through a simplistic lens of "us" vs. "them."

> **Economic self-sufficiency and a sound understanding of money are essential for girls and boys. But it's hard to get even a glimpse of that reality in the fantasyland of toy stores.**

In addition to the war toys, the male area offers word games, chess, and other challenging board games. Boys—and presumably their dads—are prominently featured on the boxes of Pavilion's Backgammon and Chess Teacher. Planetariums, globes, interactive world maps, atlases, 3-D Dino Adventure, Legos, science kits, and GeoGenius fill the shelves.

I tried to find one female—child or adult—on any of the many science kits at Toys 'R' Us. I thought my research results would look a bit questionable if, in 2005, I claimed that not one female appeared on any of the science kits. I was determined to find at least one. I found a small plastic chair and attempted to reach the top shelf to see if that very last science kit would have a female on it. A friendly—albeit skeptical—store clerk asked if I needed assistance. I told him about my research and he brought the box down. For one joyous moment I thought I had found a female. Alas, it was not to be. The boy on the back panel just had long hair.

The girls' area, or should we say, fantasyland, is well stocked with vanity mirrors, combs, brushes, nail kits, makeup, and polyester hair extensions. The focus is on being popular with boys. The shelves are overflowing with Mattel Barbies and endless paraphernalia, including Barbie's scale, set at one weight: 110 pounds.

Shopping is a focus of many of the girl toys such as Lil Bratz Fashion Mall, which warns girls "Don't forget to stop at the makeup shop." Packages provide fashion advice and tips about how to be trendy and get noticed. Crowns, pom-poms, and phones in lavender and pink hang on the separate carousels near the small, upholstered furniture. Jump ropes, umbrellas, tea sets, and sticker books are in abundance. Unlike the colors used on the panels of the boys' toys, pastels reign here. The edges of the letters are smooth and an *i* or a *t* is dotted or crossed with a heart, butterfly, or star. Glitter is on everything—from the packaging to the product itself. The copy usually includes words such as "kitten," "princess," "fairy," "precious," "wish," "dream," and "wonder."

The girls' section does not have many board games that stimulate creative thinking or require higher-order reasoning. It has bingo and simple activities such as coloring books and car or travel games. Although the female area appears to be a pink fantasyland, the dream soon ends. After getting the guy, by playing Milton Bradley's Mystery Date or through sheer vanity and competition, the girls get the brooms, mops, vacuums, diapers, and plastic food. And they are smiling in every packaging photo.

Boys are noticeably absent from any of the advertisements, promotions, store posters, or packaging for toy household cleaning products, kitchen items, or childcare toys such as baby dolls and strollers. The product lines do not model social acceptance for boys to play homemaking or parenting.

When young boys engage in dress-up, pile on the necklaces, enjoy painting their nails, or select other girl toys, cultural norms or homophobia often correct the behavior immediately. In fact, in Fisher-Price Playlab studies, where staff members observed children behind one-way glass, they found that boys will play with "girl" toys if they think they are in a safe environment.

My students frequently offer supporting evidence about boys crossing these gender lines, from their part-time jobs at after-school programs. They believe that young boys relish the chance to get their nails painted and have their hair styled when girls are doing it as a special activity. As one student told my class recently, "I think boys just like the closeness of being with a staff member, being touched while we paint their nails, and talking with us." Perhaps it is the tactile, calming aspect of this activity that draws boys and girls to it. However, sex roles are reinforced very early in boys' lives, and toys play a part in that socialization.

Jackson Katz in *Tough Guise: Violence, Media and the Crisis in Masculinity*, a Media Education Foundation video, explores the ways boys are taught to be tough and how they're encouraged to define manhood in ways that hurt themselves and others. Katz provides an insightful analysis about how boys are socialized to be solitary, independent, and often violent through toys, video games, and Hollywood movies. According to Katz, the cultural message is that emotional connections are for sissies. Beyond the obvious problems of violence and aggression that many of the toys engender, even the science-based toys are solitary and don't present opportunities for verbal or social development. Pack-

JOSEPH BLOUGH

aging hints at being the best or creating and building superior models or designs. There is little evidence that toys help boys in social and emotional development or in Katz's words, help boys to be "better men" some day.

**Boys are still blasting, crushing, striking, and pulverizing their way through playtime. And girls are cleaning, diapering, and primping through theirs.**

Toys for girls implicitly urge them to find husbands in order to get their dream lives. Girls are taught to compete with each other for male validation. One makeup kit states, "Wait 'til they see you." Female rivalries, jealousies, and other negative behaviors such as bullying and harassment pose a host of problems for girls. Yet girls' toys promote unattainable physical perfection and materialistic values and typically strengthen the cultural messages of inferiority and second-class status that have influenced and continue to affect self-image and academic performance for many girls.

The harsh reality for girls is that when they enter the labor force they will make about 80 cents to a man's dollar, according to the U.S. Department of Labor's Women's Bureau (www.dol.gov/wb). More than 90 percent of U.S. women will work during their lifetime; they comprise 47 percent of U.S. workers, and about 70 percent of moms participate in the labor force. Most women work because they have to, and girls should be aware of this fact early on in their lives. Economic self-sufficiency and a sound understanding of money are essential for girls and boys. But it's hard to get even a glimpse of that reality in the fantasyland of toy stores.

## Action Research for Students

After completing my own toy store research, I designed an exercise for my students where they navigated a store of their choice, aisle by aisle. The students were enrolled in a gender issues course in the college of education at St. Cloud State University. I had originally intended the course to be an elective for teacher education students but the course has filled with non-licensure students every time I have offered it. In the first few weeks of the course, we examine a wide range of common gender socialization practices for young children, from parental biases in decorating the nursery, to the clothes and toys selected for children, to the verbal messages given to them regarding their gender roles.

In most of my classes I favor projects that send students out into the real world and these assignments frequently send the students into retail stores. For example, I send my students to seasonal stores in the fall to determine which Halloween costumes perpetuate racism, and in the spring I ask students to analyze the colors and fabrics used in children's spring jackets. We begin the action research project in my gender issues course by reviewing class material on gender socialization. Students generate a list of things to look for in a toy store such as messages about gender expectations and general issues such as cost, quality, and amount of toys in the boys' section vs. the girls' section. The students can use the list of questions the class formulated together to complete their research or they can use their own.

Part of the action research assignment is a written and oral report to the class that summarizes their findings. Some students have asked if they can give their report as a group, and I have found these presentations to be lively and interactive. One group somehow came up with the funds—or credit card—to buy many of the toys they researched. They provided the class with an array of war toys, Barbies, and GI Joes. The men in the group were the most vociferous in their critique of the messages sent to children, particularly boys, who play with war toys. One of the students had been in the military and said he felt angry about the socialization he had absorbed from toys, like assumptions that men make war, war is exciting, and new weapons are fun to use. The students took their show on the road and shared their research with classes in the college of education, and they also provided a session at a student-sponsored conference on nonviolence on campus.

Each class has found different things to review in its research. For example, one student found that there were "twice as many toys for boys than girls." She went on to write that the smaller girls' section was located in the front of the store and shared space with seasonal toys.

Another student noticed the facial expressions on the packaging of toys. She observed this in one item in particular, a beanbag chair. She wrote the following:

> The girls' beanbag package displayed two pictures of girls sitting back in their chairs, smiling and looking very relaxed. One girl was talking on the phone and the other girl was talking to another girl. The boys' beanbag package showed two pictures of boys leaning forward in their chairs. Both boys were gritting their teeth as the one played an electronic game while the other raised his fist and cheered for a sports team.

Other packages portray girls taking instruction or baffled by some accomplishment. A student noticed that the cover of Marvin's Magic Mind Blowing Card Tricks Set shows four boys in the front row and two girls in the back row watching a card trick being performed. The facial expressions of the two girls make them look flummoxed by the trick, while the boys seem to be studying it. In addition to these observations, almost all students reported that women were highly sexualized in many marketing promotions. One student reported that Toys 'R' Us had 126 covers of video games displayed on a wall and the only women shown were in "compromising positions" with "major cleavage." The only non-sexualized female was a furry yellow "Sonic Hero."

## Toy Segregation

The effect of toys and playtime may not be as benign as some parents and educators think. Although great strides have been made in many social areas, boys are still pushed toward higher levels of unhealthy competition and stoicism during playtime while many girls are reinforced in their unrealistic beliefs that they will always be taken care of or that employment outside the home is optional. The segregation under those neon lights is a fairly good predictor for what is to come, both in terms of earning power and career choice. The power and labor inequities in homes and work places—and the damaging messages sent to boys about their roles in society—are often shaped and defined in the types of toys that are mindlessly thrown in the shopping cart.◆

---

*Sudie Hofmann teaches at St. Cloud State University in Minnesota.*

# Part 4:
# View and Analyze Representations of Teachers, Youth, and Schools

KATHERINE STREETER

# TV Bullies

*How* Glee *and anti-bullying programs miss the mark*

◆ GERALD WALTON

Bullying has captured the public imagination as the news media have focused on several high-profile cases that culminated in homicide and/or suicide of gay boys and young men. These tragic events prompted several prominent celebrities and politicians such as Ellen DeGeneres, Cyndi Lauper, Kathy Griffin, Daniel Radcliffe, President Barack Obama, and Secretary of State Hillary Clinton to speak out against homophobic bullying by posting videos in support of lesbian, gay, bisexual, transgender, and questioning (LGBTQ) children on social commentator Dan Savage's "It Gets Better" YouTube campaign. Even fictional characters such as Kermit the Frog jumped into the fray.

Another voice in the "It Gets Better" campaign is that of Chris Colfer, who plays openly gay and flamboyant Kurt Hummel in the immensely popular musical television drama *Glee,* which debuted in September of 2009. Since the first episode, bullying has featured prominently as a bitter reality for most kids in the fictional school located in small-town Ohio. Although no one would argue that the focus on "bullying" is unimportant, using the term to describe acts of homophobia hides the ways in which LGBTQ youth are subjected to unique forms of verbal and physical assaults related to their real or imagined sexual orientation. Specifically, Kurt has been the target of homophobic attacks because his gender performance is feminine. Also targeted for homophobic violence is Finn Hudson, played by Cory Monteith.

Finn has problems. He is the quarterback on the football team and is also one of the key performers in the glee club. Other football players routinely harass Finn, despite the fact that he is avowedly straight. No one utters the word "faggot," but it is loudly implied in these scenes. However, the epithet "fag" was used on the show strategically and carefully in a scene where Finn pushes Kurt away because of his discomfort with sharing a bedroom with him after Kurt's father and Finn's mother have hooked up and moved into the same house. Kurt's father overhears the slur and confronts Finn, who eventually apologizes. (See episode 20 called "Theatricality.") This scene—as well as a scene in a previous episode where Kurt comes out

ERIC HANSON

to his working-class dad who supports his son for being "who he is"—is among the most emotionally powerful in the series to date.

These scenes demonstrate powerfully that the claim "boys will be boys"—which is used to legitimize boys' behaviors such as sexual harassment of girls and homophobic assaults on other boys—has harmful if not devastating consequences. Torment-

**Since the first episode, bullying has featured prominently as a bitter reality for most kids in the fictional school located in small-town Ohio.**

ing LGBTQ children is not just fun and games that can be ignored. And yet, when one looks at research on bullying, it becomes clearer how such prominent forms of bullying can be minimized and discounted even among those who purport to study bullying and to develop school policy on it. This is an ongoing tension in *Glee*, too, as the club itself is made up of misfits who are routinely bullied because of their "differences," which range from physical disability to simply being a "geek." In this way, homophobic attacks such as those experienced by Kurt and Finn, which include linguistic violence (being called "fag") as well as physical attacks (being thrown against a locker)

**Why do so many school administrators and teachers, real and fictional ones in shows such as *Glee*, claim their schools are safe for children while homophobic harassment remains prominent and obvious?**

are undercut and made to seem less harmful. When Rachel gets a slushy thrown in her face for being an overachieving social misfit, it suggests that the homophobic violence Finn and Kurt endure is simply another form of high school bullying experienced by those who choose to be different.

The focus on bullying in *Glee* is related to a larger cultural focus on the issue. Since the early 1990s, research on bullying has blossomed into a field of its own—as have related educational policy and programming, news stories, lawsuits, public discussions, and entire careers. One result is that researchers, educational administrators, psychologists, and journalists have become "experts" through which information about bullying is disseminated. Media technologies, specifically the internet, have also proliferated, increasing the velocity by which information is spread, including stories about bullying.

On one hand, such dissemination is good, as it informs the public and draws attention to the fact that bullying is harmful. On the other hand, identifying incidents of violence in schools as "bullying" has become usual practice for behaviors that used to be accurately described as sexual harassment. In an article in the *Arizona Law Review*, for example, Nan Stein observes how the label "bullying" expunges victims' rights under human rights legislation concerning sexual harassment. In *Glee*, then, the physical violence that Kurt experiences regularly from "the Neanderthal" on the football team—who consistently body slams him in the hallway and taunts him about his lack of masculinity—as in the scene where Kurt enters the locker room to hear his tormentor say "the girls' locker room is next door," can more accurately be defined as acts of sexual harassment.

The broad representation of bullying in *Glee* can be tied to the concept's commodification. Bullying has become useful and profitable for corporations, and they have an interest in framing it in the most generic way possible, which in turn strips it of any social critique. In the past two decades, parents and others have become anxious about bullying, providing rich soil in which a robust marketplace grows. A range of products that purport to offer solutions, such as books, DVDs, and prefabricated programs, has become widely available. The growing awareness of—but also construction of—bullying as a problem, then, has generated a lucrative industry. Corporate interests are involved in keeping the public concerned and worried about bullies in schools so that anti-bullying products will fly off the shelves. In addition to books and programs that can be purchased online and in major bookstores,

# What Can Be Done?

Given the complexity of the issue, strategies to tackle homophobic bullying should aim for a combination of intervention (to address behavior) and prevention (to identify and educate about specific forms of bullying). Challenging social prejudice requires participation at all levels, including students, teachers, administrators, bureaucrats, parents, and the broader community:

◆ Policies must be developed at all levels. They provide a framework for building toward safer learning environments, and a foundation from which student-focused and student-led initiatives such as GSAs can be developed.

◆ Staff and teachers should be trained appropriately to address homophobia.

◆ School boards should work with community organizations to build and implement such training. For instance, the Ottawa-Carleton District School Board has collaborated with community organizations to form the Rainbow Coalition, which provides "students with a safe space to socialize, support each other, and discuss concerns."

◆ Preservice teachers should be trained in the prevention and management of homophobia and gender-based violence through courses on equity and social justice offered in bachelor of education programs.

◆ Students, who constitute the majority of the school population, should be consulted when drafting and implementing policy.

# Intervention Strategies

The preceding strategies are preventative in design. Intervention-oriented strategies that teachers can incorporate into their daily practice are also important. In addition to educating themselves about how homophobic violence operates in the lives of all students, teachers might also:

◆ Include age-appropriate discussion that educates students on what words such as "gay" mean. The film *It's Elementary: Talking About Gay Issues in School* provides examples of teachers doing so with students of various ages.

◆ Use films to generate discussion, such as *Tomboy*, *Trevor*, and *Breakfast with Scot*.

◆ Sponsor a Gay-Straight Alliance and act as a mentor and resource for participants.

◆ Teach about family diversity by designing lesson plans on films such as *It's Elementary: Talking about Gay Issues in School* and, especially for children in elementary grades, *That's a Family!*

◆ Educate students about words that are used in a derogatory manner such as "fag," "queer," and "dyke."

◆ Teach the use of more appropriate terms and acronyms such as "questioning," "two-spirit," and "LGBT."

◆ Challenge students' use of homophobic language in the same way that one would challenge racial slurs, and identify its use specifically as homophobia; and structure a classroom discussion on homophobic language.

◆ Organize a workshop for teachers on homophobic bullying, to be held on a professional development day.

**Educating school communities, including parents, about harassment based on perceived or actual sexual difference is crucial if we are to make serious gains toward fostering safety in school for gay, lesbian, transgendered, and questioning students.**

consider also the Reynolds Bully-Victimization Scales for Schools, which can be purchased through the 2008 Catalogue for Psychological Assessment Products published by the Psychological Corporation of Harcourt Assessment, Inc. The School Starter Kit for whole-school or district assessment costs $440.00, not including manual ($75.00) or Machine-Scorable Answer Documents (package of 30: $45.00). Corporate media also benefits by perpetually casting the spotlight on bullying in schools, especially if it involves homicide, suicide, and/or lawsuits. That *People* magazine featured Phoebe Prince, who committed suicide to escape peer bullying, on the April 26, 2010, cover was most likely a bid for magazine sales.

## The Problem with Current Approaches

It may be the case that anti-bullying products, programs, and policies are sincere attempts to help students—bullies and victims alike—cope with the violence of bullying. The problem is that such well-meaning work mostly focuses on the management of behavior. Anti-bullying strategies are typically punitive (such as so-called zero tolerance policies) or regulatory (such as codes of conduct). This kind of approach appears in *Glee*. In the episode "Never Been Kissed," Kurt visits an all-boys' school, where one of the students tells him that "this is not a gay school, we just have a zero-tolerance harassment policy. Everybody gets treated the same no matter what they are." Of course, administrators and teachers can hold a reasonable expectation of appropriate behavior from students. However, regulating behavior fails to account for social prejudices, such as homophobia, which inform behaviors that are routinely labeled as bullying.

Homophobic harassment, especially among boys, reflects ideas about how boys and men should think and act. It also means that masculinity is regulated and enforced; those who do not meet the social standards of what it means to be a "boy" or "man" face the consequences of exclusion and ridicule. In *Glee*, Kurt Hummel and Finn Hudson know all too well how homophobia operates in each of their lives to shame and exclude them and configure them as legitimate targets of violence from other boys. One gay and the other straight, Kurt and Finn mirror the damage of homophobic assaults in schools.

Although Kurt and Finn inform the viewing audience that homophobia is harmful, *Glee* has yet to demonstrate that it is a problem that the school administrators must address, even in small towns

### Resources for Teachers

**Getting Ready for Benjamin** by Rita M. Kissen (Rowman & Littlefield, 2002).
**Challenging Homophobia: Teaching About Sexual Diversity** by Lutz van Dijk, Barry Van Driel, foreward by Archbishop Desmond Tutu (Jossey-Bass, 2007).

### Books for Children

**Daddy, Poppa, and Me** by Lesléa Newman (Tricycle Press, 2009).
**Momma, Mommy, and Me** by Lesléa Newman (Tricycle Press, 2009).
**Who's in a Family** by Robert Skutch (Tricycle Press, 1997).

### Film Resources

*Ma vie en rose* (1997) directed by Alain Berliner.
*Breakfast with Scot* (Capri Films, 2008)
http://caprifilms.com/breakfastwithscot/index.html
*It's Elementary: Talking About Gay Issues in School* (Groundspark, 1996) www.groundspark.org.
*That's a Family!* (Groundspark, 2000) www.groundspark.org
*Tomboy* (Coyle Productions, 2009) an animated short by Karleen Pendleton-Jimenez.
*Trevor* (1994) writer James Lecesne, director/producer Peggy Rajski, and producer Randy Stone. www.thetrevorproject.org/about-trevor/trevor-film
*Straightlaced: How Gender's Got Us All Tied Up* (Groundspark, 2009) Directed by Debra Chasnoff. Candid interviews with teens on gender and sexuality.

### Websites

**www.thetrevorproject.org**
 An important resource on GLBTQ kids, bullying, and suicide.
**www.glsen.org**
The Gay, Lesbian and Straight Education Network works with student, teachers and the public to create healthy school climates for GLBTQ youth.
**www.itgetsbetter.org**
 A collection of videos in support of GLBTQ youth from celebrities and regular folks.

in Ohio where the fictional school is located. In *Glee*, homophobia is regarded as a personal problem rather than an institutional one that poisons school environments and leaves children emotionally and physically unsafe. For example, in the episode where Kurt visits the all-boys school to watch their glee club, he meets a gay member of the club whose advice to Kurt is not to organize, but to have "courage" in the face of harassment from the football players. He also reminds Kurt that "only you can make yourself a victim." So Kurt returns to his school, pastes the word "courage" to the inside of his locker (along with a photo of the guy from the other school) and then confronts a harasser. Kurt tells him: "You can't beat the gay out of me." Thus, Kurt must take responsibility for standing up for himself rather than relying on institutional support. When Mr. Schuester asks if there is anything he can do, Kurt says, "You, like everyone else at this school, are too quick to let homophobia slide." Even after this, Kurt confronts his harasser alone. Yet, the bullying continues.

Why do so many school administrators and teachers, real and fictional ones in shows such as *Glee*, claim their schools are safe for children while homophobic harassment remains prominent and obvious? The work of curbing bullying in schools is misguided if regulation of behavior is the raison d'être of policies and programs. Educating school communities, including parents, about harassment based on perceived or actual sexual difference is crucial if we are to make serious gains toward fostering safety in school for gay, lesbian, transgendered, and questioning students. Unfortunately, it is also more complex and difficult than regulating behavior and is usually neglected as a key strategy.

Educating about sexual difference can be controversial and difficult, but children who are vilified by their peers for not performing femininity or masculinity in normative ways and/or refusing heterosexuality deserve it if their educational success is to be enhanced. For instance, one of the most effective and widespread strategies for LGBT rights and anti-homophobia organizing in U.S. schools is gay/straight alliances (GSAs). These student-led clubs, which obviously function best when they have strong staff and administrative support, have made a huge difference in many schools. How would Kurt and Finn's harassment be dealt with differently if a GSA were part of the plot line of *Glee*? The writers of *Glee*, as well as real life school administrators, need to take the issue of bullying one step further by placing the problem of homophobic harassment at the door of school administrators and compelling them to act to support LGBT children and those perceived as such.◆

---

*Gerald Walton is an assistant professor in the faculty of education at Lakehead University in Thunder Bay, Ontario.*

## References

It Gets Better Project: www.itgetsbetterproject.com/
Stein, Nan (2003). Bullying or sexual harassment? The missing discourse of rights in an era of zero tolerance. Arizona Law Review, 41.3: 783–799.

# Kid Nation

*Creating little capitalists*

◆ ELLEN GOODMAN

RANDALL ENOS

**Will kids left to their own devices create a democratic idyll or a savage anarchy?**

When they write the cultural history of childhood in the 21st-century United States, I hope they leave room for a few unkind words about *Kid Nation*.

CBS' 2008 reality show—that wonderful oxymoron—is about 40 kids from 8 to 15 years old who are dropped into a ghost town in New Mexico with only a production crew to call their own. The kids' task, we are told in the best go-team fashion, is to "try to fix their forefathers' mistakes and build a new town that works."

Their real job, of course, is to attract viewers who want to see what happens to the "first-ever kid nation." Will kids left to their own devices create a democratic idyll or a savage anarchy?

There is nothing particularly new about the conflicting images of children as innocents and children as beasts. It's as old as mythology. It lives on in the heart of every parent who's seen her child turn from a screaming sociopath at the supermarket checkout to a philosopher king at the beach: "Who painted the sky blue?"

But the real founding fathers of *Kid Nation* leave little to chance or choice. It's the producers, not the so-called "pioneers," who determine the structure of the town called Bonanza. It's the adults who lay the cultural grid down the main street. And this makes *Kid Nation* an entry into the annals of childhood as it's now lived and argued about in the United States.

You see, this is what the adults brought with them from Hollywood to Bonanza: competition, class conflict, and consumerism. In the very first episode, the children were directed to form four armies for color war. And they did. They were told that victory would determine their class status. And it did.

In a scenario Karl Marx couldn't have made up, the winners of the war were dubbed "upper class," the runners-up were labeled "merchants," then "cooks," and finally "laborers." The little capitalists were allowed to use their very unequal paychecks for very unequal chores to pay for goodies at the town store. The producers did everything but deny the lower-income children their health coverage.

Cutthroat competition, class divisions, unrelenting consumerism. Maybe it is reality programming after all. Aren't these the basic three Cs of the culture in which we are all raising children?

Parent bashing is the favorite indoor sport on reality television. It's behind the voyeurism that makes Supernanny popular and Britney Spears unpopular. It's why we cheered the judge assigning the sinking celebrity a parenting coach.

Ordinary parents are held responsible for protecting their children from every imaginable danger. They are fed a high-anxiety diet of horror stories about lead paint in toys, Crocs on escalators, and killer cribs. If you Google "danger" and "children," you get 172 million hits of everything from online predators to takeout junk food.

Yet even the most watchful parents are not immune to criticism. The latest villains are the helicopter parents. See them hover over their children's lives! Watch them pull the invisible apron strings of a cell phone, book their children's playdates, and write their college entrance essays while squashing their sense of imagination. Parents even have to protect kids from overprotection.

The backstory is that the United States has privatized child raising. We regard children as the wholly owned subsidiary and responsibility of their families. Parents, in turn, can become so absorbed in worrying about the side rails on cribs that we lose focus on the cultural environment that encases all of us. And there is no bike helmet that can protect our children's brains from the three Cs.

Before it premiered, *Kid Nation* itself was charged with endangering the children by violating child labor laws and even child abuse laws. Indeed, the consent form that the parents signed is as creepy as the ones you don't read before you go into surgery. Even creepier was the scene when two homesick children cried and not one adult had the impulse to drop a camera and offer comfort.

**The backstory is that the United States has privatized child raising. We regard children as the wholly owned subsidiary and responsibility of their families.**

Nevertheless, the real trouble in Bonanza is not that the cast of mini-survivors was exposed to "serious bodily injury, illness, or death." It's that the children, urged to build a better town (read "world") than their forefathers, were manipulated into the copy-cat media culture. The reward is a gold star literally worth its weight in gold: $20,000.

The only hero so far is 8-year-old Jimmy, the New Hampshire boy who had the good sense to go home. As for the rest? The children of Bonanza didn't make the rules. They inherited them. It's not a kid nation. It's our nation.◆

---

*Ellen Goodman is a Pulitzer Prize-winning writer for the* Boston Globe. *This is reprinted with permission from the Washington Post Writers Group.* Kid Nation *was canceled on May 14, 2008.*

# *Freedom Writers*

## *White teacher to the rescue*

◆ CHELA DELGADO

I find it hard to put a finger on what bothers me about Hollywood's teacher movies. Is it the young white teachers saving kids of color? Is it the guilt I feel as a teacher who may not have succeeded as well as these superheroes? Is it the notion that teachers should be mother, father, college counselor, and best friend to our students, despite the incredible personal toll that takes? Or is it the movies' individualized solutions to structural problems?

It's all of that—and more. I want a teacher movie where there aren't cardboard heroes and villains, but there is a genuine analysis of how race and class play out in schools.

For now, however, we have *Freedom Writers*. Released in January 2007, the movie is based on the book *The Freedom Writers Diary* and chronicles the educational triumph of Erin Gruwell, an idealistic young white teacher who inspired the hearts and minds of her remedial students of color in her freshman English class. (Gruwell left classroom teaching after about five years and now heads a foundation promoting her "Freedom Writers" approach.)

Starring Hilary Swank as Gruwell, the film opens with footage of the violence following the 1992 Rodney King verdict in Los Angeles that acquitted four police officers who had been filmed beating King. The aquittal resulted in widespread rioting in Los Angeles. This set the scene for the tension at the Long Beach school system where Gruwell teaches, which had recently been forcibly integrated.

The story truly begins when, during class, a Latino student draws a racist caricature of a black student and passes it around. Our hero, "Ms. G," snatches the paper from the desk of the black student depicted in the drawing. The student is crying. Ms. G angrily asserts that the picture reminds her of caricatures of Jews in the years leading to the Holocaust. (Why it only reminds her of anti-Semitic caricatures and not of other racist caricatures of African Americans, I can't tell you.) At the end of her speech, she asks the students how many of them have heard of the Holocaust. Only one—the white student—has. She then asks how many students have been shot at. Slowly, each student raises his or her hand (except for the same white kid).

It's a turning point. For Ms. G, there's the realization of the violence

RANDALL ENOS

that haunts her students' lives. The students, meanwhile, begin to "connect" with Ms. G. They become involved, they read *The Diary of Anne Frank* and relate it to their lives, and they organize to stay with their teacher for the next academic year and beyond.

**The frustrated youths roll their eyes at their teacher's ignorance of hip hop, and the lesson is a failure.**

## 'Connecting' with Students

Early in the film, Ms. G uses a 2Pac song to introduce "standard" poetic devices. The frustrated youths roll their eyes at their teacher's ignorance of hip hop, and the lesson is a failure. Later, the students' study of the Holocaust successfully connects, in part because of Ms. G's passion about the issue. This raises several questions. Rather than studying their own histories—U.S. slavery, the violence of colonization and border creation, the Khmer Rouge regime in Cambodia—the students study the Holocaust. Even when the stories of students of color are brought into the classroom, they can rarely be a focus, a stand-alone issue. We teach hip-hop lessons so that students can learn Shakespeare.

**Though the audience is supposed to pity Ms. G's students, we are not supposed to sympathize with their parents—an incarcerated father, a mother who kicks out her son.**

Even where the Holocaust is a vehicle for the students telling their own stories, that connection to a white experience is key. The Holocaust should be studied in its own right—but so should the current lived experiences of youth of color in the United States.

The movie's turning point, in which Gruwell realizes the extent of violence in her students' lives, is significant only because she didn't realize it before. She doesn't come from where her students come from, and she apparently hadn't learned much about their lives before she began teaching.

There is something deeply worthwhile about Ms. G attempting to connect the oppression of her own people to the oppression experienced by her students. But the theme of white legitimization of the experiences of youth of color is one that runs throughout *Freedom Writers*, and it often precludes the kind of grappling with racism that—just once—I would like to see on screen.

### Individualistic 'Solutions'

The problem with *Freedom Writers* isn't so much the kind of cookie-cutter stereotyping that we see in Hollywood's white-teacher-as-savior genre. Rather, it's the highly individualistic nature of these stereotypes. It scares me that people will leave this film thinking: "See? You can change the system."

Sure. If, like Ms. G, you get two other jobs, neglect your personal life, isolate yourself from your fellow teachers, and rely on your white privilege to ensure you won't be fired. And, by the way, that's not changing the system. It's changing one classroom.

Don't get me wrong—changing one classroom is an accomplishment. And as far as I can tell, Gruwell and her former students are doing their best, through their foundation, to make this story bigger than what happened in room Room 203. But let's be clear: This is not a movie about the depth and breadth of racism in education; it's a movie about a white savior.

There are undeniably "saviors" of color, as well as students "saving" themselves. They just don't get movies made about them.

### Taking Race Seriously

People of color talking about racism is nothing new. And too often, when we rail against moments in which the specter of race remains invisible to white perception, white people think we're delusional. Racism can only be taken seriously, it seems, when it is championed by white allies, or by young people of color who can't *quite* be held responsible for their plight.

There is a marked absence of black and Latino adults in *Freedom Writers*, and there's a reason. They aren't youthful enough to elicit sympathy. Though the audience is supposed to pity Ms. G's students, we are not supposed to sympathize with their parents— an incarcerated father, a mother who kicks out her son. The parents' struggles, and the ways in which their lives are also held down by structures of race and class, are not part of the story.

> **There are undeniably "saviors" of color, as well as students "saving" themselves. They just don't get movies made about them.**

There's no room in *Freedom Writers* for a bigger narrative. We can't talk about adults of color "saving" themselves from racism, because that's just called living your life. We can't talk about a teacher of color "saving" her students because, apparently, it's only exciting to watch white people suddenly become aware of race and start a crusade. And we can't begin to talk about what it would take to save anybody from the "tangle of pathologies" that is structural racism. That would have meant, in addition to Ms. G's students finding a way to tell their stories, they would *also* have had to demand resources for their class so Ms. G wouldn't have to work three jobs—to say nothing of challenging the tracking system, organizing student forums to discuss the impact of the integrated school district on their lives—and on and on. Who wants to sit through a movie that long?

Watch *Freedom Writers*. Enjoy it for what it is. But afterward, take away the message of continuing to struggle against racism in education. Don't be fooled into thinking the short-lived triumph of one savior in one classroom is enough. ◆

---

*Chela Delgado is the community action coordinator at the June Jordan School for Equity in San Francisco.*

# City Teaching, Beyond the Stereotypes

◆ GREGORY MICHIE

From the opening frames, it's evident that *Half Nelson* isn't going to be a conventional "urban teacher" film. It begins on the hardwood floor of a bare apartment, where Dan Dunne sits in his underwear, legs outstretched, a scraggly beard creeping down his neck, a dazed, spacey look in his eyes. An alarm clock buzzes insistently in the background. It's time for Dan to leave for school, but he's struggling to peel himself off his living room floor. Soon, we understand why: In addition to being a social studies teacher and the girls' basketball coach at a Brooklyn junior high school, he's a crack addict, a basehead.

Dan wants to be a good teacher, and even when he's coming unglued personally—which is often—he does his best to hold it together for his students. In his classroom he ditches the prescribed curriculum and asks his black and Latino kids to wrestle with tough questions. His methods are part Socratic seminar, part didactic ramble, but his lessons push students to think, to make connections, to see history as something that can be shaped by everyday people working together and taking action.

Yet we're never tempted to see Dan as the savior, the white hero—and not just because of his drug habit. Although it's clear that he despises the forces that keep his students down ("the machine," he calls it), the filmmakers remind us that he's not an innocent. When he asks his kids during class one day to name the obstacles to their freedom, their answers come easily: "Prisons." "White people." "The school." Then Stacy chimes in from the back row: "Aren't you part of the machine then? You white. You part of the school."

As committed as Dan tries to be to his students, it's obvious that he's holding on by a thread. He succumbs to his addictions at night and is distracted and tired in class the next day. It seems inevitable that his two lives will collide, and one evening following a girls' basketball game, they do. One of his students, Drey, a player on the team, finds him cowering in a bathroom stall, soaked in sweat, crack pipe in hand. She glares at him, more hurt than surprised; he looks terrified.

"Can you help me up?" Dan finally mutters.

Drey gets him to his feet, then wipes his forehead with a wet paper towel. For a moment, we forget who's the teacher and who's the student. If anybody needs saving here, it's Dan.

ANDY PEREZ

But no miracle turnarounds or stand-and-cheer moments are to come. *Half Nelson* is too smart for that—subtle, understated, every note played in a minor key. It's a quiet film that takes the trite conventions of Hollywood teacher-hero movies and turns them inside out, revealing troubling contradictions and real-life shades of grey.

**Stacy chimes in from the back row: "Aren't you part of the machine then? You white. You part of the school."**

Dan Dunne is bright, sensitive, politically aware, and has a genuine rapport with his students. He's also immature, unfocused, impulsive, and self-absorbed. Is he a good teacher? In some ways, yes; in others, probably not. That alone makes him far more believable than the saint-like, cardboard protagonists of most urban teacher films.

Even in its smallest details, *Half Nelson* seeks complexity and plays against popular stereotypes. As Dan arrives at school one morning and gets out of his car, we don't hear sirens, gunshots, or a thumping hip-hop soundtrack. Instead, we hear the chirp of a lone songbird. Who knew the city had any? Later in the film, when Drey rides her bike past a row of desolate lots in her neighborhood, the overwhelming feeling is not one of menace or impending danger but of utter isolation and abandonment. It's the crippling aftermath of deindustrialization: factories shuttered, opportunities vanished, work disappeared.

What's freshest about *Half Nelson*, though, is its depiction of the reciprocal nature of the teacher-student relationship. Dan teaches and is taught, guides and is guided, receives as much as he gives. His students have much to learn from him, and they do—lessons about the clash of opposing social forces, about historical turning points and how change happens—but he, too, is a continual learner. Drey and the other kids help make Dan a better person than he would be without them. And in watching him, we learn that good teaching is not only about changing the world or changing the lives of others—it's about changing ourselves, a transformation from within.

For city teachers, it's also about functioning within—and challenging—a system that in many ways works to undercut and even thwart your best efforts. Although the tyranny of high-stakes testing has made life difficult for teachers from the tiniest towns to the toniest suburbs, teachers in big-city schools often face additional hurdles and hardships. They must navigate added layers of administrative responsibility, do more with fewer resources, create community in buildings where alienation and anonymity are accepted elements of school life. Teachers in city schools are far more likely than their counterparts elsewhere to have fewer desks than students, to have no planning periods (or even bathroom breaks) during an entire school day, to lack daily access to a school counselor or photocopier, or to be handed a scripted curriculum and told how and when it must be taught. To teach in a big-city school system is to recognize, as former New York City Teacher of the Year John Taylor Gatto once said, that the institution itself has no conscience. And it is to understand, as Dan tells his students, that you sometimes have to throw your body on the gears of the machine.

## The First Year

In the documentary film *The First Year*, novice teacher Maurice Rabb gets a crash course in how the needs of a child can be crushed by the entrenched bureaucratic machinations of a mammoth school system. "I feel the pain of my students," says Maurice, who is black, of his 5-year-olds in South Central Los Angeles. As we watch his futile efforts to obtain help for Tyquan, a student with a severe speech impediment, we feel it, too. Maurice agitates to get Tyquan assessed by the school's frequently absent speech therapist, but months pass with no results. Although his principal is sympathetic to his plight, she claims her hands are tied. The bigger picture, she says, is that the district is short 40 speech therapists, so their school is lucky to have one at all. Maurice makes phone calls to public clinics to try to get services for Tyquan, but there, too, he runs into a wall: The child's government insurance will cover only two hours of therapy per month. Frustrated and angry, but undeterred, Maurice begins one-on-one tutoring sessions with Tyquan three days a week after school. Progress is slow but certain. It's not enough, to be sure. But it's something.

Maurice's story demonstrates that resistance to schooling-as-usual doesn't have to take the form of grand or symbolic gestures. It can also be found in steady, purposeful efforts to make the curriculum more meaningful, the classroom community more affirming, the school more attuned to issues of equity and justice. Sometimes it means starting small: visiting the home of a troubled child, ignoring a senseless mandate, improvising to create a lesson that connects to students' lives. Other times it means joining with like-minded educators to form a study group, advocate for a policy change, or speak out at a board meeting. Either way, committed urban teachers learn that while they can't always tear down the wall that stands between their students and a truly humanizing education, they can chip away at it brick by brick.

Of course, not all city teachers face identical challenges because not all city schools are the same. In Chicago, where I taught for nine years, magnet schools and college prep academies are inundated with resumes from qualified teachers and lavished with attention from community partners and politicians. Many schools in poor neighborhoods, meanwhile, struggle to stay alive amid threats of "takeover," and strain to attract the attention of outside partners or prospective teachers. A few elite Chicago public schools boast state-of-the-art facilities and technology; many others have sparsely stocked libraries, lack functional science labs, or have no recreational space for students. These differences don't mean the selective and elite schools aren't really "urban." But they're a reminder that vast differences and inequities exist even within big-city systems, and for teachers in the most forgotten and forsaken schools, the journey toward equitable outcomes for children is an even steeper, more precarious climb.

Even so, urban teaching is not all toil and struggle—not by a long shot. It's nurturing a community among teenagers who've experienced too much pain in their young lives. It's the comfortable rhythm of Mr. B's classroom at the juvenile detention center. It's getting a surprise birthday present from 13-year-old Ellis, coming out to your 5th graders, helping Jasmine begin to heal. It's protesting against a dreadful standardized test—and winning. For teachers who remain in city schools long enough to get their bearings, the instances of utter frustration are tempered—and on the best days eclipsed—by moments of joy and transcendence.

The obstacles are no doubt formidable for city teachers but, to borrow from James Baldwin, the work is more various and more beautiful than anything anyone has ever said about it. ♦

---

*Gregory Michie has been a teacher and teacher educator in Chicago for 20 years. The author of* Holler If You Hear Me: The Education of a Teacher and His Students, *he currently teaches at Concordia University in Chicago.*

# Sticking It to the Man

◆ WAYNE AU

What's the purpose of rock 'n' roll? Sticking it to The Man. At least that's what Dewey Finn tells his students in the introductory "lesson" in the 2003 Paramount release *School of Rock*. Finn, played by comedian Jack Black, is not really a teacher but an out-of-work, out-of-band rock guitarist who impersonates his roommate in order to land a job as a substitute teacher at an elite prep school. What is surprising about *School of Rock* is that Finn, for all of his blundering, draws on students' feelings of disempowerment as the core of his curriculum.

After Finn notices a chart of gold stars and black-dot demerits marking student "progress" on the wall, he asks "What kind of sick school is this?" and proceeds to shred the chart, prompting the teacher's pet to cringe in horror. Thus begins "Project Rock Band"-an interdisciplinary, theme-based project to form the class into a band. He works with students to assign them different roles, where they are allowed to work collaboratively and creatively in small groups. As inspiration for their song material, Finn draws on the various ways that these students are alienated—from their parents, their peers, their school, and their education—as a means to connect them to the project. He says, "If you wanna rock, you gotta break the rules. You gotta get mad at The Man!" And getting mad at The Man in this case means rebelling against all authority, parents and principals included.

The audience gets to see several interesting changes take place. The classroom space shifts from neat rows to loose groupings of desks. The atmosphere changes from silent contained obedience to free-spirited classroom participation. Students also begin personal transformations as they deal with some of their individual alienation. In one poignant scene, Tomika, an African American girl with an incredible singing voice, feigns sickness to get out of performing. Finding that Tomika is insecure about being overweight, Finn reminds her of her vocal talents and how some good-looking, legendary performers are big, citing Aretha Franklin as a prime example. Finn changes too. He starts out self-absorbed, and doesn't have a clue about teaching. By the end, he shows genuine concern for the well-being of his students.

*School of Rock*'s pedagogy obviously has its limits. It is about a bunch of kids from really rich families attending an expensive, elite private school. Issues of race, class, gender, and sexuality, while hinted at, are

PARAMOUNT PICTURES

explicitly left out of the teaching. Finn exposes his multiracial students to a pantheon of white rockers, never mentioning rock's roots in the black community. It is also not clear that Finn teaches any academic skills.

**"What kind of sick school is this?"**

But throughout the movie, the students' attitudes about their education are clearly shifting—in a positive direction. In the climactic scene where the band performs, the students sing to an awestruck crowd that includes their parents: "Maybe we were making straight A's/ But we were stuck in a dumb daze/ Don't take much to memorize your lies/ Or feel like I've been hypnoticized/ You know I was on a honor roll/ Got good grades and got no soul/ Raise my hand before I can speak my mind/ I've been biting my tongue too many times"

The final lesson comes after they lose the Battle of the Bands. Finn is crushed, and a student reminds him, "Rock isn't about getting an A. The Sex Pistols never got an A." Ultimately this is what *School of Rock* is about: creating an education that is less alienating and embraces your soul instead of a system of education that dehumanizes.

In my mind, there's no question: *School of Rock* sticks it to The Man.

## The Perfect Score

According to Kyle, the protagonist of the 2004 Paramount/MTV release *The Perfect Score*, SAT actually stands for "Suck-Ass Test." To be sure, this is mainstream Hollywood schlock through and through, but in the midst of mediocre writing, acting, directing, and cinematography, *The Perfect Score* manages to provide a series of surprisingly biting critiques of the SAT, the Educational Testing Service (ETS), and the

College Board.

*The Perfect Score* is worth seeing for at least two scenes. In the movie's opening, Kyle makes some searing observations. While he narrates that the SAT "sees us all the same," the screen cycles through images of a pregnant teenager sitting down to take the exam, a typical prep school student going to a well-funded classroom, and a student who has to go through metal detectors to get into school, highlighting just how different all students are. The scene ends on an even more serious note when Kyle solemnly observes that the SAT is "not about who you are. It's about who you'll be."

Later, as Kyle is deciding whether or not to take part in the college exam caper, he comes home to his mom, who is a teacher. Mom jokingly asks Kyle if he wants to help her grade and adds with a wry smile, "We're teaching the 1st graders to bubble." Kyle responds: "Mom, 1st graders can't read." To which mom replies, "I hate to say it. There's more money in filling in bubbles than reading these days." Kyle concludes, "Standardized testing is taking over."

There are other more specific critiques of the SAT peppered throughout *The Perfect Score*. At varying points the test is labeled as "anti-girl" for underscoring women on the math sections, having a bias toward National Merit Scholars, and being racist. The script writers even managed to squeeze in the term "stereotype vulnerability," which refers to the theory that students are vulnerable to stereotypes regarding achievement: meaning, for instance, that African American students will perform more poorly on the SAT because they know that African American students traditionally score lower than white students on the test. Fortunately, when another student raises this issue with *The Perfect Score*'s only African American student, Desmond, he says he couldn't care less about the stereotype since he needs to take care of business and go to college. Later it comes out that Desmond breaks the stereotype of being a dumb, black jock because, much to the surprise of his movie-mates, he is a whiz in math.

Thankfully, as in Desmond's case, broken stereotypes are generally left strewn along the edges of the storyline by the end of *The Perfect Score*. The Asian American stoner-slacker-underachiever, Roy, proves to be quite intelligent, just unhappy and unmotivated. The "perfect" 4.0 student, Anna, suffers from test anxiety and overburdening parents, but figures out how to make her own choices. Matt, the average Joe who lives for his girlfriend who is already at college, decides it's OK to live for himself. Kyle does fine on his retake and gets into college, and the rich "bad" girl, Francesca, whose dad conveniently owns the building that houses ETS, sees that she may not need the love of her father in order to be a whole person. Hollywood or not, what *The Perfect Score* does well is effectively equate the standardized SAT with the stereotyping and external expectations placed on students. It shouts that we are not numbers, and our intelligence and worth cannot be measured and quantified by these types of tests.

*The Perfect Score* does not score perfectly though. The audience is supposed to laugh at Roy's sexist behavior, and in one joke the movie leans on criminal stereotypes of Mexicans for comedic fodder. And Desmond's mother fits all too neatly into the stereotype of the African American matriarch who not only takes care of her own kids but ends up mothering motherless Roy as well.

Finally, while I grinned ear to ear hearing all those critiques of the SAT spilling forth from a mainstream movie, most of the points came in the form of zippy one-liners and lacked any real sustained argument. Not surprisingly then, *The Perfect Score* leaves us with no sense of collective student action against standardized tests. Instead its solution relies on a small group of individual students operating mainly out of individual self-interest of varying flavors. So while their critiques of the SAT are based on real social issues, the action that grows out of that critique is ultimately self-centered.

Speaking purely in terms of film quality, *School of Rock* and *The Perfect Score* cannot compare. While *The Perfect Score* is just a plain-old badly written movie with bad acting, *School of Rock* works as a refreshingly respectful and amusing "kid power" flick with much more imaginative writing and acting. Quality aside, ETS did decide to take *The Perfect Score* somewhat seriously. In an odd, slightly paranoid move, it decided to increase building security in case students got any ideas from watching the movie.

As artistically divergent as both movies are, they do share similar political sensibilities. The moral of both is that grades and test scores don't represent real learning, and they certainly don't represent all that is human and important about students and education. This may be a surprising message coming from mainstream Hollywood, but given the current context of No Child Left Behind, budget cuts, and the continual hyper-quantification of students via high-stakes tests and GPAs, the rebellious spirit of both *School of Rock* and *The Perfect Score* is more than welcome. ◆

---

*Wayne Au, a former high school teacher, is an assistant professor at the University of Washington–Bothell Campus and is a* Rethinking Schools *editor. Most recently he edited* Rethinking Multicultural Education: Teaching for Racial and Cultural Justice *(Rethinking Schools, 2009) and authored* Unequal by Design: High-Stakes Testing and the Standardization of Inequality *(Routledge, 2009).*

# More Than Just Dance Lessons

◆ TERRY BURANT

**M**ad Hot Ballroom, a 2005 documentary about a 5th-grade ballroom dance program in New York City schools, is more than a feel-good summertime film. I use it to raise questions and teach multiple lessons in my Introduction to Teaching in a Diverse Society class.

I wasn't an immediate fan. A few minutes into the film, a white principal launches into a monologue about her students and their families that made me shift in my seat and cringe. She describes her students, mostly from the Dominican Republic, with a deficit view that highlights single-parent families, children "with issues" raised by grandparents, families where more than one generation lives in the household, and a 97 percent poverty rate. I was afraid that I was about to see a white savior narrative, one in which kids of color are saved through the heroic efforts of white teachers and the timeless discipline and grace of ballroom dance.

Then the dancing began. Four viewings later and still craving more, I now have my favorite kids, my most cherished moments, and a list of lessons this film can teach future teachers.

First, this film is a wonderful illustration of the joys of teaching and the best that learning brings. We watch children from three very different city schools as they learn to move to the beat of the tango, to follow directions ("feel the eye-to-eye connection," "take your dance position"), to care about, cheer for, and accept one another. They develop competence and a vocabulary about this activity, learn to graciously take the stage, and they perform together like magic. It is a grand testament to the privileged moments that teaching and learning bring.

We see this joy explicitly in the tears of a young white teacher, Allison, when she talks about seeing her students "turning into little ladies and gentlemen." We see it again in the cheers of all the teachers as they stand on the sidelines while their children dance in competition. We hear it in teacher Yomaira Reynoso's proud voice as she explains, "I'm not rich, but I am a teacher." And we see it yet again as the dance instructors from the American Ballroom Theater's Dancing Classrooms program thrill to their students' continuing improvement. We see it as well in the students' self-reflective critiques of themselves, their part-

ners, and their performances, and in the examples of lives turned around by participation and unexpected excellence in dance.

The film also demonstrates fine teaching. Reynoso, a dedicated Dominican teacher from P.S. 115, effortlessly shifts from English to Spanish, expects the best efforts from her dancers, gets out on the floor and dances during each class, and speaks with heart about "not knowing what is hidden in each child" and how teachers and programs like this can unearth these hidden talents. She goes beyond the classroom and takes the girls on her school's team shopping together for matching skirts when they are chosen for the final competition. Although she demands that they pick out outfits with "no belly buttons showing," she also solicits and attends to their fashion opinions.

*Mad Hot Ballroom* also made me rethink prior assumptions about the place of dance in schools to bridge cultural gaps and promote cultural understanding and respect. As a dancer myself, I've critiqued dance as just one more shallow form of feel-good cultural celebration, a surface-level approach to multicultural education. Yet here I see students from diverse cultures dancing in one another's arms and watch their teachers infuse cultural knowledge and pride into the lessons of dance. I became a little more open to the transformative and community-building potential of dance.

**Four viewings later and still craving more, I now have my favorite kids, my most cherished moments, and a list of lessons this film can teach future teachers.**

The film also raises questions about gender, sexuality, and the complexities and tyranny of competition, although not necessarily in explicit ways. The traditional gender roles inherent in ballroom dance (for example: boys lead, girls follow) aren't disrupted or challenged. In between dances, the film weaves precious glimpses of the children's lives and opinions into the mix, and many of these vignettes illustrate the pervasive heterosexual orientation in dance lessons, school, and life in general. Although the heartbreak of competition is vividly expressed in the children's tears and in their heartfelt debriefings afterward, there is an unquestioning acceptance of competition as a cultural form throughout the film. But the structure of the competition itself, with a grand parade of all the dancers and prizes for everyone, the supportive refrains of all of the instructors, and even the names of the levels in which all the teams are either bronze-, silver-, or gold-level winners, help to mitigate the potentially nastier effects of competition.

More subtly, the film raises serious and important questions about the demographics of teaching and the persistent need for more teachers of color. As a teacher educator, I present the preservice teachers in my introductory classes with statistics about schooling in the United States; this film brings these numbers and their possible meanings to light. The oft-cited cultural mismatch between an overwhelmingly white teaching force and an increasingly diverse student population is vividly illustrated when the middle-aged white women teachers of Forest Hills P.S. 144 (the school that won the previous year's competition) talk about how much they love their giant traveling trophy. In contrast, there is no doubt that Yomaira Reynoso brings priceless insider knowledge to her school or that Rodney, a Latino dance teacher in the film, has a unique ability to connect with his students, especially with some of the more reluctant boys. *Mad Hot Ballroom* is a useful tool for stimulating discussions about questions like: Can white teachers teach all children? If so, what do they need to know, or be able to do, to do this well? How can we change the face of teaching to reflect a more diverse nation?

Finally, and perhaps most importantly, the litany of ills listed by the principal in the early moments of the film, is challenged throughout. We see parents walking with their children and talking about sacrificing in order for them to have better lives. We hear children talking at length about their parents' strict rules for them. At the final competition, the dressed-up family members cheer madly, hotly, for their children. This disrupts the earlier deficit script and speaks to the importance of connecting with parents and families.

*Mad Hot Ballroom* brings to life the action and color of New York

City streets—from flower vendors to overflowing buckets of mussels and shrimp. And the children themselves take center stage, delivering insights on life as only 5th graders can: Emma, the young white girl full of statistics and explanations for every social issue imaginable ("young girls of 10 are the No. 1 target for sexual predators"); Wilson, a Dominican boy who recently immigrated to the United States and knows very little English, and the way in which dance opens the door for new friendships in an unfamiliar place; Michael, the chubby, clumsy white boy in his Batman T-shirt, commenting on life and love and gay marriage while playing endless games of foosball in his bedroom, complete with American flag bedspreads; and Amber, a Dominican girl who poignantly talks about her fears of growing up and expresses how right now "it's fun to be 10" and to still "be a children." Throughout the film, children speak freely about all that is on their minds—from drugs and gangs to boys and girls and hopes and dreams.

> I became a little more open to the transformative and community-building potential of dance.

Yes, the kids are truly the stars of this show—turning initially awkward moves into the flowing dances of the rumba, tango, fox trot, merenque, and swing. It's enough to make even the most uncoordinated dance denier find a partner, put on a little Frank Sinatra, and get out on the floor.♦

---

*Terry Burant is currently a chemistry teacher at Marquette University High School and an adjunct assistant professor in the department of educational policy and leadership studies at Marquette University in Milwaukee. She is an editorial associate at* Rethinking Schools *magazine.*

# Part 5:
# Take Action
# for a Just Society

KATHERINE STREETER

# Taking the Offensive Against Offensive Toys

◆ LEONORE GORDON

Inspired by an article from the Council on Interracial Books for Children, I took up the issue of biased toy packaging with my 5th-grade class.

At the time I was teaching at a small private school in Brooklyn, N.Y. The class was racially mixed, with an equal number of boys and girls. Economically, students ranged from lower middle class to upper middle class, with a large number living with single working mothers.

Their consciousness about racism and sexism had been raised through studies of Native Americans, working people at their jobs, and—on occasion—television commercials. They had gained some insight into class issues by discussing Studs Terkel's book *Working*. And they had furthered their knowledge by conducting interviews with working people.

Thus the group was primed for action when I brought up toys and the political implications of their packaging. Some of the questions I asked to stimulate this discussion included: If you're a boy, what kinds of presents have you gotten on holidays? What do people expect you to be like? What have girls gotten as presents? What are you expected to be like? How many girls have wanted trucks? How many boys have wanted dolls? Tell me about the TV commercials you've seen. What kinds of kids are they about?

The first products the children discussed were sneakers and jeans. When one child noted, "You wear Jordache and Pumas if you're poor," other students added: "It's because of status. It's the only way to show you have something." Status, said one student, means "belonging—it means you're part of the group."

The students then discussed the manipulative techniques of corporations, including how advertisements try to make consumers think they need a product even if they can't afford it or how they make people think they have to "belong" to larger groups.

By the end of our discussion, we had begun to plan our next step: a visit to a local branch of Toys"R"Us.

We created a checklist and I suggested that each child carry a clipboard with a copy. The list had such items as: Describe the picture on the package. Is it racist? Why? Is it sexist? Why? Is it classist? Why? What

ERIC HANSON

does the toy cost? Is it sturdy? Are people of color shown in the picture on the package? Is it a stereotypic picture? Do the kids on the package look real?

They were also asked to note the name of a toy, its manufacturer, and the firm's address.

When we arrived at the store, the students set to work enthusiastically. Some of the products they found to be the guiltiest were, of course, the kitchen toys (with pictures of little white girls), most science toys (only boys shown experimenting), and the sports equipment. I also found that although girls were being increasingly included on previously male-designated toys, the issue of racist packaging was barely being addressed.

When we returned to school, we discussed what we had seen and analyzed the students' checklists. Reporting on their experiences, they spoke of the noticeable absence of African Americans.

As part of this examination of toy packaging, I encouraged students to share their complaints with toy manufacturers. Following are

**One child noted, "You wear Jordache and Pumas if you're poor."**

samples from two of the letters written by the children.

Dear Kenner:
Your product, the X-Ray Stretch, is racist and sexist because your toy only has whites on the toy but no blacks. The toy is sexist because there's a boy in it but not a girl. I advise you to change the appearance of this toy.

Dear H-G Industries:
One of your products [an archery set] is very badly stereotyped of a Native American. The facepaint, headdress, and clothes are all stereotyped. Another thing, your toy is so badly built everything in the package is warped, so get it together and put together your toy.

The project helped make the children more aware of negative corporate mentality. They also felt more capable of judging that mentality and of identifying the tactics of some of the manufacturers. I hope they will be able to recognize similar tactics in other sectors of society. Most important, they have become children who are less gullible targets of corporate advertising. ◆

---

*Leonore Gordon is an educator, writer, certified family therapist, and social activist. Before Parkinson's forced her retirement, she taught poetry as a teaching artist in the New York City public schools with Teachers & Writers Collaborative. She is a congressional coordinator for the Parkinson's Action Network. Her poems and articles about education have appeared in numerous books and magazines.*

# Beyond Pink and Blue

*Fourth graders get fired up
about Pottery Barn's gender stereotypes*

◆ ROBIN COOLEY

CHRISTIANE GRAUERT

"Pink, pink, pink! Everything for girls in this catalog is pink," exclaimed Kate, one of my 4th graders, as she walked into the classroom one morning, angrily waving the latest Pottery Barn Kids catalog in the air.

"I HATE the color pink. This catalog is reinforcing too many stereotypes, Ms. Cooley, and we need to do something about it!"

**I asked the class: "Why did William's family and friends tease him because he wanted a doll? Why should only girls play with dolls?"**

I knew she was right. And I was glad to see that our classroom work on stereotypes resulted in my students taking action. As we finished up the school year, my students initiated a letter writing campaign to Pottery Barn, one of the most popular home furnishings catalogs in the United States.

Newton Public Schools is actively working to create an anti-bias/anti-racist school environment. In fact, beginning in 4th grade, we teach all students about the cycle of oppression that creates and reinforces stereotypes. I weave discussion of the cycle of oppression throughout my curriculum to help my students understand how stereotypes are created and reinforced, and more importantly, how we can unlearn them.

## Anti-Bias Literature

I began the year's anti-bias work in my multiracial classroom by looking at gender stereotypes. As a dialogue trigger, I read aloud the picture book *William's Doll,* by Charlotte Zolotow. This is a wonderful story about a little boy who is teased and misunderstood by his friends and family because he wants a doll.

When I finished the book, I asked the students the following discussion questions: "Why was William teased? What did William's father expect him to be good at because he was a boy?" I explained that expecting William to like sports and play with trains was an example of a stereotype, an oversimplified picture or opinion of a person or group that is not true.

Next, I asked the class: "Why did William's family and friends tease him because he wanted a doll? Why should only girls play with dolls? Where did this idea come from?" The students immediately said, "Family!" Through discussion, the students began to understand that they are surrounded by messages that reinforce these stereotypes. We brainstormed some ideas of where these messages come from, such as television shows, advertisements, and books.

Next, I asked: "Why didn't William's father listen to his son when he said he wanted a doll?" One student exclaimed, "Because William's father believed only girls played with dolls!" I explained that the father believed this stereotype was true.

One boy in my class complained: "I don't get it. I like dolls and stuffed animals. Why did William's dad care? Why didn't he buy his son what he wanted? That doesn't seem fair. Someday, I'm going to buy my kid whatever he wants!"

Finally, I asked the students: "In this story, who was William's ally? Who did not believe the stereotype and helped William get what he wanted?" The students knew that William's grandmother was the one who stood up for him. She was an example of an ally. William's grandmother bought William the doll, and she taught the father that it is OK for boys to want to hold dolls, the same way he held and cared for William when he was a baby.

Each week during the fall semester, I read a picture book that defied gender stereotypes, and we had discussions like the one on *William's Doll*. Tomie dePaola's *Oliver Button Is a Sissy* is another excellent book about a boy who wants to be accepted for who he is. Oliver really wanted to be a dancer, and all the kids at school teased him about this. Despite great adversity and risk, Oliver had the courage to do what he wanted to do, not what others expected him to do or be. After reading the book, students in my class were able to share personal stories of what their parents expected them to do, or when they were teased for doing something "different."

Another title that helped to break gender stereotypes was *Horace and Morris but Mostly Dolores*, a story about three mice who are best friends. One day, the two boy mice decide to join the Mega-Mice Club, but no girls are allowed. Dolores joins the Cheese Puffs Club for girls. She is unhappy and bored because all the girls want to do is make crafts and discuss ways to "get a fella using mozzarella." One day, the three friends decide to quit their clubs and build a clubhouse of their own where everyone is allowed, and you can do whatever you want, whether you're a boy or a girl.

> We discussed some different family structures and talked about how some families might have two moms or two dads, a single parent, or a guardian.

## Looking at Families

Next we explored stereotypes about families. The students were aware of the messages they've absorbed from our culture about what a family is supposed to look like. Ben, who is adopted, said he was upset when people asked him who his "real" mom was. "I hate that I have to explain that I have a birth mother who I don't know, and my mom lives with me at home!" he said. We discussed some different family structures and talked about how some families might have two moms or two dads, a single parent, or a guardian. *Heather Has Two Mommies*, by Lesléa Newman, is a great picture book that illustrates this point.

After two months of eye-opening discussions, the last anti-bias picture book I read to my class was *King and King,* by Linda de Haan and Stern Nijland. This picture book does not have the typical Disney ending. In this story, the queen is tired and wants to marry off her son so he can become king and she can retire. One by one, prin-

**The day my class decided that they wanted to write individual letters to Pottery Barn Kids was the day I knew my students felt they could make a difference in this world.**

cesses come, hoping the prince will fall in love with them. Each time, the prince tells his queen mother that he doesn't feel any connection. It's not until the last princess arrives with her brother that the prince feels something—but it's not for the princess. He falls in love with her brother. The queen approves, and they get married and become "king and king." My students loved this story because the ending is *not* what they expected at all! They also appreciated hearing a picture book that has gay characters because they know gay people exist. They wondered why there aren't more gays and lesbians in picture books.

Since my students were so excited about their anti-bias work, I decided we should do a project with our 1st-grade buddies and teach them about breaking stereotypes. We created a big book called "What Everyone Needs to Know." This became a coffee-table book that we left on the table at the school's entrance waiting area. The 1st and 4th graders brainstormed all the stereotypes that we knew about boys, girls, and families. Then each pair picked a stereotype to illustrate on two different pages. On one page, the heading was, "Some people think that . . ." with a drawing portraying the stereotype. On the next page, the heading would say, "but everyone needs to know that . . ." with a drawing breaking the stereotype. For example, one pair came up with, "Some people think that all families have a mom and a dad, but everyone needs to know that all families are different. Some families have two moms or two dads. Some families have one grandparent. All families are different."

Another pair came up with, "Some people think that only girls wear jewelry but everyone needs to know that both boys and girls wear jewelry."

I knew our work on stereotypes was sinking in because my students would continually share with the class examples of how they tried to speak up when they saw people acting on stereotypical beliefs. One day, a student told the class about how she spoke up to a nurse at the hospital where her baby brother was just born. "I couldn't believe the nurses wrapped him in a blue blanket and the baby girls in pink!" she said: "I asked the nurse why the hospital did that and she said it was their policy. I don't think I can change the hospital's policy, but maybe I at least made that nurse stop and think."

## Making a Difference

The day my class decided that they wanted to write individual letters to Pottery Barn Kids was the day I knew my students felt they could make a difference in this world. They wrote letters that told the truth about how they felt and why they thought the catalog was so hurtful to them. I was so proud that my students were able to explain specific examples of gender stereotypes in the catalog and why they thought the images should change. The students analyzed the catalog, front to back, and picked out things I hadn't noticed. One student wrote:

**One thing I know for sure is that my students now look at advertisements with a critical eye.**

> Dear Pottery Barn Kids,
>
> I do not like the way you put together your catalogs because it reinforces too many stereotypes about boys and girls. For instance, in a picture of the boys' room, there are only two books and the rest of the stuff are trophies. This shows boys and girls who look at your catalog that boys should be good at sports and girls should be very smart. I am a boy and I love to read.

The boys in my classroom felt comfortable enough to admit out loud and in writing that they wished they saw more images of boys playing with dolls and stuffed animals. Another boy wrote:

> Dear Pottery Barn Kids,
>
> I am writing this letter because I am mad that you have so many stereotypes in your magazine. You're making me feel uncomfortable because I'm a boy and I like pink, reading, and stuffed animals. All I saw in the boys' pages were dinosaurs and a lot of blue and sports.
>
> Also, it's not just that your stereotypes make me mad but you're also sending messages to kids that this is what they should be. If it doesn't stop soon, then there will be a boys world and a girls world. I'd really like it if (and I bet other kids would too) you had girls playing sports stuff and boys playing with stuffed animals and dolls.
>
> Thank you for taking the time to read this letter. I hope I made you stop and think.

The day we received a letter from the president of Pottery Barn, my students were ecstatic. The president, Laura Alber, thanked the students for "taking time to write and express your opinions on our catalog. We'll try to incorporate your feedback into the propping and staging of our future catalogs and we hope that you continue to see improvement in our depiction of boys and girls."

I knew the students would expect the fall 2003 Pottery Barn Kids catalog to be completely void of pink and blue and I reminded them that change is slow. The most important thing is that they made the president of a large corporation stop and think. I pointed to two of the quotes I have hanging in my classroom, and we read them out loud together:

> Never doubt that a small group of thoughtful, committed citizens can change the world. Indeed, it's the only thing that ever has.
> —*Margaret Mead*

> Each of us influences someone else, often without realizing it. It is within our power to make a difference."
> —*Deval Patrick*

## Epilogue

The fall 2003 Pottery Barn Kids catalog arrived in my mailbox in late August, and the first thing I noticed was the cover: There's a picture of a boy, sitting at a desk, doing his homework. Another picture shows a boy talking on the phone, instead of a girl, which was something one of my students had suggested. The boy is also looking at a *Power Puff* magazine, something that is typically targeted to girls. When I asked one of my former students what she thought, she said, "Well, the catalog sort of improved the boys, but not really the girls. They still have a lot of changes to make."

One thing I know for sure is that my students now look at advertisements with a critical eye, and I hope they have learned that they do have the power to make a difference in this world. ◆

*Robin Cooley taught 4th grade for 12 years in Newton, Massachusetts. She currently teaches 5th grade.*

### Resources

**King and King** by Linda de Haan and Stern Nijland (Tricycle Press, 2002).

**Oliver Button Is a Sissy** by Tomie dePaola (Voyager Books, 1990).

**Horace and Morris but Mostly Dolores** by James Howe (Aladdin Library, 2003).

**Heather Has Two Mommies** by Lesléa Newman (Alyson Publications, 2000).

**William's Doll** by Charlotte Zolotow (HarperTrophy, 1985).

# Taking Action Against Disney

*A teacher struggles with encouraging direct student action*

◆ STEVEN FRIEDMAN

To protest or not to protest, that was the question. After showing my 7th- and 8th-grade Judaic studies class *Mickey Mouse Goes to Haiti,* a 28-minute documentary about the exploitation of workers in factories contracted to Disney, I once again faced this dilemma.

By showing the video, produced by the National Labor Committee (NLC), I hoped to encourage some activism. But I was afraid of getting in trouble for influencing the students on what some would consider a political issue. Instead of boldly proposing direct action, I suggested the class write letters to Disney headquarters.

THE WALT DISNEY COMPANY

My student Lizzie Louis had another idea. She asked if we could organize a demonstration outside one of Disney's stores in San Francisco. I told her it was a great idea but that the school would never sanction such an activity. My parting words to her were, "Let me see if I can arrange something for after school."

I was stalling.

**I knew I was on solid ground with respect to the extent of injustices in Disney's sweatshops. But I was still afraid.**

As the school's community service coordinator, I had never shied away from raising political or moral issues. In fact, I'd helped students get involved in a variety of important causes or projects: corresponding through art and letters with patients who have life-threatening illnesses (mostly cancer and AIDS); serving meals to the homeless; tutoring and mentoring children in one of the county's poorest neighborhoods; collecting food, toys, and clothing for area shelters and food banks; volunteering at a prison day care center. So why was I reluctant about my students protesting against Disney?

Disney contracts with factories in Haiti, Honduras, Indonesia, Thailand, and China. Independent monitoring groups (sponsored by unions, religiously affiliated groups, or organizations in those countries) as well as U.S. journalists have confirmed widespread abuses and horrendous working conditions at many of these factories. I knew I was on solid ground with respect to the extent of injustices in Disney's sweatshops. But I was still afraid.

My apprehension was partly because of a past experience. The previous year, my 5th graders viewed *Zoned for Slavery,* NLC's video about the inhumane working conditions in Central American factories that make Disney and other products. Afterward, my 5th graders and I wrote letters of protest to Disney CEO Michael Eisner. After tepid responses from one of his vice presidents, the students suggested we provide the school community with a list of which clothing manufacturers used sweatshop labor in countries such as Haiti and El Salvador. The students and I felt that if people knew which manufacturers relied on sweatshops, they might boycott these companies.

After I published the list of the guilty companies twice in the school's weekly newsletter, the school's director told me to stop. He said that by becoming a political activist, I was perilously close to muddying my role as a neutral educator.

The accusation was strange because I teach at a private Jewish school where we spend a significant portion of time learning about ethics and values and relating them to our lives. We go beyond teaching about biblical precepts—such as the commandment to leave the corners of your field or portions of your harvest for the poor—and stress modern applications of these ancient laws, such as helping at soup kitchens or stocking food at local food banks.

But now I had been told that I had crossed a line.

I printed the list once more. The director then told me that my future community service columns would need his prior approval. Apparently, it was OK to advertise clothing drives or ask for money to help an inner-city school purchase supplies, but it was "too political" and "too activist" to provide people with information about companies that routinely deny basic rights to workers, many of them children who labor for U.S. markets.

Why, I asked myself, is it too political to highlight the exploitation and repression of workers who earn 7 cents to sew a *101 Dalmatians* outfit that retails for $19.95? How can anyone remain neutral when workers, mostly teenage women, are forced to work 12 to 16 hours a day making Disney toys in dusty, sweltering factories using dangerous chemicals?

The director failed to tell me the real reasons I'd been reprimanded. The school was afraid to offend board members who might own stock in Disney; it wanted to be able to attract donations without appearing too political or too controversial. In other words, we had to remain neutral to protect investments in Disney and to secure funding for the school.

I realize there are complicated issues involved in trying to determine when and how it is appropriate for a teacher to guide student activism. For instance, teachers need to be sensitive to the importance of letting students discuss, analyze, and make up their own minds about social issues—rather than merely allowing them to regurgitate what they perceive to be the teachers' views. And, as is true with any field trip or out-of-classroom activity, communication with parents and parental permission is essential.

But the complexities of the issue should not be used to hide the reality that teaching is never politically neutral. Everything educators do or don't do can be classified as political. If it's OK to promote progressive behavior by students (food drives, meals to the homeless), why shouldn't we guide students into social activism against inhumane working conditions that help cause poverty and homelessness? And I doubt that a group of middle school students protesting against Disney is the revolutionary straw that will break the back of the empire.

I knew I had to answer Lizzie's question. When word leaked out that I might organize an action against Disney, more students in her class asked about helping and attending. Then the class studied a unit on hunger and poverty and connected the dire conditions of the poor in the Third World with the policies of U.S. corporations subsidized by the U.S. government. The issue of a protest resurfaced. Then some of my former 5th-grade letter writing activists questioned me about pursuing the topic of sweatshop labor this year (I do not teach the 6th-grade Judaica class). How could I dodge the issue any longer?

The answer came when the NLC announced an international week of action against Disney. A gift had landed in my lap: The NLC was sponsoring the demonstration I'd been afraid to organize. All I had to do was invite my students to the rally on a non-school day and we'd have our opportunity to get involved.

I sent a letter about the rally with some background information on Disney's behavior to each middle school family (we have only 36 kids) and requested that anyone who was interested join me on the first Saturday of protest.

Most responses were positive. One parent phoned to say that even though she and her daughter would be away during that weekend, she appreciated my organizing the parents and students; three more parents pledged to attend; two other parents took me up on my offer to transport students.

Not everyone was pleased. Soon after the letter was mailed, two of my colleagues and friends felt I'd sealed my fate and would be fired. Although I'd paid for the mailing, they reasoned that involving the school community in political activity—even in an indirect way—would be a direct challenge to the director's admonition from the previous school year. They feared the fallout resulting from my termination would hurt the school's reputation. Another co-worker told me that her boyfriend, a superintendent of schools in another county, had seen the letter (her son is a student of mine) and remarked that if I'd worked for him, he would have had my head on a platter. Two parents felt I'd abandoned my role as a neutral educator by leading students to protest. They were worried that I hadn't presented both sides of the story.

What are the two sides when people working in factories contracted by U.S. corporations in Asia and Central America don't earn enough to feed their families, are routinely beaten and abused, and have no legal options to remedy their situation? Balance and other perspectives have their utility, but I completely eschew moral relativism. It's one thing to strive for balance (and we should) by teaching, for example, that no civilization or religion has a corner on superiority. It's likewise important to present as valid other perspectives, such as those of indigenous populations, women, and other groups whose stories are often marginalized and distorted by traditional accounts. But certain issues do not have two equally valid sides.

We don't teach the Civil Rights Movement by equating the views of the Bull Connors of the South with the views of Rosa Parks and Martin Luther King Jr. And we don't teach the Holocaust by presenting the Nazi viewpoint as anything other than evil. Why should our approach to the issue of U.S. companies using sweatshop labor be any different?

I believe educators, parents, and students have a responsibility to expose injustice and oppression, and the call for "balance" can be used to cloud the real issues. Why shouldn't we be forced to look outside our proverbial windows and help make the world a better place?

## Outside the Disney Store

Two students initially joined me in the protest outside the Disney Store in downtown San Francisco on a cold, blustery Saturday morning nearly three weeks before Christmas. The two students, Jessica Whyman and

Natalie Shamash, and I handed out leaflets and asked for signatures on petitions to Michael Eisner. We held placards that said: "Boycott Disney" and "Disney Supports the Repression of Workers in Central America."

Throngs of shoppers and tourists crowded the streets in search of the latest bargain or the perfect gift, but amid the din of holiday traffic, we felt invisible. Many people passed us with blank stares, few words, and the look of indifference.

Jessica and Natalie were becoming chilled and disillusioned, but their mood changed dramatically after Lizzie arrived. Although none of the other students had ever attended a "formal" protest before, Lizzie had experience at political gatherings. Two years ago, for instance, she and her father, Jerry, had gone to Washington as part of an Oxfam-sponsored youth meeting to pressure President Clinton on meaningful aid to those ravaged by war and famine in Africa. Lizzie had also won Oxfam's postcard-drawing contest and had spoken at several functions as a result.

Lizzie's presence reenergized Jessica and Natalie. People started talking to us, mostly to the three of them, and signing our petitions. Before long we were joined by Lizzie's father, two more of my students, Samantha and Ian, and their mother, Pam. By noon, our kernel of eight had grown into a crowd of nearly 75 protesters, including members of the Bay Area Haitian-American Council, political activists, several local union representatives, and members of a Unitarian Meeting House. There was also a group of striking workers, mostly Latina women, who had walked out against a Disney licensee over unfair working conditions, intimidation, and discrimination.

What happened when I returned to school on Monday? Luckily, not much. Colleagues who feared there would be repercussions, such as my getting fired, were wrong. As it turned out, the director's only stated concern was whether I'd improperly used the school directory for the mailing to parents telling them about the protest. The school guarantees that the directory will not be used for business or nonprofit purposes, and he was worried that someone might accuse the school of violating that binding agreement.

For my part, I know we did the right thing by attending the rally, just as I know that teaching for social justice is critical to every classroom. By putting social action at the center of learning, we join those who challenge injustice in our schools and in our communities. ◆

---

*Steven Friedman taught at Brandeis Hillel Day School in California.*

# Why We Banned Legos

*Exploring power, ownership, and equity in the classroom*

◆ ANN PELO AND KENDRA PELOJOAQUIN

Carl and Oliver, both 8-year-olds in our afterschool program, huddled over piles of Legos. They carefully assembled them to add to a sprawling collection of Lego houses, grocery stores, fish-and-chips stands, fire stations, and coffee shops. They were particularly keen to find and use "cool pieces," the translucent bricks and specialty pieces that complement the standardissue red, yellow, blue, and green Lego bricks.

"I'm making an airport and landing strip for my guy's house. He has his own airplane," said Oliver.

"That's not fair!" said Carl. "That takes too many cool pieces and leaves not enough for me."

"Well, I can let other people use the landing strip, if they have airplanes," said Oliver. "Then it's fair for me to use more cool pieces, because it's for public use."

Discussions like this led to children collaborating on a massive series of Lego structures we named Legotown. Children dug through hefty-sized bins of Legos, sought "cool pieces," and bartered and exchanged until they established a collection of homes, shops, public facilities, and community meeting places. We carefully protected Legotown from errant balls and jump ropes, and watched it grow day by day.

After nearly two months of observing the children's Legotown construction, we decided to ban the Legos.

## The Investigation Begins

Our school-age childcare program—the "Big Kids"—included 25 children and their families. The children, ages 5 through 9, came to Hilltop after their days in elementary school, arriving around 3:30 and staying until 5:30 or 6:00. Hilltop is located in an affluent Seattle neighborhood, and, with only a few exceptions, the staff and families are white; the families are upper middle class and socially liberal. Kendra was the lead teacher for the Big Kid program; two additional teachers, Erik and Harmony, staffed the program. Ann was the mentor teacher at Hilltop,

DAVID McLIMANS

working closely with teachers to study and plan curricula from children's play and interactions.

A group of about eight children conceived and launched Legotown. Other children were eager to join the project, but as the city grew—and space and raw materials became more precious—the builders began excluding other children. Occasionally, Legotown leaders explicitly rebuffed children, telling

**Other children were eager to join the project, but as the city grew—and space and raw materials became more precious—the builders began excluding other children.**

them that they couldn't play. Typically the exclusion was more subtle, growing from a climate in which Legotown was seen as the turf of particular kids. The other children didn't complain much about this; when asked about Legos, they'd often comment vaguely that they just weren't interested in playing with Legos anymore. As they closed doors to other children, the Legotown builders turned their attention to complex negotiations among themselves about what sorts of structures to build, whether these ought to be primarily privately owned or collectively used, and how "cool pieces" would be distributed and protected.

These negotiations gave rise to heated conflict and to insightful conversation. Into their coffee shops and houses, the children were building their assumptions about ownership and the social power it conveys—assumptions that mirrored those of a class-based, capitalist society. As we watched the children build, we became increasingly concerned. Then, tragedy struck Legotown and we saw an opportunity to take strong action. Hilltop is housed in a church, and over a long weekend, some children in the congregation who were playing in our space accidentally demolished Legotown.

When the children discovered the decimated Legotown, they reacted with shock and grief. Children moaned and fell to their knees to inspect the damage; many were near tears. The builders were devastated, and the other children were deeply sympathetic.

We gathered as a full group to talk about what had happened; at one point in the conversation, Kendra suggested a big cleanup of the loose Legos on the floor. The Legotown builders were fierce in their opposition. They explained that particular children "owned" those pieces and it would be unfair to put them back in the bins where other children might use them. As we talked, the issues of ownership and power that had been hidden became explicit to the whole group.

We met as a teaching staff later that day. We saw the decimation of Legotown as an opportunity to launch a critical evaluation of Legotown and the inequities of private ownership and hierarchical authority on which it was founded. Our intention was to promote a contrasting set of values: collectivity, collaboration, resource sharing, and full democratic participation.

We knew that the examination would have the most impact if it was based in engaged exploration and reflection rather than in lots of talking.

We didn't want simply to step in as teachers with a new set of rules about how the children could use Legos, exchanging one authoritarian order with another. Ann suggested removing the Legos from the classroom. This bold decision would demonstrate our discomfort with the issues we saw at play in Legotown. And it posed a challenge to the children: How might we create a "community of fairness" about Legos?

## Out with the Legos

Taking the Legos out of the classroom was both a commitment and a risk. We expected that looking frankly at the issues of power and inequity that had shaped Legotown would hold conflict and discomfort for us all. We teachers talked long and hard about the decision.

**Children moaned and fell to their knees to inspect the damage; many were near tears. The builders were devastated, and the other children were deeply sympathetic.**

We shared our own perspectives on issues of private ownership, wealth, and limited resources.

One teacher described her childhood experience of growing up without much money and her instinctive critical judgments about people who have wealth and financial ease. Another teacher shared her allegiance to the children who had been on the fringes of Legotown, wanting more resources but not sure how to get them without upsetting the power structure. We knew that our personal experiences and beliefs would shape our decision-making and planning for the children, and we wanted to be as aware as we could about them.

We also discussed our beliefs about our role as teachers in raising political issues with young children. We recognized that children are political beings, actively shaping their social and political understandings of ownership and economic equity—whether we interceded or not. We agreed that we want to take part in shaping the children's understandings from a perspective of social justice. So we decided to take the Legos out of the classroom.

We had an initial conversation with the children about our decision. "We're concerned about what was happening in Legotown, with some kids feeling left out and other kids feeling in charge," Kendra explained. "We don't want to rebuild Legotown and go back to how things were. Instead, we want to figure out with you a way to build a Legotown that's fair to all the kids."

The children had big feelings and strong opinions to share. During that first day's discussion, they laid out the big issues that we would pursue over the months to come.

Several times in the discussion, children made reference to "giving" Lego pieces to other children. Kendra pointed out the understanding behind this language: "When you say that some kids 'gave' pieces to other kids, that sounds like there are some kids who have most of the power in Legotown—power to decide what pieces kids can use and where they can build." Kendra's comment sparked an outcry by Lukas and Carl, two central figures in Legotown:

> Carl: "We didn't 'give' the pieces, we found and shared them."
> Lukas: "It's like giving to charity."
> Carl: "I don't agree with using words like 'gave.' Because when someone wants to move in, we find them a platform and bricks and we build them a house and find them windows and a door."

These children seemed to squirm at the implications of privilege, wealth, and power that "giving" holds. The children denied their power, framing it as benign and neutral, not something actively sought out and maintained. This early conversation helped us see more clearly the children's contradictory thinking about power and authority, laying the groundwork for later exploration.

Issues of fairness and equity also bubbled to the surface during the animated discussion about the removal of the Legos:

> Lukas: "I think every house should be average, and not over-average like Drew's, which is huge."
> Aidan: "But Drew is special."
> Drew: "I'm the fire station, so I have to have room for four people."
> Lukas: "I think that houses should only be as big as 16 bumps one way, and 16 bumps the other way. That would be fair." ["Bumps" are the small circles on top of Lego bricks.]

This brief exchange raised issues that we would revisit often in the weeks ahead. What is a fair distribution of resources? Does fairness mean that everyone has the same number of pieces? What about special rights: Who might deserve extra resources, and how are those extra resources allotted?

After nearly an hour of passionate exchange, we brought the conversation to a close, reminding the children that we teachers didn't have an answer already figured out about Legotown. We assured them that we were right there with them in this process of getting clearer about what hadn't worked well in Legotown, and understanding how we could create a community of fairness about Legos.

We'd recorded the discussion so that we'd be able to revisit it during our weekly teaching team meeting to tease out important themes and threads. The children's thoughts, questions, and tensions would guide us as we planned our next steps. We weren't working from carefully sequenced lessons on ownership, resource sharing, and equity. Instead, we committed to growing an investigation into these issues, one step at a time. Our planning was guided by our goals for social justice learning, and by the pedagogy our school embraces, inspired by schools in Reggio Emilia, Italy. In this approach, teachers offer children a provocation and listen carefully to the children's responses. These responses help teachers plan the next provocation to challenge or expand the children's theories, questions, and cognitive challenges.

> **"We don't want to rebuild Legotown and go back to how things were. Instead, we want to figure out with you a way to build a Legotown that's fair to all the kids."**

## What Does Power Look Like?

A few days after we'd removed the Legos, we turned our attention to the meaning of power. During the boom days of Legotown, we'd suggested to the key Lego players that the unequal distribution of power gave rise to conflict and tension. Our suggestion was met with deep resistance. Children denied any explicit or unfair power, making comments like, "Somebody's got to be in charge or there would be chaos," and "The little kids ask me because I'm good at Legos." They viewed their power as passive leadership, benignly granted, arising from mastery and long experience with Legos, as well as from their social status in the group.

Now, with Legotown dismantled and the issues of equity and power squarely in front of us, we took up the idea of power and its multiple meanings.We began by inviting the children to draw pictures of power, knowing that when children represent an idea in a range of "languages," or art media, their understandings deepen and expand. "Think about power," said Kendra. "What do you think 'power' means? What does power look like? Take a few minutes to make a drawing that shows what power is."

As children finished their drawings, we gathered for a meeting to look at the drawings together. The drawings represented a range of understandings of power: a tornado, love spilling over as hearts, forceful and fierce individuals, exclusion, cartoon superheroes, political power.

During our meeting, children gave voice to the thinking behind their drawings.

> Marlowe: "If your parents say you have to eat pasta, then that's power."
> Lukas: "You can say no."
> Carl: "Power is ownership of something."
> Drew: "Sometimes I like power and sometimes I don't. I like to be in power because I feel free. Most people like to do it, you can tell people what to do and it feels good."

Drew's comment startled us with its raw truth. He was a member of the Legotown inner circle, and had been quite resistant to acknowledging the power he held in that role. During this discussion, though, he laid his cards on the table. Would Drew's insight break open new understandings among the other members of the inner circle?

## Exploring Power

To build on Drew's breakthrough comment about the pleasure and unease that comes with wielding power, and to highlight the experience of those who are excluded from power, we designed a Lego trading game with built-in inequities. We developed a point system for Legos, then skewed the system so that it would be quite hard to get lots of points. And we established just one rule: Get as many points as possible. The person with the most points would create the rules for the rest of the game. Our intention was to create a situation in which a few children would receive unearned power from sheer good luck in choosing Lego bricks with high point values, and then would wield that power with their peers.

We hoped that the game would be removed enough from the particulars and personalities of Legotown that we could look at the central Legotown issues from a fresh perspective.

This was a simple game about complicated issues.

We introduced the Lego trading game to the children by passing a bin of Legos around the circle, asking each child to choose 10 Legos; we didn't say anything about point values or how we'd use the bricks. Most children chose a mix of colored Lego bricks, though a few chose 10 of one color. Liam took all eight green Legos, explaining that green is his favorite color; this seemingly straightforward choice altered the outcome of the game.

When everyone had their Legos, the teachers announced that each color had a point value. The more common the brick color, the fewer the points it was worth, while the scarcest brick color, green, was worth a whopping five points.

Right away, there were big reactions.

> Liam: "I have all the green! I have 40 points because I have all the green!"
> Drew: "This isn't fair! Liam won't trade any green, I bet, so what's the point? What if you just want to quit?"
> Carl: "I don't want to play this game. I'll just wait for Liam to give me a green. If he doesn't, it's hopeless."

We didn't linger with the children's reactions, but carried on with the game, explaining that the object of the game was to trade Lego pieces in an effort to get the most points. Kids immediately began to calculate how they'd trade their pieces, and dove into trading. Several children shadowed Liam, pleading with him to give them a green—but he refused.

After a few minutes of trading, we rang a bell and children added up their scores. Liam and Kyla had scores that far out-totaled those of the other children. Kendra asked them each to create a rule, explaining that we'd play another round of the game, following the new rules and aiming for the same goal: to get the most points possible.

**We were struck by the ways the children had come face-to-face with the frustration, anger, and hopelessness that come with being on the outside of power and privilege.**

We expected that the winners would make rules to ensure that they would win the next round—for instance, "All greens are worth 50 points" or "You can only win if your name starts with a K." We were surprised at what happened.

Liam instituted this rule: "You have to trade at least one piece. That's a good rule because if you have a high score at the beginning, you wouldn't have to trade, and that's not fair."

Kyla added this rule to the game: "If you have more than one green, you have to trade one of them."

With these new rules on the books, we held a second short round of trading, then rang the bell and added up points. Liam, Kyla, and Lukas won this round. The three winners grinned at each other as we gathered in a circle to debrief the game. Before we could launch a conversation as teachers, the children's raw emotion carried us into a passionate exchange:

> Drew: "Liam, you don't have to brag in people's faces."
> Carl: "The winner would stomp his feet and go 'Yes' in the face of people. It felt kind of mean."
> Liam: "I was happy! I wasn't trying to stomp in people's faces."
> Carl: "I don't like that winners make new rules. People make rules that are only in their advantage. They could have written it simpler that said, 'Only I win.'"
> Juliet: "Because they wanted to win and make other people feel bad."
> Kyla: "I wasn't trying to make other people feel bad. I felt bad when people felt bad, so I tried to make a rule that would make them feel better. It was fun to make up the rule—like a treat, to be one of only three people out of the whole group."

When the teaching staff met to reflect on the Lego trading game, we were struck by the ways the children had come face-to-face with the frustration, anger, and hopelessness that come with being on the outside of power and privilege. During the trading game, a couple of children simply gave up, while others waited passively for someone to give them valuable pieces. Drew said: "I stopped trading because the same people were winning. I just gave up." In the game, the children could experience what they'd not been able to acknowledge in Legotown: When people are shut out of participation in the power structure, they are disenfranchised—and angry, discouraged, and hurt.

To make sense of the sting of this disenfranchisement, most of the children cast Liam and Kyla as "mean," trying to "make people feel bad." They were unable or unwilling to see that the rules of the game— which mirrored the rules of our capitalist meritocracy—were a setup for winning and losing.

Playing by the rules led to a few folks winning big and most folks falling further and further behind. The game created a classic case of cognitive disequilibrium: Either the system is skewed and unfair, or the winners played unfairly. To resolve this by deciding that the system is unfair would call everything into question; young children are committed to rules and rule making as a way to organize a community, and it is wildly unsettling to acknowledge that rules can have built-in inequities. So most of the children resolved their disequilibrium by clinging to the belief that the winners were ruthless—despite clear evidence of Liam and Kyla's compassionate generosity.

In Legotown, the children had constructed a social system of power where a few people made the important decisions and the rest of the participants did the grunt work—much like the system in the trading game. We wanted children to critique the system at work in Legotown, not to critique the children at the top of the Legotown hierarchy. At the same time, we wanted them to see that the Legotown system was created by people, and, as such, could be challenged and reformulated.

The children's reaction to the winners of the trading game was a big warning flag for us: We clearly had some repair work to do around relationships, as well as some overt teaching about systemic fallibility. The Lego trading game presented core issues that would be our focus for the months to come. Our analysis of the game, as teachers, guided our planning for the investigation into the issues of power, privilege, and authority that spanned the rest of the year.

## Rules and Ownership

In the weeks after the trading game, we explored questions about how rules are made and enforced, and when they ought to be followed or broken. We aimed to help children see that all rules (including social structures and systems) are made by people with particular perspectives, interests, and experiences that shape their rule making. And we wanted to encourage them to consider that there are times when rules ought to be questioned or even broken—sharing stories of people who refused to "play by the rules" when the rules were unjust, people like Rosa Parks and César Chávez.

**Young children are committed to rules and rule making as a way to organize a community, and it is wildly unsettling to acknowledge that rules can have built-in inequities.**

We added another thread to our investigation of power as well, by turning our attention to issues related to ownership. In Legotown, the builders "owned" sections of Legotown and protected them fiercely from encroachment. We were curious to explore with the children their beliefs about how ownership happens: How does a person come to own something? How is ownership maintained or transferred? Are there situations in which ownership ought to be challenged or denied? What are the distinctions between private and public ownership?

We looked at ownership through several lenses. With the children, we created an "ownership museum," where children displayed possessions they brought from home—a Gameboy, a special blanket, a bike helmet, a baseball card, jewelry, dolls—and described how they came to own them. And we visited Pike Place Market, the farmers and artisans market in downtown Seattle, and asked questions to provoke kids to think about ownership, like: Does a farmer own her produce? Or does the consumer own it?

In their reflections during these explorations, the children articulated several shared theories about how ownership is conferred.

◆ **If I buy it, I own it:**
Sophia: "She owns the lavender balls because she makes them, but if I buy it, then it's mine."

◆ **If I receive it as a gift, I own it:**
Marlowe: "My mom bought this book for me because she thought it would be a good reading book for me. I know I own it because my mom bought it and she's my mom and she gave it to me."

◆ **If I make it myself, I own it:**
Sophie: "I sewed this pillow myself with things that my teacher gave me, like stuffing and fabric. I sewed it and it turned into my pillow because it's something I made instead of something I got at the store."

◆ **If it has my name on it, I own it:**
Alex: "My teacher made this pillow for me and it has my name on it."
Kendra: "If I put my name on it, would I own it?"

Alex: "Well, Miss S. made it for me . . . but if your name was on it, then you would own it."
Sophie: "Kendra, don't put your name on it, OK?"

◆ **If I own it, I make the rules about it:**
Alejandro: "I own this computer, because my grandpa gave it to me. I lend it to my friends so that they can play with it. But I make the rules about it."

## The Return of the Legos

Throughout the investigation, the staff continued to meet weekly to study our notes about the activities we took up with the children, watching for moments when children identified contradictions in their own thinking, took on new perspectives, or questioned their own assumptions. In late spring, we decided it was time to challenge the children to wrestle their theoretical understandings into practical shape and apply their analysis of individual and collective ownership to a concrete project. After five months of naming and investigating the issues of power, rules, ownership, and authority, we were ready to reconstruct Legotown in a new way.

We invited the children to work in small, collaborative teams to build Pike Place Market with Legos. We set up this work to emphasize negotiated decision-making, collaboration, and collectivity. We wanted the children to practice the big ideas we'd been exploring. We wanted Lego Pike Place Market to be an experience of group effort and shared ownership: If Legotown was an embodiment of individualism, Lego Pike Place Market would be an experiment in collectivity and consensus.

We offered the children some guidelines to steer them into a new way of interacting with each other and with the Legos: "Create teams of two or three people, decide as a team on some element of Pike Place Market that you'll build, and then start constructing." The first day or two, children created signs warning the other teams "Do Not Touch" their collaboratively constructed vegetable, fruit, and crafts stands. As they settled into this construction project, though, the teams softened the rigid boundaries around their work and began to leave notes for each other describing their work and proposing next steps for Pike Place Market. We celebrated this shift, seeing it as a sign that the children were beginning to integrate the thinking of the last months into their interactions.

## A New Ethics for Legotown

This "practice" round of Lego construction served as a foundation for a full-fledged return of Legos to their front-and-center place in the classroom, but with a new location in the consciousness of the group. In preparation for bringing Legos back, we held several meetings with the children to generate a set of key principles for Lego play. We met with small groups of children over snack or as we walked to and from the park, posing questions like "If you were going to play with Legos, what would be important to you?" "What would be different if we bring the Legos back to the classroom?" "How could we make it different?" "What could we do if we fall into old habits with the Legos?" From our conversations, several themes emerged.

> **We were excited by these comments. The children gave voice to the value that collectivity is a solid, energizing way to organize a community—and that it requires power-sharing, equal access to resources, and trust in the other participants.**

- ◆ **Collectivity is a good thing:**
  "You get to build and you have a lot of fun and people get to build onto doesn't have to be the same way as when you left it.... A house is good because it is a community house."

- ◆ **Personal expression matters:**
  "It's important that the little Lego plastic person has some identity. Lego houses might be all the same except for the people. A kid should have their own Lego character to live in the house so it makes the house different."

- ◆ **Shared power is a valued goal:**
  "It's important to have the same amount of power as other people over your building. And it's important to have the same priorities." "Before, it was the older kids who had the power because they used Legos most. Little kids have more rights now than they used to and older kids have half the rights."

- ◆ **We should strive for moderation and equal access to resources:**
  "We should have equal houses. They should be standard sizes.... We should all just have the same number of pieces, like 15 or 28 pieces."

As teachers, we were excited by these comments. The children gave voice to the value that collectivity is a solid, energizing way to organize a community—and that it requires power-sharing, equal access to resources, and trust in the other participants. They expressed the need, within collectivity, for personal expression, for being acknowledged as an individual within the group. And finally, they named the deep satisfaction of shared engagement and investment, and the ways in which the participation of many people deepens the experience of membership in community for everyone.

From this framework, the children made a number of specific proposals for rules about Legos, engaged in some collegial debate about those proposals, and worked through their differing suggestions until they reached consensus about three core agreements:

◆ All structures are public structures. Everyone can use all the Lego structures. But only the builder or people who have her or his permission are allowed to change a structure.

◆ Lego people can be saved only by a "team" of kids, not by individuals.

◆ All structures will be standard sizes. Kids won't build structures that are dramatically bigger than most folks' structures.

With these three agreements—which distilled months of social justice exploration into a few simple tenets of community use of resources—we returned the Legos to their place of honor in the classroom.

Children absorb political, social, and economic worldviews from an early age. Those worldviews show up in their play, which is the terrain that young children use to make meaning about their world and to test and solidify their understandings.

We believe that educators have a responsibility to pay close attention to the themes, theories, and values that children use to anchor their play. Then we can interact with those worldviews, using play to instill the values of equality and democracy. ◆

---

*Ann Pelo worked as a teacher and teacher mentor for 16 years at Hilltop Children's Center in Seattle. She is the editor of* Rethinking Early Childhood Education *(Rethinking Schools, 2008).*

*Kendra Pelo Joaquin is the pedagogista at Peabody Terrace Children's Center, a Reggio Emilia-inspired child care center serving infants, young children, and their families in Cambridge, Massachusetts.*

*This piece resulted in a great deal of media coverage and reader correspondence after it appeared in* Rethinking Schools *magazine (vol. 21, no. 2) in 2006.*
*To read a response written and published by the editors, see next page.*

# 'Lego Fascists' (That's Us) vs. Fox News

◆ THE EDITORS OF RETHINKING SCHOOLS

DAVID McLIMANS

The winter 2006-07 issue of *Rethinking Schools* featured "Why We Banned Legos" by Ann Pelo and Kendra PeloJoaquin, teachers at Hilltop Children's Center in Seattle. We had intentionally given the article a provocative title, and knew that many people's first reaction would be: No, not Legos! What could possibly be wrong with Legos? We also knew that those readers who probed beyond the playful headline would be rewarded with an extraordinary piece that recounted how a group of teachers investigated children's play in order to discover the lessons children were absorbing about power, ownership, authority, and cooperation—and how those teachers responded. And by the way, Legos are not banned at Hilltop and never were; Hilltop teachers simply removed them temporarily to help focus students' attention on issues of fairness.

Then the emails began to pour in:

> You Teachers Are Fascists!!! To Ban Legos and Brainwash Them Like This!…

> You don't want us to defend ourselves against the Islam-o-fascist Terrorists you just want us to roll over and die or convert to Islam…

> If this does NOT prove once and for all that the Teachers' Unions are full of Socialist S.O.B's! Nothing will! Break Up the Damn Teachers' Unions!!!

**We need a curriculum that honors children's potential, rather than the scripted lessons of memorization and correct answers, favored by so many conservatives.**

A woman writing from Augusta, Georgia, offered her opinion more economically: "Y'all are just plain NUTS!"

Right-wing bloggers, evidently taking a break from defending the Iraq war, began the "Legos" assault. Rush Limbaugh and other AM radio talk show hosts picked up the story. And finally, Fox television ran a segment on an evening newscast, "Big Story, Big Outrage." (A Google search of "Why We Banned Legos" in late April 2007 pulled up more than 17,000 entries.)

Many of the critics appeared to read no further than the headline and offered passionate testimonials on the benefits of Legos. But others, like John J. Miller writing in the *National Review Online*, inferred deeper implications. In a March 27, 2007, posting, Miller expressed outrage that youngsters at Hilltop sometimes use Legos to construct "community meeting places." Miller declared that his kids would never dream of something so "rotten," as he put it. "Instead, they make monster trucks, spaceships, and war machines. These little creations are usually loaded with ion guns, nuclear missiles, bunker-busting bombs, force-field projectors, and death-ray cannons. Alien empires have risen and fallen in epic conflicts waged in the upstairs bedrooms of my home." If children don't play war and empire then evidently the "latte-sipping guardians" in Seattle have led kids astray.

Common to Miller et al.'s critiques is an aversion to the notion that everything that goes on in school—including play—teaches values. Our critics appear content to let children absorb without reflection the values from the broader society—competition, militarism, consumerism, aggression, selfishness. By contrast, "Why We Banned Legos" tells the story of the Hilltop teachers who seek opportunities to help children reflect about "the meaning of power and ways to organize communities that are equitable and just."

Critics also derided Pelo's and PeloJoaquin's insistence that children can be encouraged to question inequality in the worlds they create in their play and consider alternatives. One blogger was indignant: "What happens when [children] grow up and not everyone wins?—i.e., injustice happens, deal with it; children should not be taught to question it, to think of democratic alternatives, but should simply see unfairness as a natural state of affairs." Another blogger at a site called "The Sixth Column" wrote: "[C]hildren will not be prepared to face brutal competition that makes up real life outside of the carefully constructed feel-good environment found in many of today's classrooms… In the real world, not everyone will be able to participate in 'the power structure.'" Like these attacks on the article, many writers insisted that injustice was eternal and that questioning it was not merely futile, but misled children about human nature and the world that they would inherit.

Underlying much of the blog and email commentary was a profound disregard for children's capacities to reflect together about their own interactions and to thoughtfully discuss notions of fairness. As one blogger wrote, the conversations among children described in "Why We Banned Legos" revealed "willful manipulation of young minds"—presumably because in the real world, kids could never think like this on their own. This was a revealing criticism. Because what if kids are indeed *always* making meaning about their world and, with good teaching, are more and more able to express their insights with sophistication? Then we need a curriculum that honors children's potential, rather than the scripted lessons of memorization and correct answers, favored by so many conservatives.

If these right-wing attacks were confined to the Lego article then we might dismiss them as mere annoyances, reminders of the tenacity of conservative views of schooling. But they seem to be part of a pattern—an emerging attack on social justice teaching itself. For example, when Fox News went after the Legos issue, they turned to Jim Copland of the Manhattan Institute as the sole outside "expert." (Fox: "How ridiculous is this?" Copland: "Preposterous.") The Manhattan Institute is a free market-oriented think tank whose education mission is to promote vouchers, charter schools, and more testing—in public schools only, of course, not private schools. Sol Stern, a Manhattan Institute senior fellow, is waging a smear campaign against social justice education work. He has attacked the El Puente Academy for Peace and Justice in Brooklyn, Eric Gutstein (University of Illinois-Chicago professor and co-editor of our book *Rethinking Mathematics*), the New York Collective of Radical Educators, and a New York City math and social justice conference ("Creating Balance in an Unjust World"). Writing in the Rupert Murdoch-owned *New York Post* ("Math and Marxism: NYC's Wack-Job Teachers," March 20, 2007), Stern first caricatures social justice teaching and then complains that it "violates every commonly accepted standard of ethical and professional responsibility for public school teachers," and laments that "the city's Department of Education has so far turned a blind eye."

Some of these attacks represent nothing new. They are simply part of the right wing's ongoing attempt to discredit public schools, and push more "accountability" (read testing), vouchers, and school privatization. (Even though Hilltop Children's Center is not a public school and its teachers are in the Service Employees International Union, not

> **With greater frequency, educators seem to recognize that at this crucial juncture in world history, schools need to address the issues of our time.**

one of the two teachers' unions, neither fact deterred critics, who used the Legos article to attack both public schools and teachers' unions—as exemplified in the excerpt from our antifascist friend, above.)

But there may be something else afoot. It's become increasingly difficult to ignore social and environmental ills—whether it's the climate change crisis, the Iraq war, or growing global inequality. More and more educators now talk about "social justice teaching"—albeit not always with clarity around what this means. With greater frequency, educators seem to recognize that at this crucial juncture in world history, schools need to address the issues of our time; and that at all educational levels, we need a conversation and literature describing how educators can respond effectively.

Inevitably, this curricular exploration calls into question existing cultural patterns and systems of ownership and control that are at the root of today's crises. And this will step on some powerful toes. This teaching may take the form of early childhood programs encouraging children to reflect on the implications of their play. Or it may take the form of high school math teachers analyzing the concept of "peak oil" in algebra class, or 5th-grade teachers prompting students to evaluate the manifold costs of the Iraq war.

This is important and exciting work. Rethinking Schools is committed to helping nurture a grassroots literature of social justice teaching. And we're committed to defend this teaching wherever and whenever it comes under attack. This is no time to be meek. The world is becoming more perilous by the day. Schools can either be part of the problem or part of the solution. ◆

# Tuning In to Violence

*Students use math to analyze what TV is teaching them*

◆ MARGOT PEPPER

Six years into the "War on Terror," my 2nd-grade Spanish immersion students found that aggression, selfishness, and insults have exploded on national television.

For the last decade, I've had my students at Rosa Parks Elementary School in Berkeley, California, analyze television shows preceding National TV Turnoff Week (www.tvturnoff.org). I ask the 7- and 8-year-old students to collect all the data themselves. For seven days, students study a random sampling of about 35 English and Spanish-language children's television shows—and one or two soap operas or reality shows.

MICHAEL DUFFY

The first day of the study, as homework, students shade in a square on a special graph sheet each time they see hitting, hurting, or killing on half-hour segments of the shows they regularly watch, viewed from beginning to end. The second day, they focus on acts of selfishness; the third day, on instances of put-downs; and the fourth day, on the number of times a typical class rule is broken. Finally, in class, four groups of students compile the data produced by the homework, each focusing on one of the four variables in the study. But in April 2007, when I pulled out model graphs compiled by a class in April 2002—year one of President George W. Bush's "War on Terror"—the contrasts between their graphs and those produced five years prior shocked my students.

"In a half hour of [the cartoon] *Jackie Chan Adventures* in 2002 you

**Many of these students seemed eager to learn more about the television implants I implied existed in their brains; others appeared enchanted with the excuse to watch the boob tube as homework.**

would see hitting 10 times at most," wrote 7-year-old Flynn Michael-Legg in the essay I assigned summarizing the findings of our study. "In 2007, shows of *Jackie Chan* had [up to] 34 hitting scenes." For the 2001-02 season, nearly one-fourth of the television shows my students watched had one or no acts of violence at all in one half-hour. Now of the shows they watch, only *That's So Raven* continues to have no violence, and all other shows have at least three instances of hitting or violence in one half-hour. Today, nearly half the shows randomly viewed by my students contain seven to 34 instances of hitting or other violent acts each half-hour.

The maximum number of put-downs or insults has nearly doubled since 2002, going from 10 in *That's So Raven* to 18 in *Dumb and Dumber*—more than one put-down every two minutes. In *SpongeBob SquarePants*, Flynn pointed out, one would hear at most two put-downs in 2002. Today it's 16. No shows had more than 10 put-downs in 2002. Now three shows did—*SpongeBob* (16); *Dumb and Dumber* (18); *Betty la fea* (13). Very few shows have no insults at all any more.

All the shows my students watched in 2007 showed people or characters being selfish at least once per half-hour segment. From our class rule to "be considerate and cooperative," my students interpreted "selfish" to mean that characters did something that put themselves first at the expense of someone else. In 2002, only three shows had more than three acts of selfishness in a half-hour. Now, 10 did. Half of the 2007 shows contained five to nine instances of selfishness in each episode.

Students also found that in April 2002, only one show depicted the violation of ordinary class rules—making good decisions: no hitting, put-downs, being unsafe, etc.—12 or more times. In April 2007, the number of such programs rose to six. In 2002, the maximum times class rules were broken on a given half-hour show was 17. In 2007 the number of such shows quadrupled with the maximum number of rules broken on a given show doubling or reaching more than 35. The worst offenders, with 18 or more broken rules, were *SpongeBob*, *Dumb and Dumber*, *Jackie Chan*, and *Phil of the Future*— the latter two topping the hitting and selfishness categories as well.

Whenever students exhibit disruptive behavior, appearing to ape television—pretend shooting, arms flailing, mouth ceaselessly chattering gibberish, etc.—I ask them to please turn off the television in their head if they happen to have left it running. Students often chuckle and, following my lead, turn off an imaginary knob around their ear. As we embarked on our study, many of these students seemed eager to learn more about the television implants I implied existed in their brains; others appeared enchanted with the excuse to watch the boob tube as homework. (Every year, one or two students are excused from the homework due to parental objections to television viewing or, like their teacher, the absence of a set at home. They serve as positive role models and still participate in the class data analysis.)

**My aim was to get these young philosopher-scientists in the habit of asking "why" about their world instead of merely consuming it.**

After sorting the completed television homework graphs into four piles, I assigned one variable or "change" (e.g., "violence") to student groups to compile into one of four large rainbow colored graphs like the 2001–02 model I had on the board in front of them.

"Which homework graph sheet recorded the highest number of hitting or hurting instances?" I asked the "blue group" in Spanish. Students sifted through to find the greatest number of shaded-in squares. *"¡Mira! ¡Jackie Chan' tiene 34!"* (Look! *Jackie Chan* has 34!) Leah Abramsom voiced her discovery in perfect Spanish, though her multi-ethnic roots, which include African American and Jewish, do not include Latina.

For the sake of easy comparison, I wrote *Jackie Chan* on our Violence Graph in the same color and position relative to its appearance on the 2002 graph. Then I had a student take a turn to color in 34 squares.

"Let's put a check by every *Jackie Chan* you see on other homework sheets because we're done looking at that program," I reminded them. "Now which homework has the next largest number to 34 of violent acts?"

Just as my students had in 2002, the students proceeded through the pile under my supervision to record the top 16 violent shows, assigning each a particular color. Regardless of discrepancies in student perceptions of violence of up to three instances for the same program, date, and variable (the margin of error over the years), just as in 2002, students recorded the highest number of aggressive acts for each of these shows. After each group of five students completed its specific group bar graph of findings, and students saw it next to the colorful 2002 graph of the same variable, they were visibly horrified. Gisell González clasped hands over her mouth, while others gasped, "Ieeew!"

Ever since the first month of school when we studied opposing points of view about the so-called discovery (or not) of the Americas, I've encouraged my students to turn to other sources like library books and the internet to answer questions or prove social studies and science hypotheses and, for the most skilled, to question the sources of their answers. So when I proposed searching the internet to support our findings, many were delighted.

The next day, I rotated each group of five through my English internet research station around a large computer. The class had decided on the preliminary Google search terms: "television violence increase." Though students controlled the mouse and keyboard, I helped weed out irrelevant sites and urged them to explore promising ones. We'd scroll through these until we found something that related to our hypothesis about increased violence. Next, I'd give them time to read paragraphs on the screen to each other. "Puppies" (native standard-English speakers) would read the material to the "Kittens" (standard-English language learners), explaining if necessary. When they got to a finding, they would let me know so I could record it on chart paper in the color that corresponded to their group.

Traditionally, in this way, virtually all students have been able to discover something to share with their group. Usually two students in each group alight on juicy, complex information and, perhaps because of the immersion program's need for translation, are able to simplify explanations for the rest. The overall quality of research and writing vocabulary has been extraordinary in part, I think, because of each group's heterogeneous composition—ranging from one to two high-skilled students to one or two who are currently performing well below grade level. Typically, my two-way Spanish immersion classes have been composed of one-third children of college-educated professionals, while half qualify for free lunches. About a third are native Spanish speakers or Latino children; up to one-fifth African American children, and the rest European American and other minorities.

I had the "green group" explore the TV Turnoff Network site. The students clicked on the Real Vision study. Maeve Gallagher was shocked. "Wow! Kids will have seen 200,000 violent acts on television by age 18…and 16,000 murders." Some wondered if the increase in television violence highlighted on the site had led to more real-life killing.

"What words do you think you might see in a report that says killing is related to television?"

They decided on "television + violence = killing."

"Oh my gosh! 'TV shows and Video Games Teach Children to Kill!' Look, down there!" Ceilidh Welsh was pointing to the screen of search results. The note turned out to be a footnote in a report from the Parents Television Council (PTC). I showed the group how important it was to trace primary sources and helped them type in the name of the author of the study, which turned up in a Senate Judiciary Report.

"This is a report by our own government!" Now I was excited, too. We typed in the report's title and got the full report titled "Children, Violence and the Media."

"Video Games and TV are 'teaching kids to kill,' and 'teaching them to like it!'" Maeve read aloud for us from the report.

"Violence on TV is over 300 times more than before the war!" Students in the subsequent yellow group were jumping up and down. Well, not exactly. I darted to the board and shaded parts of pizzas to explain percentages. This made the concept more understandable to some, but for most, I had to translate. Using both the internet and fact sheets, children in the "yellow group" found that, according to a 2007 study by the PTC called "Dying to Entertain," since 1998, violence on ABC TV has quadrupled (a 309 percent increase—a huge rise, though not quite the "300 times" increase students had mistakenly proclaimed).

> **Violence in all television shows has shifted to being more central to the story—with more graphic autopsy or torture scenes—than it was five years ago.**

They found that in 1998 the network had about one act of violence per hour (.93). By 2007, it was almost four (3.8) on average. CBS, according to the PTC study, had the highest percentage of deaths during 2005-06, with more than 66 percent of violent scenes after 8 p.m. depicting death (www.parents.org). Incidentally, the study points out that, in general, violence in all television shows has shifted to being more central to the story—with more graphic autopsy or torture scenes—than it was more than five years ago. It indicates that the 2005-06 season was one of the most violent ever recorded by the PTC.

After each group read its findings aloud, facts discovered by students in the "red group" persuaded the rest of the class, through a show of hands, to agree to limit their television viewing, turning it off completely during TV Turnoff Week—something they were reluctant to do when our television unit began. What this group had discovered, thanks largely to the TV Turnoff Network's website is that there are more televisions (2.73) in the average home than people (2.55), according to USA Today. The average home keeps a television turned on eight hours a day, according to Nielsen (2006). Children who watch six or more hours a day perform worse on reading tests than do those who watch one hour a day or don't play video games, reports the Center for Screentime Awareness. And by the time they finish high school, children will have spent more hours watching TV than in school.

I knew students would brainstorm both absurd and frighteningly astute reasons to justify the increase of violence and selfishness on television. My aim was to get these young philosopher-scientists in the habit of asking "why" about their world instead of merely consuming it—of making educated hypotheses then requiring multiple sources of supporting evidence.

During the group discussion, I learned that they were most troubled by the Senate report statement that television was teaching them to "like killing." The Senate report also claimed that 10 percent of crimes committed are caused by violence seen on television. The study, though predating ours, related the violence they saw on television directly to their present world.

I asked students if they had noticed an increase in violence in their world with the increase in television violence. Jacobo McCarthy and several others fiercely nodded: "Three years ago, I'd only see one or two kids in trouble in the office now and then; now there's up to six or seven," Jacobo commented. I too have noticed an increase in behavior problems at the school since 2001, despite better leadership and more effective intervention. However, increasing poverty and less spending on social services leading to a rise in domestic or neighborhood violence could be as equally valid contributors.

"What do you think the reason is behind the increase in television violence?" I asked.

"For brainwashing. TV advertises or sells violence. It influences us to vote for a president who uses war to solve problems," Flynn said.
"I suspect the increase in television violence has something to do with the war on terror," English-learner Andres Ventura wrote, emulating his classmate Sebastian Anderson's elevated vocabulary in his summarizing essay. "By scaring kids and parents and pushing violence, people are more likely to vote for war. The TV makes you dumb because if you see a lot, it makes you forget things. It makes parents forget how things were when they were kids."

One of the most shocking facts my students found was that according to the TV Turnoff Network's Real Vision project, parents spend only 38.5 minutes a day with their children in meaningful conversation. And more than half of 4- to 6-year olds (54 percent) would rather watch TV than spend time with their parents.

This finding inspired Alejandro González's conclusion: "I think George Bush wants to make people more scared. We know George Bush likes war. And? TV makes you like more war. What's scary is kids spend more time seeing TV than being with their dad. Since our study, I turn off the TV more and go play with my dad. Maybe the president used to watch more TV than being with his dad."

"And if Bush isn't responsible? Why would television stations or their advertisers want us to like war?" I asked after reading Alejandro's essay aloud.

"To make money, to sell things and make rich people richer like the people selling guns," Ceilidh said.

"To steal stuff from other countries to make our own country the richest!" Jacobo asserted.

What impact did the students think this increase in television violence and selfishness was having on the world around them?

"TV makes people want violence by making it seem cool," Ceilidh said.

Sebastian added: "Then they want to be part of the Army. It's a cycle. TV affects the world, then the world affects the TV, which affects world violence. It's a 'chain reaction of evil,'" Sebastian said, borrowing from a Martin Luther King Jr. quote I had them memorize for King's birthday.

"Yeah, TV leads to more fighting. Fighting leads to war," added Jacobo. He evoked King to finish his thought: "'Hate begetting hate. Wars producing more wars.' We need to stop or 'we shall all be plunged into the dark abyss of annihilation.'"

It was a peak teaching moment. Students were assimilating valuable things they had learned earlier in the year to shape their thinking about the world. Although some of the conclusions tended toward hyperbole, I can't argue with the soundness of my students' hypothesis that television selfishness and violence are part of a propaganda campaign to foment war and enrich certain sectors. But more importantly, my students are learning to think for themselves, to question the sources of their information.

One of my former students, Daniel Hernandez-Deras, once commented that "watching television replaces your imagination with television thinking and there's not much space left after that." Now my current students had begun to turn off the televisions in their own brains and turn on their imagination and curiosity. At last, they had begun to internalize the insight contained in Maeve's essay: "If you watch too much TV, you lose the kid that is inside you," wherein lies our higher inner wisdom.♦

---

*Born in Mexico City, Margot Pepper is a bilingual educator, journalist, and author. Her memoir,* Through the Wall *(Freedom Voices, 2005), was a finalist nomination for the 2006 American Book Award.*

# Examining Media Violence

*How can we help students to think about the relationship between media images and violence?*

◆ BAKARI CHAVANU

"Overwhelming Hate," "Why I Like Disturbing Music," "Eminem: Rapper or Hypocrite?": These are not necessarily typical titles of student English essays.

My students wrote these essays as part of a nine-week unit in my 11th-grade English class on violence in society. In the unit, we address a variety of topics—from domestic violence, to urban poverty, to racist police policies in communities of color. One of the unit's more popular sections involves violence and the media, in particular sexist violence. The most useful resource I have found for this section is the program *Beyond Blame: Challenging Violence in the Media*, produced by the Center for Media Literacy in Los Angeles.

The producers of *Beyond Blame* recognize that "media violence is not the sole cause of violence in society." But they go on to note that "more and more we're coming to understand that they [the media] do reinforce the myths and images, beliefs and attitudes that support a culture of violence."

*Beyond Blame* is not a single resource but is a comprehensive packet of articles, lesson plans, and worksheets, and a video of excerpts pulled from films, television, documentaries, and other media texts. These materials provide sufficient background and resources for a week to two-week presentation by teachers, parents, or community organizers. (In the two times I've used this program, I have yet to cover all the material.)

Some of the most provocative debates in my class have grown out of the program's discussions about media violence and sexist images of women, and about the media's glorification of violent solutions to conflict.

One especially useful activity, "Damsels in Distress: Women and Violence," centers on a selection of videotaped images of women in music videos typically found on popular cable channels such as MTV and

JONATHON ROSEN

BET. Before showing the clips, I use the program's handout, "Beauties and Brutes," which asks students to circle the adjectives that describe how men and women are depicted in music videos.

Students identified both genders as "sexy," "hot," "crazy," and "active." But for the women in the videos, my students mostly circled "teasing," "sweet," and "provocative." For the men they circled "tough," "angry," and "strong," with few students describing

**What is the role of the media in perpetuating the view that all cultures are violent in one way or another and that violence is part of human nature?**

the men as "passive" and "remote." Helping the students to recognize these different depictions became an important lesson in itself.

After an initial showing of the video selections, I replay them without sound. Although this irritates some students, I point out that they might "see" more without the music to distract them. I then have the students pair up, one male and one female together, to discuss the video clips and answer questions from the *Beyond Blame* program guide.

One student, Haniyyah, told a particularly interesting personal story in her essay "Are Women Disrespected in Music Videos?" She wrote: "After the release of the music video 'Holla Holla' in the summer of 1998 or 1999, my three brothers changed tremendously in their attitudes towards women. They watched this sexually provocative video and would run around the house singing the lyrics, talking about sluts and whores. On one occasion, I stopped them to tell them to watch their mouth and attitude, especially toward the women in their life."

What is the role of the media in perpetuating the view that all cultures are violent in one way or another and that violence is part of human nature?

To address this issue, I use the *Beyond Blame* activity titled "Media Heroes, Real Heroes." The activity begins by having students call out descriptions of a typical media hero. Their descriptions include: "good looking," "strong," "fearless," "always wins in a battle," "saves people," "good at using a gun," and so on. Next I ask them to describe people they consider heroes or heroines in real life. That list includes: "caring," "always there when you need them," "provides good advice," "supportive," "a mother, a father, a friend," and "helps keep you out of trouble." They could easily see a contrast between media heroes and real heroes.

As a follow-up, I show an extended segment from the 1994 TV special *Kids Killing Kids*. The excerpt illustrates how a violent resolution to a conflict between two young men might have been resolved nonviolently. I then ask the students what it means when the media rarely presents dramatic stories in which conflict is resolved without violence. One of the questions that came up is whether the media can make nonviolent films that are dramatically satisfying. Opinions varied. One student wrote: "I think the media could make nonviolent dramatically satisfying films. I think they should. It would teach people how to resolve things without violence. Children could learn how to communicate instead of fight." Another student, who disagreed, perhaps unwittingly realized that relationship between violence and ratings and wrote: "Without violence, TV would be boring. And the media would not have any ratings."

Above all, the unit showed the need for increased study of such a powerful institution. As the founder of the Center for Media Literacy Elizabeth Thoman explains in her essay "TV Violence: It's Time to Break the Circle of Blame," In the past 20 years, we've learned to make different choices around smoking and cholesterol and buckling up your seat belt. Critical media literacy proposes that, with different information, viewers might make different choices or engage in different behaviors.◆

---

*Bakari Chavanu is a freelance writer and photographer. He taught high school English for 12 years, including a course in popular culture and media.*

**Resources**
*Beyond Blame: Challenging Violence in the Media* is available from www.medialit.org.

# Part 6:
# Use Popular Culture
# and Media to Transgress

KATHERINE STREETER

# 'And Ya Don't Stop'

## Using hip hop in the language arts classroom

◆ WAYNE AU

*Livin' in these last days and times,*
*check yourself, and what you feed your mind.*
*I know you can't be blind livin' in the future...*
                              —Boogiemonsters,
                        "The Beginning of the End"

*I first wrote "And Ya Don't Stop" back in 1995 as an expression of my merging identities as a teacher, education activist, and DJ/hip-hop head. It should thus come as no surprise that all of the artists used and discussed in the article are quite dated, and most kids today don't know them.*

*Since this article was first written, however, hip hop has gone global and gone big capital. Hip hop has also become a subfield in academia, and there are now many books, articles, studies, and curricula about the use of hip hop in classrooms.*

*Given the age of this article and the growth of "hip-hop education" and "hip-hop pedagogy," I would encourage readers of "And Ya Don't Stop" to see the teaching ideas used here as more of a general model—one that could easily be updated with more contemporary artists and songs. Also, just as with any other subject matter, making good use of hip hop in classrooms requires that teachers be knowledgeable about hip hop. So I hope teachers read up on the history and politics of this cultural form before they begin developing curriculum with it (for example,* Can't Stop Won't Stop *by Jeff Chang).*

A few years ago I attended a workshop where a colleague was presenting a teaching method he uses to get his high school students more connected to their math work: using popular, mainstream rappers as the subjects of word problems. In particular, I remember a word problem where the object was to see if Snoop Dogg (a real-life platinum-selling rapper originally known as Snoop Doggy Dogg) who supposedly was in one time zone, could have committed a murder in another time zone without having to travel through time. I'm sure my colleague's intentions were to find a way to reach students, but I couldn't help being critical of his approach. Not only was this a stereotypical linking of young African American men to violence, but the patronizing tone and tokenistic sentiment of this idea

STEPHEN KRONINGER

lacked a respectful understanding of urban youth and their music.

## Breakdown

Technically speaking, the term "hip hop" describes a culture as a whole, which includes DJing/MCing, B-boying/B-girling, and Graff. Mainstream society

**The beauty of hip hop as a culture lies in its ability to absorb anything in its path, take what it can use, and make it into something new.**

knows these terms as rap music, breakdancing, and mural/graffiti art (not to be confused with tagging or gang graffiti), all of which make up the music, dance, and visual art, respectively, of hip-hop culture. According to Steven Hager, author of *Hip Hop: The Illustrated History of Break Dancing, Rap Music, and Graffiti,* hip-hop culture developed in the late 1970s and early 1980s as a positive alternative to violent gangs that were developing in New York at the time. B-boys and B-girls, and DJs and MCs would form crews and battle each other on the dance floors and in the parks instead of fighting out their differences in the streets.

The beauty of hip hop as a culture lies in its ability to absorb anything in its path, take what it can use, and make it into something new. Take for instance the art of DJing. At the core of hip hop is the idea that the DJ, using a snippet of music called a break beat, can use two copies of one song and put them on two different turntables. Then he or she can play that break beat over and over by switching between the turntables. The DJ, having reconstructed a "new" song by extending and mixing up the original break beat, creates a musical space for the MCs to move the crowd with their words and the B-boys and B-girls to move their bodies to the music. (This is the origin of the term B-boy or B-girl—break-boy or break-girl.)

Rap music has a rich and varied history and has always been a vital form of communication. Chuck D, front man for the iconic group Public Enemy, once stated that rap is like the "black version of CNN" because it is a medium of communication that is created by, and reaches to inner-city African American youth. The core sentiment of his statement still holds true today, but because of the rapidly changing demographics of the inner cities, and because rap music reaches national and international audiences, one could say that rap is the CNN of many youth worldwide. (For example, Japanese B-boys are well respected for their breaking skills and have been accepted as members of the Rocksteady Crew, Latinos are actively involved as MCs and rappers, and Filipino Americans have won worldwide DJ competitions.)

One of the first widely distributed songs in this genre to address social issues was Grandmaster Flash and The Furious Five's "The Message." It presented the realities of poverty and street life, unromanticized and unrelenting, and unfortunately, it was also laced with intermittent homophobia and misogyny.

This mix of political flavors, although certainly not representative of all that rap music has to offer, has been a point of constant struggle within hip-hop culture as it has tried to work out the growing pains associated with its marketable, mainstream appeal. For instance, I have always been critical of rap music's treatment of women. From my vantage point as a DJ, I have studied and watched the portrayal of women go through leaps and bounds as well as bumps and recessions over the last decade. When I was in high school, I remember Queen Latifah stepping out in her Afrocentric clothing and commanding respect, as she stood with her head held high and rapped her hip-hop anthem, "Ladies First." It was a powerful image.

Queen Latifah is still around, but the current top-40 hits are full of female rappers like Foxy Brown and Lil' Kim in heavy makeup, high heels, fishnet stockings, and tight dresses who rap about how they will be good to you as long as you buy them diamond rings, fancy cars,

STEPHEN KRONINGER

clothes, etc. This type of artistic "dialogue" mirrors a continuous political ebb and flow within hip-hop culture, if not within society itself. Although bragging about being a street hustler may make a platinum-selling record, you can still find lyrics about police brutality and poverty on almost any full-length album today.

**Even for those students who don't feel the harshness of working-class, urban life, these issues beg us to question why people in different neighborhoods are treated differently.**

## Speaking Poetry

My intent here is not to endorse bringing any old rap recording in and playing it for your class. What I am suggesting is that teachers use rap music with a clear understanding of how to meet their educational objectives through the music. There are an infinite number of ways to do this, and as a teacher I personally have just barely begun to scratch the surface. One of the most effective methods I have found is to examine lyrical content for poetic device, imagery, and style. More creative rap artists make use of complex metaphors and word plays in their rhymes.

One of my favorites, for both its perspective and accessibility to those new to the music, is the group Spearhead. Spearhead's debut album, *Home*, addresses a wide range of issues, from homelessness to AIDS, to contemporary gender relations, all the while making use of poetic metaphor. An especially well-done piece titled "Hole in the Bucket" uses the familiar children's song as a basis to talk about homelessness, poverty, and society at large. Here lead vocalist Michael Franti launches into the psychology of how he feels as someone asks him for spare change:

> He's starin' in my eyes just as I'm walkin' past
> I'm tryin' to avoid him cause I know he's gonna ask
> me about the coinage, that is in my pocket,
> but I don't know if I should put it in his bucket.
> Walk right past him to think about it more,
> back at the crib, I'm opening up the door.
> A pocketful of change, it don't mean a lot to me.
> My cup is half full, but his is empty....

Tragically, by the time he decides to go back and give his change to the man on the street, he finds that all his money has fallen through a hole in his pocket. This song is both politically astute and metaphorically sound because it draws on the glaring connection between the "hole in the bucket" and a society that creates poverty on one hand, yet refuses to deal with it on the other.

In addition, rap can be taught as a poetic form along with sonnets and the blues, as well as analyzed for vocal rhythm, varying rhyme schemes, and other literary techniques. Recently, to illustrate personification, I used an excerpt from a song titled "I Gave You Power" by Nas, where he takes on the characteristics of a gun:

> I seen some cold nights and bloody days
> They grab me bullets spray
> They use me wrong so I sing this song 'til this day

This rap is not just a diatribe in favor of glorified violence. In addition to the personification in this rhyme, Nas touches on a humanities theme by literally and metaphorically leading us through a tale about black-on-black crime and the pain that poverty and gun violence have wrought in his community. In the end, the gun decides it doesn't want to contribute to the violence, gets jammed up, and won't fire for his owner—who subsequently gets shot and killed because of this "decision." This isolated attempt to stop the violence does not work and soon another person picks up the gun, and the cycle begins again.

In the same vein of discussing the complexities of being poor and trying to survive, KRS-One tells a story in his song titled "Love's Gonna Getcha (Material Love)":

> See there in school, I'm made a fool.
> With one and a half pair of pants, you ain't cool,
> but there's no dollars for nothing else.
> I got beans, rice, and bread on my shelf.
> Everyday I see my mother struggling,
> now it's time I've got to do something!
> I look for work, I get dissed like a jerk.
> I do odd jobs and come home like a slob.
> So here comes Rob, his gold is shimmery.
> He gives me two hundred for a quick delivery.
> I do it once, I do it twice.
> Now there's steak with the beans and rice.

**I used this song to prompt students to think about what they saw going on in their neighborhoods.**

In the song, school doesn't work for him and he's mistreated on the job, so in order to make ends meet, he turns to delivering drugs. You can feel the frustration of his position and the sacrifice that he makes, but as he says, "Now there's steak with the beans and rice...." I use this opportunity to ask the students about how they define a "crime," and inevitably I have to pose the question to the class, "Is the main character in the song a criminal?" The issues at hand are complex, and after some lengthy class discussion, many students identify with the rapper and acknowledge that if you're poor and are just trying to provide for daily things like food and clothing, it is understandable why you might turn to illegal means to achieve your ends—especially if no other opportunities to remedy the situation are presented.

What I found remarkable in using this song in my classroom was the near universality with which the students accepted KRS-One's message. The school that I taught in was mainly for "drop-out retrieval and retention." The students were mostly from low-income families and they had left their traditional schools for one reason or another. Some were former gang bangers, some were teen mothers, some were in group homes, and some just decided they needed a change. But regardless of their varying backgrounds (approximately 85 percent students of color) and experiences, the one thing that bound our student body together was that all had felt alienated by their schools and/or society at one time or another. So even though not all students were fans of rap music, they were still able to identify with the content of "Love's Gonna Getcha."

In addition, rap music can be applied to almost any humanities and social sciences theme because of its intense political discourse.

There are a number of rap groups with political agendas, and you can find songs with content ranging from nonsensical party lyrics to left-wing revolutionary political outlines. For example, the Boogiemonsters released a cut titled "The Beginning of the End" that reflects on the realities of life in their neighborhood.

> As the crackdown begins
> intensity reaches to the maximum
> and you really get to see who is your friend.
> The same sneakers dangle from the telephone cable
> 5-O forever patrolling
> my neighborhood is never stable these days
> This appears to be a concentration camp
> Eliminating welfare and still fishing for a victim
> 'cause from 200th down to 95th street is all blackly populated
> then go further downtown,
> it ain't debated who inhabitates the rest
> C'mon! We segregated
> But that's a'right,
> somebody's comin' like a thief in the night
> The police state technique is the practice on the cattle
> on the humble for that worldwide battle….

In this piece, the Boogiemonsters give the listener a news brief on the crackdowns that have occurred in ghettos and poor neighborhoods all over the United States. In addition, the roadblocks and welfare cuts are connected directly to the broader, more historical concepts of concentration camps and a rising police state. In class, I used this song to prompt students to think about what they saw going on in their neighborhoods. Many students at my school felt like the police harassed them daily. They felt the injustices of racism, misogyny, anti-immigration laws, and welfare reform acts on a firsthand basis. Depending on what neighborhood they were from, the song may or may not have matched their experience. But even for those students that don't feel the harshness of working-class, urban life, these issues beg us to question why people in different neighborhoods are treated differently.

## Rhyme, Rhythm, and the Politics of Language

Outside of examining rap music for content and style/form, using it in the classroom has another very important function: It forces students to analyze a form of media that they listen to and support regularly. I don't know how many times I've asked students why they liked a song and they've replied: "I don't know. I just listen to the beats." Rap has become something that they take for granted, a standard, just something to listen to. When I hear students rattling off lyrics they've memorized—about women, about gays and lesbians, about extremely violent behavior, about selling drugs—I always push them to try and step back and really think about what they are saying. This can sometimes get sticky, because as a teacher, I know that students can take such criticism very personally, especially when the critique targets areas they are so connected to like music or culture. The process is long and difficult, and I have yet to find an effective way to get students to be critical of something so close to home. What I try to keep in mind as I engage them is that the misogyny, homophobia, violence, gangs, and material values are all being supported by mainstream culture in the United States, and that the struggle in the classroom is representative of the struggles over larger social issues.

Traditionally, schools marginalize youth by taking an oppositional stance to their clothing styles, language use, and music. This oppositional stance comes under the guise of policies like dress codes, Standard English, and censorship.

So when hip hop is acknowledged or even validated in the classroom we take steps toward a pedagogy that is based on cultural relevance and student-centered education. When I've used rap music in my lesson plans, I've been deeply impressed with the students' responses. If the boom box comes out and the beats begin to thump, students offer me and the music their rapt attention (no pun intended).

Teens know their music intimately, and if given the chance to discuss and share their views about it, they are generally open and enthusiastic. In addition, students can gain a deeper sense of self-worth when they see their music acknowledged as an art form that holds cultural and technical validity.

For those students who love rap music, writing a rap usually comes easily. They've listened to it, heard and read enough lyrics to know what raps sound and look like, and odds are they've written them before. But, when it comes to the students who don't listen to rap regularly, the first stumbling block is always, "I don't know how to write a rap!" In response, I have not forced students to write raps as a poetry form, but have left it up to them to decide how they wanted to handle their writing. This has resulted in students producing work in a variety of forms —free verse, couplets, interior monologues, raps—as well as any hybrid in between. Joel, a Chicano student, wrote the following poem after a workshop where I used a rap titled "Fat Cats and Bigga Fish" by The Coup as a writing prompt:

Oh dios,
all I ask for forgiveness, though I live a simple lifestyle
hoping that you hear me out right now
You know the truth ever since I was a little kid, all the sins
I committed, evil things that I did to live
is kind of hard in this land of temptation,
Taking it day by day, but I still pray
for my salvation or am I facing total darkness,
dissing—stop between heaven and earth still stressing,
progressing, to live my life around people with fake smiles
caught up in the mista lie, betrayal, denial.
I've been informing situation that had let you down
and I know that things are gone, it's gonna come back around.
I've been humiliated with a few two-elevens with one eight-sevens
damaging my sho' way to heaven
but I know that the moment is coming
cause I feel it in my soul. When it's time for me to go,
then it'll be time for me to go
and I'll be waiting, waiting.
It doesn't faze me,
the way I was brought up in my dayz be starting at
my neighborhood gangs got me crazy,
living off the scraps of life, ain't that astounding,
and I feel the way I feel influenced by my surrounding,
refused to take a bowing
never can I be a brain when it's time to be taking
gin roll with the Mexican prege.
Hoping that things don't have to be like that
without no trust, it's a definite must
the bust, cops.

Joel's poetry is pointed in its honesty about his life and his feelings about the world. In terms of poetic form, you can feel Joel's subtle rhyme and rhythm laced throughout the piece, even if it doesn't match a 4/4 timed beat or a strict, coupled rhyme scheme.

What I feel is most important here is that Joel is not afraid to use his own language—his home language—in his work. Standard English, and its enforcement as the only correct or proper way to speak English, can serve to linguistically handcuff students. Using hip hop in the classroom challenges the notion that Standard English is the only legitimate form of English, and supplants it with the idea that the language spoken at home, with friends, or even on the streets is a valid, viable form of communication. Because rap music uses English in particular ways, with its own adaptations and vocabulary, it reflects a sense of language that is noninstitutional, nonstandard, and nontraditional. It therefore can help pave the way for students to express themselves in forms that are true to their lived experiences and cultures, while increasing their potential creativity, learning, and development.

Whether you enjoy it or not, you will hear rap music every day bumping down the street in the car next to you or see it on your TV pushing the latest soft drink. It is a powerful form of cultural communication that deserves our attention and use in the classroom, particularly if we are to be student-centered in our teaching. Even more important is the idea that using rap in the classroom can serve to decriminalize popular images of youth by providing us with a window for understanding their lives, cultures, and music. So the next time you see students with their headphones on their heads, try asking them about what they're listening to and call it research. ◆

*Wayne Au, a former high school teacher, is an assistant professor at the University of Washington-Bothell Campus, and is a* Rethinking Schools *editor. Most recently he edited* Rethinking Multicultural Education: Teaching for Racial and Cultural Justice *(Rethinking Schools, 2009) and authored* Unequal by Design: High-Stakes Testing and the Standardization of Inequality *(Routledge, 2009). He would like to thank Mira Shimabukuro, Alonzo Ybarra, and Jack Thompson for their assistance.*

# Stenciling Dissent

*Political graffiti engages students
in the history of protest for social justice*

◆ ANDREW REED

A couple of summers ago I was racking my brain to come up with new lessons for my U.S. history classes. I wanted the format of the projects to reflect the content of our unit on the power of protest. I finally came up with the idea that my students would create stencil images. Stencils are often used as a form of street protest, not just in the United States, but throughout the world as well, because they're easy to make, quick to apply, and can be used over and over.

Because most of my students here in Wichita, Kansas, are immigrants or children of immigrants and from lower socioeconomic households, I stress in my history classes how dissent, strikes, and protest have given the poor, minorities, and immigrants a voice when the vote hasn't. When my students learn about people like Sacco and Vanzetti, Emma Goldman, and Malcolm X, and events like the 1892 Homestead Strike and the United Farm Workers' grape boycotts of the 1960s, it gives them an understanding of the struggles and achievements of those in the past who have faced obstacles similar to those my students and their families face today.

The relevance of this kind of curriculum was apparent in April 2006. After learning about the 1968 Chicano student walkouts, some of my students organized a walkout in solidarity with the nationwide immigrant rights rallies and walkouts going on at that time. My students' walkout involved about 500 young people from different Wichita high schools; it ended up on the front page of the *Wichita Eagle* and was the top story on all three local evening newscasts. I took no part in organizing the student walkout and, contrary to the superintendent's claims, no other adults organized it either; it was all led by students. However, I do believe that the history curriculum they learned in my class gave them a sense that they were capable of doing it. The following year, I wanted to do something to keep alive my students' spirit of protest.

Our power of protest unit dovetailed with a school district requirement for a research-based persuasive essay. I decided to ask students to choose an individual, group, or event essential to the history of dissent in the United States. Their project would entail researching their chosen topic, writing the essay, creating and printing a stencil, and dis-

ANDREW REED

tilling the essence of their topic into a paragraph to accompany the stencil.

The list of topics I gave students included individuals like Emma Tenayuca (labor organizer for Mexican migrant workers in the 1930s), Fred Korematsu (Japanese American who resisted relocation to an internment camp during World War II), and Philip and Daniel Berrigan (Catholic priests who protested against the Vietnam War); organizations like the Brown Berets (Chicano rights activists in the 1960s who were inspired by the Black Panthers); and events like the Ludlow Massacre (famous labor strike in 1914) and even the recent immigration rights rallies.

I foreshadowed the stencil project by including lessons throughout the school year on the general use of art (fine art, music, video, and other types of media) as a means of protest in the past. For example, we listened to and analyzed songs of the Industrial Workers of the World (IWW), connecting the lyrics to the importance of uniting workers and giving them a voice during the early 1900s. Then, while learning

**Stencils are often used as a form of street protest, not just in the United States, but throughout the world as well, because they're easy to make, quick to apply, and can be used over and over.**

about the 1920s Red Scare, the students interpreted the messages about injustice in a Diego Rivera mural.

## One Step Ahead of the Class

While the students researched their topics and wrote and rewrote their essays, I prepared for the stencil piece of the project. I knew that before I could ask my students to create these stencils, I would have to make some myself to get an idea of how difficult and time-consuming it might be. Being artistically challenged, I figured if I could make a decent stencil any of my students could, too. My first stencil was of the abolitionist Henry David Thoreau. I spray-painted it on my podium along with one of his quotes: "It is not desirable to cultivate a respect for the law so much as a respect for the right." (Thoreau was jailed for refusing to pay a tax to support the U.S. war against Mexico—a war he believed was launched to spread slavery.) Next was an image of Emma Goldman, then Subcomandante Marcos of the Zapatista movement, and on and on. By the time I was ready to show my students how to create the stencils, many of them already had an idea just from watching me so many times.

Before students started their stencils, we watched video clips on stenciling. I found a couple of five-minute clips on YouTube to show as a visual introduction to stenciling. One video was a tutorial on creating stencils. Another showed that stencils were used throughout the world as a form of protest, especially in Latin America.

## The Stencils Take Life

First, students searched for an image on the web to make their stencil. Some students found ready-made designs, while others had to modify the images. The easiest way to modify an image to create a stencil is to load the image into Microsoft Word, adjust it to higher contrast, and experiment with the brightness until it looks more like a stencil. Once we reviewed the basic concepts, the students were able to design their images fairly easily.

The next stage was to create the actual stencil. I provided each student with a piece of 8.5- x 11-inch transparency film. Students laid the transparency over the printed images and traced them onto the transparencies. Transparency film is good to use because it's easy to cut, it's thin, and paint won't bleed through. If students wanted to make a stencil larger than 8.5 x 11, they used an 11- x 17-inch file folder. I then gave students small utility knives to cut out their stencils, along with stern warnings about safety. (I'm happy to say that not one student had an accident; I wish I could say the same for myself.)

Students had to make a stencil image to represent their topic and also a stencil cutout of the name of the person, group, or event they chose. Given the time constraints, some students used the stencil fonts preinstalled on the computers, while others made their own by hand. A variety of interesting stencil fonts can be downloaded for free from the web. After students found their images, manipulated them, traced them to transparency, and then cut them out, they were ready to paint.

**As people looked at the display and read the information, they began to think: "Who else should be up there? Who else have I learned about whose protest was important to U.S. history?"**

Instead of having students make individual posters, I bought a giant 7- x 12-foot canvas as a "wall." We used spray paint to apply the stencil images, although other kinds of paint can be used. I chose spray paint to give my students more of a feeling of making street art. Because stenciling on public spaces without permission is illegal and, of course, I was not advocating that my students do that, I figured painting the stencils on one big canvas would be the closest we could get to doing it on the streets.

There was a sense of nervous anticipation as students applied their stencils to the canvas. They would only get one shot to get it right. Too much paint would cause a stencil to run; too little paint would make it look blurry. We worked outdoors and wore masks because spray paint fumes are dangerous. Each student laid a stencil onto the canvas, applied the paint, and slowly removed the stencil to reveal the image on the canvas. I loved seeing my students' eyes light up, watching them smile, and listening as they bragged about the quality of their images.

Some moments were magical: Pedro was fairly new to the school and didn't know many people yet. When it was his turn to spray his stencil he did it with ease, as if he had done it many times before. I asked him if he had painted stencils previously. He explained that he works with his brother in a body shop airbrushing cars, which is a similar skill. He then spent the next 15 minutes teaching the other students and me the proper techniques for applying spray paint. That seemed to be the icebreaker between him and the rest of the students; from then on he was more social in class.

Another student, Ricardo Valdez, an amazing graffiti artist who has done a lot of street art in Mexico City, painted additional art on the canvas to give it more of a street art look.

I have never had students so into doing a history class project as they were into this. They loved it. Some students wanted to make more than one stencil. They would show up in class with the stencil of Che Guevara or a Zapatista that they made at home. Even though protesting the Iraq war was not on the list of topics, some students made anti-war stencils on their own time to put on our class canvas.

## Stencils for Justice

We displayed the canvas in the school's hallway for all to see. Next to the canvas, each student posted a paragraph distilling the significance—in terms of the history of dissent in the United States—of the person, group, or event represented in his or her stencil. This one-paragraph description was a big challenge for many students, taking pages worth of research and condensing the most important parts down to five or six sentences. In a hallway display, students don't have time to stand and read a lengthy report about, say, César Chávez; they have to be able to get information about him as they walk by. My students realized that in describing why César Chávez was an important figure in U.S. protest history, they couldn't start with where he was born, what schools he attended as a child, and so forth. They had to stick to the boycotts, hunger strikes, arrests, and lasting impact of his actions. It was the students, not me, who figured out what to teach to others.

For example, my student, Odalis Sosa, distilled Emma Goldman's life into this summary:

> **Emma Goldman, 1869–1940** Anarchist, feminist, antiwar activist. Emma Goldman made [it] her life to fight for the rights of women, immigrants, and all others in the United States who were being oppressed. In 1893, Emma was put into prison for "inciting a riot" when she wanted unemployed workers to stand up for their rights. In 1911, she was imprisoned for distributing birth control literature. In 1917, Emma was imprisoned for a third time for protesting against World War I and wanting people to refuse the draft. Emma Goldman's protest influenced many people during her time and later to fight for the rights of the oppressed.

The canvas display was the eye-catcher, while students' paragraphs posted to the side of the display were the education for onlookers. As my students watched others studying their "wall," they recognized how art can be an effective means to reach other people. A former student, Alma, told me how much she wished we'd done this while she was in my class. But she asked, "Why isn't Martin Luther King Jr. or Rosa Parks on the display?" I told her that those historical figures definitely fit into the theme of the project, but they were not on the list because I wanted to shine a light on great people who were lesser known. Other students, and teachers, too, talked to me about the people or events we failed to put on the display. I wasn't offended; it made me feel that the project served its purpose. As people looked at the display and read the information, they began to think: "Who else should be up there? Who else have I learned about whose protest was important to U.S. history?"

**Especially in an urban school where students appreciate graffiti and other street art, stencils hold the potential to engage students.**

A week after the display went up, my classes discussed the project and what they observed. Eduardo, an immigrant from Durango, Mexico—and proud of it, as he reminded others all the time—said, "It was nice to see some people learning about Mexicans for a change." I asked the students if they thought others would have paid as much attention to the display if we had used more traditional visuals instead of stencils. They gave a resounding no. They said that the purpose of using political stencils on the streets was to get people's attention.

The display was well received by students and staff at the school. Students stopped in the halls to observe and talk to each other about why images of Dolores Huerta or the Freedom Riders looked so cool. I received emails from teachers praising the project. I even received emails from the art teachers praising students' work. With antiwar stencils on the canvas, the project did not completely escape negative reactions. One staff member told me that he wanted to go home and get his paint so he could paint over the whole thing. A couple of others decided the display was un-American, but most seemed to understand that dissent is what gives the people of the United States our identity. Some staff members had preconceived notions about street art. They felt that any street art is graffiti and any graffiti is gang related. But when they saw how street art was used for an educational purpose, many told me they gained a new appreciation for it.

Especially in an urban school where students appreciate graffiti and other street art, stencils hold the potential to engage students. Youth can create something that might get them in trouble on the streets but an A in the classroom. And students can use stencils in other ways: to create their own shirts, posters, book covers, or postcards. Whether in a school or on the streets, stencils—at least political ones—can catch onlookers' attention and make them think. ◆

*Andrew Reed teaches at the Global Leadership Academy in the Mapleton Public School District in Colorado. When this project was created, he taught at East High School in Wichita, Kansas.*

**Resources**
**www.stencilrevolution.com**
Stencil Revolution: A Stencil Art Community Resource.
**www.justseeds.org**
To see how history has been represented in street art, check out Justseeds: Visual Resistance Artists' Cooperative.

# The Murder of Sean Bell

*From pain to poetry*

◆ RENÉE WATSON

"I'm afraid that one day I'll be shot by the cops for no reason," a 7th-grade student blurted out in our class discussion. My teaching partner and I had asked students to call out their hopes and fears. "What do you hope for your community? What is it about your community that makes you afraid?" we asked. I wrote their answers on chart paper and by the end of the discussion, our class list included better schools, more parks, peace, and safer neighborhoods. Our list also included violence, drugs, bullying, and police brutality.

One student, Felix, passionately talked about the mistreatment from the police he'd seen with his own eyes just outside his Bronx apartment window. "They always shoot us," he said. "It makes me angry."

"Me too," students in the class shouted. "They do us wrong."

Us. The word was so alive, so inclusive. Even the students who just last week had been outsiders to the cliques that often form in middle school classrooms were a part of Us. Everyone who lived in the Bronx, agreed among themselves that there was an Us and Them. Ninety-five percent of the students were of Latino or African decent. Their school was one of many New York public schools that was under corrective action from the state because of low test scores.

Felix continued: "Nobody cares about what happens to us. And there's nothing we can do. You ask us to write poems about how we feel, but words don't have no power to change things." Felix wasn't being disrespectful. I believe he honestly felt helpless.

I asked the class, "Are words powerless?" Some agreed with Felix. But others pointed out that song lyrics have caused people to fall in love, that speeches have healed nations, that storybooks have calmed sleepless, crying children.

I believe deep down Felix knew this. I wondered if maybe he thought his words were powerless because he'd never been heard. Never truly been listened to. I wanted him, and the rest of the class, to know that their angry, hurt, questioning words mattered. I wanted them to know that for centuries poets and writers have put ink to paper to celebrate, encourage, heal, challenge, teach, and even chastise their world.

I hoped they'd join that legacy.

It was our 10th creative writing workshop together. As teaching-

I asked the class, "Are words powerless?" Some agreed with Felix. But others pointed out that song lyrics have caused people to fall in love, that speeches have healed nations, that storybooks have calmed sleepless, crying children.

DUANE SMITH

artists who came in only once a week to teach a poetry residency with the theme of community and social justice, my co-teacher Nikki Westfall and I were careful to build trust and mutual respect. Each day served as a building block for the next lesson, which deepened in content and encouraged students to become more vulnerable in their writing.

First, we wrote prose about our names, using Sandra Cisneros' piece "My Name" (*House on Mango Street*). Students also celebrated their community by writing "Where I'm From" poems, inspired by Willie Perdomo's poem "Where I'm From" (*Smoking Lovely*) and Linda Christensen's lesson in her book *Reading, Writing, and Rising Up*.

We turned to Perdomo again when we realized police brutality was a concern for youth living in the Bronx. Perdomo's poem, "41 Bullets Off Broadway," was written about Amadou Diallo, an unarmed West African who was shot 19 times in a hail of 41 bullets by the police in the Bronx. The year was 1999. These 7th-grade students were only 3 or 4 years old then. Most of them had never heard about Diallo. But now, at 12 and 13, they were introduced to Sean Bell.

Bell, 23, was shot by the police in Queens and died the morning of his wedding. In total, 50 bullets were fired. Bell and his friends were unarmed. It was 2006. In the year and a half that led to the final ruling—acquittal for all five officers—Bell's picture, along with photos of his fiancée and their two children, were constantly on the news. New Yorkers talked about the case on the subway, in coffee shops, in churches, and now in classrooms.

We began the Sean Bell unit by bringing in a CD of Perdomo performing "41 Bullets Off Broadway." I gave students copies and they followed along as they listened. Bringing the poet's voice into the classroom was a powerful tool and is something I try to do often. It is important to me to provide students several entry points to the lessons. I layer lessons not only with printed words for students who have strong verbal skills, but I also bring in music, movement activities, and visual components to help address the multiple intelligences of all students. It is one thing for me to read the poem to the students, but to have Perdomo perform it like only he can, brought the stanzas to life:

> ...From the Bronx to El Barrio we heard you fall face first into the
> lobby of your equal opportunity forty-one bullets like silver push
> pins holding up a connect-the-dots picture of Africa forty-one bullets
> not giving you enough time to hit the floor with dignity and justice for
> all forty-one bullet shells trickling onto a bubble gum-stained mo-
> saic where your body is mapped out.

. . . Before you could show your I.D. and say, "Officer"
—four regulation Glock clips went achoo and smoked
you into spirit and by the time a special street unit
decided what was enough another dream submitted
an application for deferral.

 By the time you hit the floor the special unit forgot
everything they learned at the academy The mayor told them to take
a few days off and when they came back he sent them to go beat up a
million young black men while your blood seeped through the tile in
the lobby of your equal opportunity from the Bronx to El Barrio there
were enough shots to go around.

**"It won't bring Diallo back, but it will let his mother know that someone cares."**

 My teaching partner and I, along with the classroom teacher, led
a discussion. We asked the class, "Does anyone know who this poem
is about?" Most of them answered Sean Bell. "Why do you think this
poem is about Sean Bell?"

 "Because it's about a man who was killed by the police," many answered.

 I wrote on the board: Amadou Diallo. "Unfortunately, Sean Bell
is not the only person who was shot by the police. This poem is about
an incident that happened in 1999." We then asked students to turn
their poems over. On the other side there was a *New York Times* article
about the Diallo case. My teaching partner read the article to the class
as they followed along. We encouraged students to read critically. "Star
any questions you have or words you don't understand and underline
the similarities between Diallo and Bell."

 There were many similarities. Students called them out:

 "It happened in New York."

 "They were both black men."

 "He was in his 20s, too."

 "They were both unarmed."

 We then asked students to look back over Perdomo's poem. "Where
does the poet use facts from the case in his poem? Where does he use
his own imagination? What parts of the poem show Perdomo's feelings? What are some of the images that come to your mind as you read
the poem?"

 We recorded their answers on the board in three columns: Facts,
Emotions, Images. Many students focused on the lines in the poem
where Perdomo describes the bathroom and lobby of Diallo's apartment. They pointed out that Perdomo probably never saw it, but used
his imagination to add these descriptive images. After our list was complete, I asked, "Why do you think Willie Perdomo wrote this poem?"

One student responded, "Because he thought what happened was unfair."

Another added, "Because he wanted to speak for Diallo since he couldn't talk for himself."

A girl in the back of the class thought Perdomo wrote it for Diallo's mother. "It won't bring Diallo back, but it will let his mother know that someone cares about what happened to her son."

We asked the students, "What emotions do you think Willie Perdomo feels in this poem?"

In unison the class replied, "Anger." Some answered, "Sad, frustrated, confused."

We then talked about how Perdomo chose to handle his emotions: He wrote.

"How many of you are angry about the Sean Bell case?" All the students raised their hands.

"Well, today, we're going to write about it."

At this point, we passed out an article about Sean Bell. After reading it as a class, students were given the assignment in three steps.

First, they were to complete their own chart, like the one on the board, about the Bell case using the article. I gave students a worksheet that had three columns—Facts, Emotions, Images—and asked them to write at least four words under each column.

Second, they were asked to choose which voice they wanted to write in. I asked, "Who was talking in Perdomo's poem?" He was. "Who was he speaking to?" He was speaking to Diallo. We gave students a choice. They could write in their own voice to Sean Bell, or they could write as Sean Bell. They could write as his fiancée or mother. Or they could choose to be one of the bullets or an officer.

By this point in our creative writing residency, students were equipped with several literary devices and we wanted to push them to be as creative as possible, especially since most of their poems up to this lesson were autobiographical. We reminded them of their Literary Tool Box. Their toolbox included anaphora, alliteration, metaphor, simile, personification and sensory detail. These literary devices were taught in prior lessons and we'd reviewed them throughout the residency.

I reminded the students, "Willie Perdomo didn't just say: 'Diallo was shot by the police. I'm

## Literary Tool Box

**Anaphora:** When the beginning of a line repeats.

**Alliteration:** Words that begin with the same sound.

**Metaphor:** Comparing two unlikely things without using like or as.

**Simile:** Comparing two unlikely things using *like* or *as*.

**Personification:** Giving human attributes to an animal or nonhuman thing.

**Sensory Detail:** Images described using the five senses.

mad. It wasn't fair.' Be creative and use the tools you have to add sensory details to your poem."

Step three was to begin writing. "Use the words from your chart to get started and if you get stuck, refer to Willie Perdomo's poem as an example."

Then, we reviewed the assignment guidelines and handed out their Poetry Checklist. "You'll know your poem is complete when you have at least three or more stanzas, you've used three or more phrases from your chart, and you've applied one or more of the literary devices from your toolbox."

During class time, students finished the chart and decided from which point of view they wanted to write. The following week, students wrote their poems. Volunteers shared their poems in class and several students submitted their Sean Bell poem to our end-of-the-year anthology.

Belkis wrote from the point of view of Bell's fiancée:

> My expectation on that day
> was for me to walk down the aisle to you,
> but instead I walked down the aisle towards your casket…
> My expectation on that day was to be next to you saying, "I do."
> But instead, I stood next to your body, crying…
> You are the love of my life. We miss you. We hope you're doing
> better where you are than how we're doing here.

Mokhtar imagined what it would be like for a mother to lose a child. He made a list of all the things a mother might remember and feel. "Am I doing this right?" he asked, showing me his first stanza:

> To everybody else it's just a news story. To me, it's different because
> he is my son. Twenty-three years old. I remember when I changed his
> diapers.

Johnny, the class clown in the group, took this assignment seriously and wrote from the perspective of one of the bullets:

> I struck you in the neck and arm. If it was up to me, I would have never
> even touched you. I felt really shocked when the guy that took control
> of me pulled the trigger.
> I didn't know what to do. I couldn't change my direction once I was
> in the air. I'm sorry, man. I'm sorry I caused your death.
> Twenty-three years old. Two baby girls. I had no right to keep you
> in shock like that. It was really wrong. The day of your wedding. Man,
> I'm sorry.

**I encourage students to see poetry as a container that is strong enough to hold their rage, questions, and wildest imaginations.**

It is important for me to say that although I want students to use their writing to empathize with others, release their anger, and celebrate their cultures, I don't do this work at the expense of teaching basic literacy skills. I make sure my workshops are aligned with the classroom teacher's curriculum. I find that when students care deeply about the topics presented in the lesson plans, they work harder to revise and hone their writing.

My goal is to create balance in the classroom, where creative writing serves as a vehicle to heighten social awareness and academic success. I hope that my creative writing residencies provide a safe place for students to let out everything they are holding in. I encourage students to see poetry as a container that is strong enough to hold their rage, questions, and wildest imaginations.

After completing the Sean Bell unit, we continued with the theme of telling someone else's story. Using Martín Espada's poem "Jorge the Janitor Finally Quits," we moved forward to lessons about empathy and giving voice to invisible communities. Our residency ended with a reading and celebration of our anthology.

Almost a year after working at MS 279, the verdict for Sean Bell's case was announced. Every officer was acquitted. I thought about my students at MS 279. By then, I was no longer at their school. I was now working with freshmen students at Bronx High School for Writing and Communication Arts. They had just finished the unit on Sean Bell and the assignments on Invisible Communities. There had been heated discussion and debates, including students who understood the officers' point of view, students who brought up the perceived deviant pasts of Bell and his friends, and students who believed people of color were overreacting. Some believed it was sad that Bell died, but didn't think the police were negligent.

"If those officers don't get no punishment, there's going to be a riot," one student said. "People are going to be so angry."

The city of New York thought so, too. The day of the verdict police were out in full force. But there were no riots.

Citizens marched.

Actors performed in Bell's honor.

Artists painted murals, designed shirts and buttons.

Writers wrote poems and recited them at open mic poetry slams in remonstration of the acquittal.

On the afternoon of the verdict, I watched the live broadcast of the acquitted officers making their statements. Occasionally, pictures would flash on the screen—Bell with his fiancée and two daughters, the yellow tape that sectioned off the block. Then, the camera would pan across the large crowd of New Yorkers who'd come out to the courthouse to hear the verdict themselves. There was so much interest in this case. So much support for the Bell family. I wondered what it meant to them to see New York show up for them, for Sean Bell. I was reminded of a question Felix asked the day we read Perdomo's poem. "Do you know if Amadou Diallo's mom ever read this poem?" he asked. I told him I didn't know. Now, sitting in front of my television watching those same images that were shown almost two years ago, I wanted to make sure Sean Bell's mother and his fiancée and his friends read these poems. A fellow teaching-artist, Nanya Goodrich, and I created a booklet of the students' tributes to Sean Bell—both from MS 279 and Bronx High—and we sent them to the family.

People thought there'd be riots. They thought young people would join in and loot and burn up buildings. Instead the young people I know joined the legacy of Perdomo and Espada. They protested through poetry. They gave voice to a grieving family and an angry, disappointed community.

The young people I know turned their pain into poetry. ◆

---

*Renée Watson lives in New York City and is the author of the picture book* A Place Where Hurricanes Happen *(Random House) and the middle-grade novel* What Momma Left Me *(Bloomsbury).*

**Resources**
**The House on Mango Street** by Sandra Cisneros (Arte Publico Press, 1984).
**Smoking Lovely** by William Perdomo (Rattapallax Press, 2004).

# Knock, Knock

*Turning pain into power*

◆ LINDA CHRISTENSEN

Too often today, schools are about standards and common curriculum: *Scarlet Letter* and *Huck Finn* first quarter, move on to *Great Gatsby*. And too often, I get caught up in that land too. Then my heart gets cracked open by students, and I remember that first I must teach the child who is in the class. By structuring a curriculum that allows room for students' lives—and by listening to their stories—I can locate the right book, the right poem that turns pain into power while I teach reading and writing. Unless I consciously build these opportunities into the curriculum, there is little hope of getting authenticity from students.

Daniel Beaty, poet and playwright, came to life for me one New Year's Eve when my husband, Bill, and I watched hour after hour of the HBO show *Def Poetry Jam*. I fell in love with many poets that night, but when I watched Daniel Beaty perform "Knock Knock," I knew I was witnessing a poet whose performance and words would inspire my students. I bought the *Def Poetry* DVD, transcribed the words, and carried Beaty with me to class. Partly autobiographical, the poem speaks directly to many of my students because Beaty's drive-home message in everything he does is that in order to heal ourselves, our society, and our world, we must turn our pain into power. (Beaty's *Def Poetry* performance of "Knock Knock" is posted on YouTube and other video-sharing sites.)

I taught the poem to several classes at Portland's Jefferson High School days before Barack Obama was elected president. I'd spent 24 years teaching high school language arts at this predominantly African American school, and I returned this year to work with the faculty. I left each class in tears because when poetry, like Beaty's, touches students' lives in real ways, I am reminded of both the pain and the hope that schools harbor.

"Knock Knock" is constructed in three parts. Beaty begins with the story of the father's imprisonment, moves to a direct address to the father, "Papa, come home 'cause I miss you," and ends in a letter that the poet writes to "heal" and "father" himself. The poem and Beaty's performance are so powerful that I didn't want to interrupt it with instruction or teacher talk before they watched it the first time. I wanted

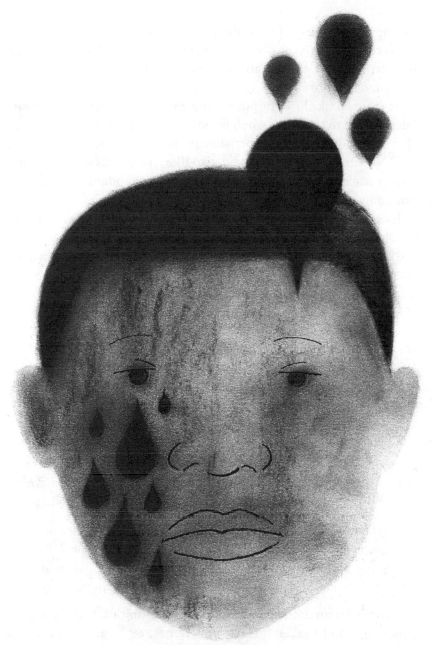

SCOTT BAKAL

them to feel the poem. My only instruction was: "As you watch the poem, notice what works for you or doesn't work. Just jot notes, so we can talk about it after we watch it a couple of times."

After students watched the video of the performance twice, I asked them to take a few silent minutes to write their thoughts about the poem. "Look

**I left each class in tears because when poetry, like Beaty's, touches students' lives in real ways, I am reminded of both the pain and the hope that schools harbor.**

at the copy of the poem. Think about what you notice about the poem, how you connect with the poem, what poetic devices Beaty used." Students started off by talking about what they liked about the poem—from content to form.

Greg said, "I like how the poem progresses from when he was young and dependent to the point when he got older and stronger."

Jerome said: "He used repetition by repeating the words 'knock knock.' Nothing was sugarcoated. I also like that it tells a story of pain. The story wasn't a nice-feeling, sweet one talking about love or flowers and moonlight. I connected to the story."

Theresa liked "how the end of the poem is like a letter from his father that he wrote himself."

When Shontay said, "I loved the line, 'Knock, knock down the doors of racism and poverty that I could not,'" many students nodded in agreement.

Demetrius spoke up: "This last part makes me think of how much positive things our generation can do. How much potential we have."

Harriet said: "You know, I really like the part during the letter where he says 'We are our fathers' sons and daughters/But we are not their choices.' We aren't the reason they made bad choices. We aren't part of their choices, and their decisions aren't our fault."

I was stunned. I had taught this poem for several years with my classes at Grant High School, and I'd never thought about how children might feel like they might bear the burden of guilt for their parents' choices. But Harriet's comment reminded me that as a child I shouldered a lot of fear about my future based on my family's history:

> Would I graduate from high school? Would I go to college when no one else in my family had? Would I get pregnant and be chained to a minimum wage job? Was my father's alcoholism a genetic stain that could explode my dreams and shackle me to relive my parents' story?

Harriet's comment prompted me to share my fears from when I was their age, and I asked: "What are your fears? What chains of the past do you drag around with you? What are you afraid of? What do you worry about?" Students wrote lists of their fears. Then we shared.

Harriet said, "The women in my family have all had children before they graduated from high school, and I'm going to break that cycle." When one student opens the door for an honest conversation, others follow, especially if I create the space by responding to the student's remark instead of rushing past it. So I said, "Yes, I was afraid of that too. Does anyone else have that fear?" A few other young women raised their hands.

Mark said: "My father went to jail, so I can relate to how he felt when his father never came home. A lot of black men could relate to this poem. Like having to teach themselves things because of an absent father."

Larry said: "My dad went to school at Jefferson. He never graduated, and now he's in prison. I'm going to break that cycle." Another student added: "My mother went here too. She had a bad temper, and she got expelled for fighting. I don't want to get expelled for fighting." Other students shared their fears: Getting shot, becoming a drug addict, not graduating, losing a parent, not measuring up to their parents' expectations.

**Harriet's comment prompted me to share my fears from when I was their age, and I asked: "What are your fears? What chains of the past do you drag around with you? What are you afraid of? What do you worry about?"**

## Writing the Poem

To move students to write the poem, I asked students to look at these three parts of the poem: "Read back over each part and write in the margin what the poet is writing about, how you connect to that part, and why you think it changes his writing style in each section." With a little nudging, students picked up on the story: the direct address and the letter format of the poem. I didn't labor over this part of the lesson. I wanted to call attention to it, so students could build their poems in a similar style.

I gave them the following assignment:

Taking a page from Daniel Beaty, write a letter poem to yourself, giving yourself the advice you need to hear. Notice how Beaty begins with a story, then moves into the letter part of the poem that he writes to heal himself. In his letter, he lists advice to himself: 'Shave in one direction, dribble the page with your brilliance.'"

What advice do you need to hear? What do you need to do differently to succeed in school? In life? Beaty writes of the obstacles that need to be knocked down in his life: racism, lack of opportunity. Are there obstacles in your life? Perhaps you have your school, friend, and home life together, then think of someone else who might need to hear a few words of advice.

As an adult, there are things I wish my mother would have told me. This is not an indictment against her. Sometimes, children aren't ready to hear their parents. Also, we grow up in different times, different social periods.

Then I shared the beginnings of my poem and showed how I started with the apology, then moved from the negative to the positive in the second stanza. I also highlighted Beaty's lines to use as a frame for the poem:

> Dear Linda, I'm sorry for the nights I left you alone after your father died. I'm sorry for the solitary dinners you ate those nights I chose a man over you. **For every lesson I failed to teach, hear these words:** Don't marry a man who drinks. He'll spend money on booze instead of the family. If a man hits you once, he'll hit you again. Pack your bags and leave. Move on. When school gets hard, remember your brilliance. Diamonds require hard work.

Although most students wrote to themselves, a few wrote poems to other people who they thought needed advice. Andrew wrote from his father's point of view:

> As I sit in a tiny cell, it amazes me how the two of us can hardly ever speak or see each other in 16 years, and yet still go through so much together. Don't do the same idiotic decisions as me. Don't let the girls, gangs, and drugs ruin both of our lives. I apologize for choosing the streets over my own son.

Another student's father had died the night before our assignment. Lester wrote:

> I'm sorry for leaving you five years ago without saying goodbye....Son, do all you can to be better than me. Go to school and learn until your skull cracks. Grow up to be a wonderful father to your kids. Be there for them before they walk to the edge....Son, I'm glad you're not here because I'm on a bed with wires attached to me and a machine that beeps every 3 seconds. I have to go because heaven is open, and I got to get in because this is the only way I can see you from a different angle.

Another student wrote a paragraph in response:

> It's crazy how you love a man who was never there. I just learned not to care. When you say you're going to come to my games and you don't come, there's no disappointment. When you don't call on my birthday, there's no disappointment. Don't get me wrong, I love you, but you showed me everything I don't need to do....Can you imagine the look on a little boy's face when the man he looks up to goes to the store for milk and never comes home....Because of all those broken promises, I love you because you showed me how not to cry. I'm no longer weak.

Noah's poem below followed the format and broke it at the same time. I love the way he played with the credit card commercial:

Dear Father,

Pay me! Pay me well and pay me now. Not with your hundreds of thousands of millions of dollars. Pay me some damn attention!

My first bike: $87.00 Varsity basketball: $175.00 Having a care: Priceless.

Charge to your card, a hug or even a pat on the back. Write me a check for some words of encouragement.

Send me a money order for the missed birthdays. Your dollars will never be enough, but your time is priceless. Your love is priceless.

—Noah Koné

Students need opportunities to hone their skills, to write essays, to practice becoming academics. They also need opportunities to write about the tough issues in their lives that rarely surface in schools. Beaty's work opened their veins, so they could write with the blood of their lives. ◆

---

*Linda Christensen directs the Oregon Writing Project at Portland's Lewis & Clark College and is a* Rethinking Schools *editor. She is the author of* Reading, Writing, and Rising Up: Teaching About Social Justice and the Power of the Written Word *(Rethinking Schools, 2003) and* Teaching for Joy and Justice: Re-Imagining the Language Arts Classroom *(Rethinking Schools, 2009).*

# Haiku and Hiroshima

*An animated film and haiku poetry raise awareness about the events of August 1945 and the atomic bomb*

◆ WAYNE AU

Some classroom materials invariably work, no matter the group of students. *Barefoot Gen* is one of them.

*Barefoot Gen*, a Japanese animation full-length feature, tells the story of Gen (pronounced with a hard G, like the word "go"), a young boy who, along with his mother, survives the bombing of Hiroshima.

The story chronicles their struggles as they try to rebuild their lives from the bomb's ashes. It is based on the critically acclaimed, semi-autobiographical Japanese comic book series *Hadashi no Gen*, by Keiji Nakazawa. Both the comic strip and the feature film oppose the Japanese government's actions during World War II and include criticism of the intense poverty and suffering forced onto the Japanese people by their government's war effort.

The film's critical eye points to one of the lessons I want students to draw from *Barefoot Gen*: that it is important to scrutinize the relationship between the people of a county and the actions of their government—ours included. I want my students to understand that as thinking human beings, we have the right to disagree and protest when a government's actions are not in the interests of humanity, as Gen's father does or as many U.S. people do in condemning the bombing of Hiroshima and Nagasaki.

I also find the film useful to help students look beyond the demonized and often racist images of the Japanese, particularly in the context of World War II, and see actual people living, dying, and protesting their government's actions. High school students enjoy the disarming and playful nature of *Barefoot Gen*'s cartoon medium. Some students are even familiar with the film genre of Japanese animation, or anime.

The film's effect is hardly playful, however, and students quickly realize that this is a serious film with character development, plot, and very real emotion. Its animation allows the intense imagery of the atomic explosion and its aftermath to take shape on screen, in front of our eyes.

The atomic detonation of the bomb named "Little Boy" over the city of Hiroshima killed almost 120,000 civilians and 20,000 military personnel. The explosion reached into the millions of degrees centi-

An eyewitness account
of the bombing of Hiroshima

"One of the most
important animated
films ever made!"
— Richard von Busack, SAN JOSE METRO

BAREFOOT
GEN

ORION HOME VIDEO

The images in *Barefoot Gen* are powerful and devastating to watch. Thankfully, the film ends on an upbeat note of survival, because like Gen, humanity can and will triumph over devastation.

grade and obliterated an area of 13 square kilometers. Three days later "Fat Man" was dropped on Nagasaki, killing 74,000 people. These astounding numbers do not include the estimated 130,000 who died within five days of the bombings or those who survived the initial explosion but suffered or died from long-term genetic damage and radiation sickness. In offering students a broader context for the events of August 1945, I've found historian Howard Zinn's work especially valuable. See the chapter "Just and Unjust Wars" from his 1990 book *Declarations of Independence* and his article "The Bombs of August" in *The Progressive* magazine, August 2000.

The images in *Barefoot Gen* are powerful and devastating to watch. Thankfully, the film ends on an upbeat note of survival, because like Gen, humanity can and will triumph over devastation.

For the post-film discussion, I mainly ask students to share their feelings and thoughts about the movie. Some say that they've never cried watching a cartoon before, and most remark that they can relate to Gen's personal struggles of losing loved ones or fighting to survive in a harsh world. Across race, gender, and nationality, students consistently develop emotional empathy with Gen.

I like to follow up the discussion with the class using the traditional Japanese poetry forms of haiku and tanka to express their responses to the film. This works best if it can be done the same day as watching the movie. First we read aloud some haiku and tanka written by survivors of the bombings from *White Flash/Black Rain: Women of Japan Relive the Bomb*.

> Reality
> is this and only this—
> the one bone I place in the bent and burned
> small school lunch tin.
>   —Shoda Shinoe

> grabbing sand
> beneath the flaming sky
> is to be alive
>   —Kingyo Humiko

> looking for her mother
> the girl still has strength
> to turn over corpses
>     —Shibata Moriyo

After discussing the imagery and themes of the haiku and tanka examples, I go over the syllabic requirements to match those traditional Japanese forms. Line by line, haiku requires three lines, with five, seven, and five syllables in each line respectively, totaling 17 syllables. With five lines, tanka similarly requires five, seven, five, seven, and seven syllables respectively, totaling 31 syllables. The examples are translated from Japanese so they do not make good syllabic models in English, but their content is powerful enough for students to get the idea.

From there, we write. Expressing emotions through poetry is hard work, and trying to make poetry fit into a limited syllable space is even harder. Fortunately because haiku and tanka are relatively short compared to essays or other writing assignments, students don't feel too intimidated and, however frustrating, have fun fitting their words into the puzzle that the traditional forms present. Students' writing has been outstanding, demonstrating their abilities to empathize with the Japanese people who suffered the bombing.

> screams the sound of souls
> being devoured, banished
> from all existence
>    —Joseph Tauti

> red sky floats above
> starts to drip the blackness down
> towards the drying deathbed
> now scorched by the liquid fire
> bleak chariots move the dead
>    —Amanda O'Conner

> Little children scream
> They look for their families which they will not find
>    —Shanique Johnson

Understandably, the feeling of dread and despair evident in the student examples underscores the immense amount of human suffering. Dropping an atomic bomb on real, live people is serious, and it is important that students recognize this fact.

In the end, the mushroom clouds left by "Little Boy" and "Fat Man" towered over more than just the two cities of Hiroshima and Nagasaki. Those explosions cast their shadows over Asia and Europe, signaling to the rest of the world, especially the Soviet Union, that the United States was indeed the dominant global military power with the devastating firepower to back it up. More important, and more frightening, U.S. officials were willing to use that firepower. ♦

---

*Wayne Au, a former high school teacher, is an assistant professor at the University of Washington-Bothell Campus and is a* Rethinking Schools *editor. He edited* Rethinking Multicultural Education: Teaching for Racial and Cultural Justice *(Rethinking Schools, 2009) and authored* Unequal By Design: High-Stakes Testing and the Standardization of Inequality *(Routledge, 2009).*

**Resources**
**Barefoot Gen, Vol. 1: A Cartoon History of Hiroshima** by Keiji Nakazawa (Last Gasp, 2004).
**Declarations of Independence** by Howard Zinn (Harper Perennial, 1990).
**White Flush/Black Rain** edited and translated by Lequita Vance-Watkins and Aratani Mariko (Milkweed Editions, 1995).
**www.theblackmoon.com/ BarefootGen/bomb.html** A valuable web site with more information about Barefoot Gen.

# Resources: Books and Multimedia

*We asked the contributors to* Rethinking Popular Culture and Media *to recommend resources they find useful. Below are their recommendations. Readers can find additional resources at the end of some chapters.*

**The Big Box**
Toni Morrison (with Slade Morrison), Illustrated by Giselle Potter
New York: Jump at the Sun, 1999.
In this provocative and complex picture book, Morrison addresses issues of freedom, expression, and noncompliance in a "simple" rhyming tale. Three children are locked inside a giant room with all the material comforts they could ask for, but without the freedom to leave. This story can spark great discussion of consumer goods and human rights issues at any grade level.

**The Black Image in the White Mind**
Robert M. Entman and Andrew Rojecki
Chicago: University of Chicago Press, 2001.
The authors provide a critical analysis of how the media frames race issues.

**Can't Stop Won't Stop: A History of the Hip-Hop Generation**
Jeff Chang
New York: St. Martin's Press, 2005.
This is a must-read for anyone wanting to understand hip hop.

**The Children Are Watching:**
**How the Media Teach about Diversity**
Carlos Cortés
New York: Teachers College Press, 2000.
The author provides a framework for thinking about media as "societal curriculum" and offers strategies for analyzing media impact on children.

**Color by Fox:**
**The Fox Network and the Revolution in Black Television**
Kristal Zook
New York: Oxford University Press, 1999.
This book examines popular '90s black sitcoms like *The Fresh Prince of Bel-Air*, *Living Single*, and *Sindbad*. Zook's analysis can be applied to many of today's black sitcoms.

**Consuming Kids:**
**The Commercialization of Childhood**
Media Education Foundation, 2008.
This informative documentary details  how children have become a key
demographic for corporations. The film pushes viewers to ask hard questions
about marketing and its effects on children.

**Corporations in the Classroom $**
Make Believe Media, 2007.
www.movingimages.ca/catalogue/Individual/corporations.html
This engaging documentary, also available through the National Film Board
of Canada, focuses on the influence of corporate funding of public schools.

**CultureJam: Hijacking Commercial Culture.**
Reel-Myth Productions Inc., 2001.
www.culturejamthefilm.com/ordervideo.php
This documentary film introduces viewers to culture jamming as activism
and details the work of artists and other pranksters as they take over and
talk back to corporate culture in the United States and Canada.

**Feed**
M. T. Anderson
Cambridge, MA: Candlewood Press, 2002.
Anderson explores the consequences of corporate- and media-driven culture
in this compelling young adult science fiction novel.

**Get the Picture? The Movie Lover's Guide to Watching Films,**
**2nd Edition**
Jim Piper
New York: Allworth Press, 2008.

**In Your Face: The Culture of Beauty and You**
Shari Graydon
Toronto: Annick Press, 2003.
Written for teens, educator Shari Graydon unpacks the beauty myth,
questions the beauty industry, and offers a range of critical media strategies
for critiquing representations of beauty in magazines and other media.

**Literacy in a Digital World:**
**Teaching and Learning in the Age of Information**
Kathleen Tyner
New York: Routledge, 1998.
Tyner explores why media literacy needs to be taught and what its
implications are for the future.

**Made You Look:**
**How Advertising Works and Why You Should Know**
Shari Graydon
Toronto: Annick Press, 2004.
This must-read book offers an important resource in which readers learn
the language and tactics of advertisers. The book is fun to read (for adults
and kids) and includes lots of information to help readers decode and
critique advertisements.

**Media/Cultural Studies:**
**Critical Approaches**
Rhonda Hammer and Douglas Kellner
New York: Peter Lang, 2009.
This is an outstanding academic resource for educators and parents
who would like to read more about critical approaches to media/culture
studies.

**No Sense of Place:**
**The Impact of Electronic Media on Social Behavior**
Joshua Meyrowitz
New York: Oxford University Press, 1986.
A classic work that shows how media influences and impacts society.

**Reel to Real:**
**Race, Sex, and Class in Movies**
bell hooks
New York: Routledge, 1996.
Hooks critiques movies like *Pulp Fiction*, *Hoop Dreams*, and *Waiting to Exhale*
and writes about movies as a form of pedagogy about race, class, and sex.

**The Rise of the Image, the Fall of the Word**
Mitchell Stephens
New York: Oxford University Press, 1998.
This is one of the first books I read to describe the power of the image and
why it's more appealing than text.

**The Schooling Biographies Project:**
**Re/Writing Our Lives Through Counter-Storytelling**
Available online: www.edliberation.org/resources/records/the-schooling-
biographies-project-re-writing-our-lives-through-counter-storytelling/view
This curriculum resource guide is intended for progressive educators who
want to develop a better understanding of decolonizing curricula and
pedagogy.

**Packaging Boyhood:**
**Saving Our Sons from Superheroes, Slackers,**
**and Other Media Stereotypes**
Lyn Mikel Brown, Sharon Lamb, and Mark Tappan
New York: St. Martin's Press, 2009.
A companion to *Packaging Girlhood*, Brown, Lamb, and Tappan analyze
common stereotypes about boys found in popular media, including comics,
video games, and movies. The authors offer strategies that encourage
youth and adults to resist the narrow definitions of masculinity offered in
mainstream media.

**Packaging Girlhood:**
**Rescuing Our Daughters from Marketers' Schemes**
Sharon Lamb and Lyn Mikel Brown
New York: St. Martin's Griffin, 2006.
Lamb and Brown critique common stereotypes about girlhood through an
insightful analysis of commercially produced media marketed to girls. The
book includes suggestions for how adults and youth might "rebel, resist, and
refuse" marketers' best efforts to sell a limited image of girlhood.

**Reel Conversations:**
**Reading Films with Young Adults**
Alan B. Teasley and Ann Wilder
Portsmouth, NH: Boynton/Cook, 1996.
A great way to encourage students to analyze media is to do a course unit
on "reading" and critiquing movies. These two books are great resources
for building a unit that would involve students in visual media skills and
enlighten students and teachers about the movies they view.

**The Wizards of Media Oz:**
**Behind the Curtain of Mainstream News**
Norman Solomon and Jeff Cohen
Monroe, ME: Common Courage Press, 2002.
Coauthored by two investigative journalists—Jeff Cohen founded the media
watchdog group Fairness & Accuracy in Reporting (FAIR)—the writers
expose bias in mainstream media.

---

*Contributed by Wayne Au, Bakari Chavanu, Rachel Cloues, Elizabeth Marshall,*
*Özlem Sensoy, and Ruth Shagoury.*

# Organizations and Websites

*We asked the contributors to* Rethinking Popular Culture and Media *to recommend some of the organizations and websites they find useful. Below are their recommendations. Readers can find additional resources at the end of some chapters.*

**About-Face**
**www.about-face.org**
This website equips women and girls with tools to understand and resist harmful media messages that affect their self-esteem and body image.

**Adios Barbie: The Body Image Site for Everybody**
**www.adiosbarbie.com**
This website advocates for positive body images for all sizes and cultures. The authors critique idealistic messages about the body offered in mainstream media and embrace a wide range of body types usually erased or negatively portrayed in popular culture.

**American Indians in Children's Literature**
**americanindiansinchildrensliterature.net**
This site offers analysis of portrayals of Indigenous peoples in media (books, film, music) for children and young adults. Teachers using the site will gain skills in recognizing biased and stereotypical imagery, and read about research studies that document the effects of images on Native and non-Native students.

**Center for Media Literacy**
**www.medialit.org**
This site offers a solid introduction for novices and experts interested in media literacy. It offers teachers a framework as well as research-based activities, including a critical media literacy kit. The site encourages critical analysis as well as the production of media.

**Education for Liberation Network**
**www.edliberation.org**
The network is a coalition of teachers, community activists, youth, researchers, and parents who believe a good education should teach people—particularly low-income youth and youth of color—to understand and challenge the injustices their communities face.

**Everyone's Books for Social Justice and the Earth**
**www.everyonesbks.com**
This is the website for a family-owned, independent bookstore in Brattleboro, Vermont. They specialize in books about social change, the environment, and multicultural children's books.

## National Association for Media Literacy Education
**www.namle.net**
An organization based in the United States that focuses on media literacy education.

## New Mexico Media Literacy Project
**www.nmmlp.org**
Founded in 1993, this site is dedicated to media justice. The site offers numerous media literacy resources, including multimedia materials, a media literacy toolbox for teachers, and contests that encourage youth to talk back to media.

## Media Awareness Network
**www.media-awareness.ca**
This Canadian-based organization offers resources and support for anyone interested in media and information literacy for youth.

## Campaign for a Commercial-Free Childhood
**www.commercialexploitation.org**
A coalition of educators, activists, health care workers, and other professionals committed to fighting the corporatization of childhood. The website has critical resources for understanding the ways corporate culture encroaches into kid culture, and it offers strategies for both understanding and action against marketers' assault on children.

## Media Education Foundation
**www.mediaed.org**
A nonprofit associated with the University of Massachusetts Amherst that produces documentary films on media literacy and popular culture for classroom use. The website has descriptions of the documentaries as well as resources (such as study guides and handouts) to provide pedagogical support when using the films.

## Rethinking Schools
**www.rethinkingschools.org**
A critical resource for educators committed to fostering the vision that public schooling is central to the creation of a caring, informed, and equitable society. The magazine, website, books, and other resources published by Rethinking Schools make it an important site of conversation and ongoing analysis about issues addressed in this book.

---

*Contributed by Bakari Chavanu, Elizabeth Marshall, Swapna Mukhopadhyay, Debbie Reese, Özlem Sensoy, and Ruth Shagoury.*

# Index

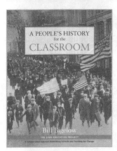

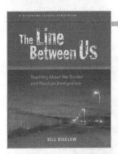

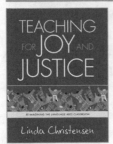

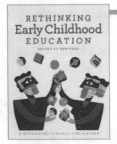